THE TRUTH OF THE RUSSIAN REVOLUTION

To Mr Chuck Johnson —

Thank you for your interest in this major period of Russian history.

Vladimir Marinich

THE TRUTH OF THE RUSSIAN REVOLUTION

THE MEMOIRS OF THE TSAR'S
CHIEF OF SECURITY AND HIS WIFE

Konstantin Ivanovich Globachev

and

Sofia Nikolaevna Globacheva

Translated by

Vladimir G. Marinich

Published by State University of New York Press, Albany

For information, contact State University of New York Press, Albany, NY
www.sunypress.edu

Production, Ryan Morris
Marketing, Michael Campochiaro

Library of Congress Cataloging-in-Publication Data

Names: Globachev, K. I. (Konstantin Ivanovich), author. | Globacheva, Sofia Nikolaevna,
  co-author.
Title: The truth of the Russian Revolution : the memoirs of the Tsar's Chief of Security
  and his wife / by Konstantin Ivanovich Globachev and Sofia Nikolaevna Globacheva ;
  translated by Vladimir G. Marinich.
Description: Albany : State University of New York Press, 2017. | Includes
  bibliographical references and index.
Identifiers: LCCN 2016031451 (print) | LCCN 2016053682 (ebook) | ISBN
  9781438464633 (hardcover) | ISBN 9781438464626 (paperback : alk. paper) | ISBN
  9781438464640 (ebook)
Subjects: LCSH: Globachev, K. I. (Konstantin Ivanovich) | Globacheva, Sofia Nikolaevna.
  | Soviet Union—History—Revolution, 1917–1921—Personal narratives. | Soviet
  Union—History—Revolution, 1917–1921—Influence. | Nicholas II, Emperor of Russia.
  1868–1918—Friends and associates. | Russia. Okhrannȳia otdieleniïa—Biography.
  | Secret service—Russia—History—20th century. | Political culture—Russia
  (Federation)—Saint Petersburg—History—20th century. | Political corruption—Russia
  (Federation)—Saint Petersburg—History—20th century. | Saint Petersburg (Russia)—
  History—20th century.
Classification: LCC DK265.7.G56 A3 2017 (print) | LCC DK265.7.G56 (ebook) |
  DDC 947.084/1—dc23
LC record available at https://lccn.loc.gov/2016031451

10 9 8 7 6 5 4 3 2 1

This work is dedicated to three Babas:
Oleg's and Vladimir's Baba
Their children's Baba
Pax and Thea's Baba

Contents

Illustrations

Maps

Figures

Translator's Preface

Over a decade ago, I was home in the evening when the telephone rang. I answered, and the voice on the other end introduced himself and asked if I had any information on General K. I. Globachev. I responded that I knew a lot about the general because he was my maternal grandfather. Thus began my acquaintance with Dr. Jonathan Daly, Professor of History at the University of Illinois at Chicago. His call prompted me to search through family materials, most of which were in boxes not opened in years. I discovered a treasure trove of photos and letters, some of which were faded with age, but others still in good condition, and also the memoirs of my grandmother, who was the wife of General Globachev.

Dr. Daly recommended that I contact Dr. Zinaida Peregudova, a renowned historian who worked in the Government Archives of the Russian Federation in Moscow. She and I exchanged information and materials about Globachev and his wife. All this inspired me to translate both of their memoirs into English, to make their adventurous and traumatic experiences more available to the greater public.

Let me begin with some background information. Konstantin Ivanovich Globachev was the last Chief of the Petrograd Okhrana. His memoirs and those of his wife, Sofia Nikolaevna Globacheva (*née* Popova), are now in the Bakhmeteff Archives of Columbia University in New York (BAR), and also at the Government Archives of the Russian Federation (GARF) in Moscow. His memoirs were written in the early 1920s while he was working in the Russian Embassy in Constantinople. His manuscript was organized into untitled chapters, each of which was headed by a short summary. I have kept that structure, but have added titles to his chapters to make them more immediately visible to the reader. The chapter titles are also more consistent with my having added titles to his wife's chapters, as I explain below.

Globachev's memoirs are political. He writes about the organization of the Security Bureau (Okhrannoe Otdelenie), its functions and activities, and the prominent events and people of the time: the Miasoedov Affair, the Ministers of the Interior, Assistant Ministers, leaders of the Duma, revolutionaries, Directors of the Department of Police, the royal family, Rasputin, and many more.

Globachev's wife presents us with a personal reflection of the times: her anxiety for her husband's safety, her efforts to free him after his arrest in March, 1917, their flight south, their life and living conditions in the south of Russia, and finally their evacuation and life in Turkey. Her memoirs were written much later, around the very end of the 1940s and finished in 1950, shortly before her death. She wrote her recollections by hand in the black-and-white composition notebooks that were popular in those days. These have been lost; however, her son typed them in several copies, and they are now at Columbia University and at GARF in Moscow. Her manuscript was written with no chapter breaks or paragraph breaks—one hundred or so pages constituted one paragraph. I broke this up into chapters that seemed to fit appropriately, not only in terms of their own content, but also as they fit in with Globachev's chapters. I also added titles to her chapters to clarify when the narrative was transitioning from him to her. It needs to be noted that in the last few chapters of her memoirs several passages are very similar to passages in Globachev's later chapters. It is not known whether Sofia merely copied some appropriate paragraphs from her husband's narrative because they matched what she wanted to convey, or if she had perhaps collaborated some years earlier in some of her husband's writing.

The memoirs are primary sources of value. They paint a rich picture of the tumultuous days leading up to the Russian Revolution of 1917, the revolution itself, the several years following that include the Civil War, and the Globachevs' evacuation to Constantinople.

Both of their memoirs end with their departure from Constantinople to the United States; however, both are supplemented by the recollections of their daughter, Lydia Konstantinovna Marinich, who was the mother of the translator of this manuscript, and her recollections include the family's life in the United States in the late 1920s, their life in Paris between 1930 and 1934, and again their life in the United States in the late 1930s and up to Globachev's death in 1941. Her information is purely anecdotal; its value lies in the fact that she lived through what is described here. Lydia Konstantinovna died in 1997 at the age of ninety-six. Having been born in 1901, she was already in her late teens when the February and October Revolutions erupted, and the subsequent Civil War broke out. Her memories, as I have incorporated them into this manuscript on Globachev's life, are perhaps the last live-witness accounts to these events. That other witnesses to the events described are alive today is highly unlikely.

In addition to the memoirs, four letters have survived that constitute correspondence from Globachev to his wife in 1919. These letters are from Kostia (the diminutive of Konstantin) to his wife Sonia (the diminutive of Sofia). It was difficult for the two to maintain communication since Globachev was moving from one place to another, often with no postal system to speak of. He had to send his letters to Sonia via friends who might be going to where Sonia and the children were staying. The content and tone of the letters range from political assessment of the situation to Kostia's seeking employment in an environment that was not friendly to ex-gendarme officers, and to the cost of everyday items such as clothing and food. Sonia kept Kostia's surviving four letters to his loving wife for the rest of her life. These letters have been incorporated into his memoirs, as they fit chronologically, as part of his narrative.

A few words about words and dates. All of the dates that Globachev refers to correspond to what is called the Old Style, Julian calendar. The dates used once the family is in the United States, and then later in Paris and back to the States, are Gregorian calendar dates.

I have used the accepted method of spelling Russian last names as one finds them in nearly all the history books—for example, Uritskii rather than Uritsky, which is the older spelling. In a few instances, however, I continue to spell the name of a major player of the February Revolution—Alexander Kerensky—with a "y" rather than "ii." This is because most people would probably recognize his name spelled this way. The books Kerensky wrote show his name spelled that way, and he himself spelled his name in English with a "y."

The agency for which Globachev was the chief between 1915 and 1917 had the official name of "Bureau for the Public Security, Safety, and Order in Petrograd." There were two other such major offices in the Empire, one in Moscow and the other in Warsaw. Different authors have translated this lengthy title to "Political Police" or "Secret Police," and sometimes have added "Department." I have chosen to refer to these offices as "Security Bureaus" and, in a few places, I use the term Okhrana Bureau, or just Okhrana, in order give the reader the Russian word that is found in so many English-language writings. I use "Bureau" to be clear that this was not the Department of Police, which had supervisory authority over these bureaus. In addition, these Security Bureaus had a connection to the city administration where they operated.

Russian cities had administrative heads called *Gradonachal'nik*. In most cases this person was a military man, a general officer. Again, various authors have translated this title in different ways, which can be confusing. Some use the title "Commandant," "Mayor," "City Governor," or "Urban Prefect," and there are probably others. I have chosen to use the term City Prefect, if for no other reason than this: the *Gradonachal'nik* was not the commander of a military district, nor was he an elected mayor, nor was he a Governor, because there is a very exact title, *Gubernator,* for Governor. "City Prefect" seems slightly less confusing than the other terms. The use of the term is not original with me. Sir Bernard Pares, a highly respected historian in the early part of the twentieth century, used the term in his book, *The Fall of the Russian Monarchy.* One final word—literally one word. When Globachev describes the efforts of his organization in fighting the activities of revolutionaries, he speaks of "liquidating" them. Today, probably because we know more about modern authoritarian regimes and their clandestine operations, the word "liquidate" tends to be associated with murder or assassination. Globachev's efforts were to neutralize revolutionary organizations through detentions and arrests.

Globachev's and his wife's memoirs are primary sources, of course. Much of the biographical information (especially his) comes from his military record that is on file at the GARF, and from various letters, visa applications, passports, and letters that are part of his family's archives. An important part of the personal side of the Globachevs comes from their daughter's recollection of her experiences and years of discussion with her parents, much of which she passed on to me over the years.

The book's introduction has been written by two scholars expert in the history of Tsarist political investigative agencies. Dr. Zinaida Ivanovna Peregudova is an emeritus scholar of the Government Archives of the Russian Federation. Dr. Jonathan Daly is Professor of History at the University of Illinois at Chicago. What follows Peregudova's and Daly's introduction is Globachev's overview (in his own words) about his reasons for writing his memoirs. After that, we have the early life of the Globachevs. This gives the reader a sense of who the Globachevs were before Konstatntin Globachev became a more major figure in security operations, and certainly before they were both caught up in the revolution and civil war. What then follows are the alternating recollections of the Globachevs, with occasional background information I have added to give a clearer picture of what was going on. Finally, there is an epilogue, written by me, which continues the Globachevs' story from the time their memoirs end to the remainder of their lives.

Translator's Acknowledgments

It is now time to thank people. A number of years ago I was involved in research in the area of Ancient Russian history that required my being able to access some rare books that could be found only in the New York Public Library and the Library of Congress. This required me to spend entire weekends in New York and Washington, DC. During this time, Ginny Marinich encouraged me to continue my research. I finished the project, and that put me on the road that led to a fulfilling career as a college teacher. I extend my gratitude to Ginny.

My brother, Oleg, was helpful in locating photos from the family's quite old albums, and making sure that I got them in the best shape possible.

A number of people have made this book possible. I've already mentioned Jonathan Daly and Zinaida Ivanovna Peregudova. But I have more to say about them. Dr. Daly was a major impetus in getting me started on this project. You will recall my mentioning his phone call. He was also kind enough, as our acquaintanceship developed, to share information with me—and he had a lot of information because he was researching and writing his book, *The Watchful State*. He got the ball rolling. I owe him many thanks. He put me in touch with Dr. Peregudova. And what a great help she was. She is a superb scholar and a wonderful person. Over the years, we exchanged information, and I certainly got the better of the deal. When I visited the GARF, she not only gave me access to materials, but before my arrival she located filed materials for me so I would not have to rummage around. So, to dear Zinaida Ivanovna I offer my sincerest respect and admiration.

Dr. Richard Robbins, a highly respected scholar of Russian history was very helpful in communicating with me about my project and some of the challenges of dealing with memoirs and issues of translation. As a result of these chats, I thought of interleaving the two memoirs so that readers could get the perspectives of both Globachev and his wife.

Some of the Russian language documents I had to deal with were faded, typed with overstrikes, or handwritten with all the problems that a reader has with someone else's penmanship. Fortunately, some of my Russian friends were able to help me considerably. Inna and Alexander Adamovich did a lot of deciphering of written materials. This was no small matter, as some of the letters and documents were over a hundred years old, written in the old orthography, and faded. But they were so helpful, so happy to do it. My young friend Mila Hanauer was always willing to give me a hand. Her knowledge of translation, especially of technical and official types of documents, was really useful. We occasionally spent time discussing the meaning of a particular word that could change the point of a sentence. She was so helpful.

Thank you, my friends. This book has a part of you in it.

My thanks to "Royal Russia" for allowing me to use the photos of Tsar Nicholas in Nizhni Novgorod. Elodie Nowodazkij was very encouraging in my efforts. Carolyn Males gave me good advice on preparing the manuscript. Lorna Mattern put me in touch with Carolyn, and encouraged me. Thanks to you all.

Tania Chebotareff, the Curator of the Bakhmeteff Archives, allowed me access to read the memoirs of General Shatilov. It was a very delicate document that had to be handled with great care. This was a valuable source for me, and I'm grateful for the opportunity to have had access to it.

My thanks to the folks at SUNY Press for their advice, keeping me on task, and the care with which they were able to shape the book. Thanks to Ryan Morris, Rafael Chaiken, and John Wentworth whose editing with all those Russian names and terms must have been quite a chore.

My family encouraged me all along the way. They are my Harrigan, Lamb, Livieratos, Marinich, and Yardley clans. I thank you and love you all.

My wife Barbara is, and was, my Muse. Her observations, questions, suggestions, and organizational ability were valuable in every way. The responsibility for the translation and my commentaries are mine, but Barbara kept me focused on accuracy, style, and the integration of the two memoirs. Barbara kept me going. Without her this book would not have been written.

Introduction

ZINAIDA I. PEREGUDOVA AND JONATHAN DALY

"The Truth of the Russian Revolution"—this is the title of the memoirs of the last Chief of the Petrograd Security Bureau, Konstantin Ivanovich Globachev. He was one of the first representatives of the political police who began to describe the events of those years, while "the trail was still hot," and he finished his account in one year (1922) with the possibility of having them published. Evidently, he was also pushed to writing his memoirs by the prevailing conditions that he found himself in—those conversations and arguments among the emigrants who blamed each other for what happened in February 1917. The publication of A. A. Blok's "The Last Days of the Old Regime" in 1919, reprinted by G. V. Gessen in an edition of "The Archive of the Russian Revolution," might have also inspired Globachev to put pen to paper. Blok had participated in the work of the Extraordinary Investigative Commission of the Provisional Government and "investigated the activities of former ministers and other responsible persons; thus Blok had access to archival documents of the last days of the Russian Empire, and he attended the interrogation of ministers and heads of the political police. In his book, Blok repeatedly cites Globachev's reports to the Minister of the Interior and the Department of Police, in which Globachev reports on the mood in the capital and the necessity to take firm action against the growing revolutionary movement.

Globachev comments on his motives to take up the pen. He writes, "I must state that I had absolutely no intention of setting forth a history of the Russian revolution in making these memoirs available to the public nor to examine in any broad terms the reasons behind this pernicious event,—this is too complex a task at the present time and will be the lot of a future dispassionate historian. I only wanted to present this information, which with other material might serve in the drafting of such a history." He continues somewhat later: "As someone who was close to senior government officials and, by the nature of my work having direct contact with various sectors of the population, I was able to communicate with various people, observe and note that which might escape the attention of an ordinary citizen or a person of little experience in internal political affairs."

Globachev's memoirs are interesting from several perspectives. These are the writings of an official who observed directly the growing wave of revolutionary activity, a testimony of the head of an organization that was called upon to fight against opposition movements. He knew well the mood of every element of Russian society, understood that the empire was collapsing, and tried to use all his authority to oppose these forces. Globachev's sharp sense of the oncoming danger can be seen in his reports and in the documents filed in the Department of Police.

No less important is the information he brings forth about the structure of the Security Bureau, the number of its staff, and the activities on the eve of the revolution. From this perspective, his memoirs about Russia's internal politics, the history of its governmental institutions, and political investigations are beneficial to researchers and general readers alike. The significance of this work is even greater because scholars of the history of the Petrograd Security Bureau have access to precious few documents that survived February 1917.

At present, the document files of the Petrograd Security Bureau are preserved in the Government Archives of the Russian Federation (GARF), and they number about 6,058, the major part of which are the daily logs of the surveillance over individuals of opposition leanings, but they also regard the security of highly placed persons and buildings; documents related to investigative service (the status of the central investigative detachment, programs and schedules of the investigators, their itinerary and missions), and other materials pertaining to the Security Command.

The activities of the chancellery, through which basic documents passed during the years (1866–1894) have not survived; for the later years there are, at least, documents concerning departmental matters. The scale of lost materials can be evaluated through comparison to the number of files held at the Moscow Security Bureau, which was established fifteen years after the Petrograd Bureau. The Moscow Bureau was subjected to the same fate at that time. Numerous files of the Moscow Bureau were also destroyed, but 51,226 files survived

If data existed that caused employees of the Petrograd Security Bureau to participate in destroying their own files, neither the archival sources nor Globachev's memoirs indicate that this occurred. But, since there was a secret directive about destroying top-secret files in the event of the possibility that revolutionaries seized political investigative organizations, especially those related to secret agents, those files were to be destroyed by officials themselves.

Some researchers consider that the Security Bureau was burned down by a mob sympathetic to the revolution with the help of representatives of the Department of Police.

Materials from the secret agents' department have not survived at all. However, their absence is filled in to a certain extent by the reports of the Security Bureau to the Department of Police, which are on file in the archives.

In this connection, debate springs up frequently among historians regarding G. E. Rasputin's personality and surveillance over him, which deserves mention because Globachev's memoirs devote a short chapter to Rasputin. The author presents his point of view on Rasputin's personality and his relationship to the royal family. "Rasputin's influence on the empress [in Globachev's view] was exclusively based on her faith in Rasputin as the intercessor and guardian of the precious health of her son, the heir to the throne. . . ."

It is very likely that Globachev knew of Rasputin's behavior and influence better than anyone else. Globachev notes, "his relationship to members of the royal family, even during his wildest debauchery, was very correct. . . ."

Globachev was neither a friend nor an enemy of Rasputin; rather, Globachev was directly responsible for Rasputin's security and at the same time for surveillance over him. A good number of logs on the external surveillance of Rasputin between 1906 and 1916 have been preserved, and are now in the GARF. Code names for Rasputin were "the Russian" and "the dark one." The peculiarity of these logs is that they are typed copies of the surveillance logs. The original handwritten logs have not been found. Thus, some maintain that the typed logs are a forgery. Some researchers believe there never was surveillance of Rasputin—it was all fabrication by the police. Do the memoirs bring anything new to this issue?

Globachev was an unequivocal witness of the systematic shadowing of Rasputin conducted by the Petrograd Security Bureau. This is confirmed by the testimony of other representatives of political investigative agencies, including the Director of the Department of Police and the Deputy Interior Minister, S. P. Beletskii, in testimony to the Extraordinary Investigative Commission of the Provisional Government in 1917. As Globachev writes, the Minister received reports on the surveillance of Rasputin practically every day that included a list of people whom Rasputin visited and met. It stands to reason that the Minister did not get handwritten reports of the surveillants, who were generally semiliterate; rather, he received typed copies. The documents that are preserved in the archives are secondary and tertiary copies of the logs that were sent to the Minister. Similar typed copies regarding the surveillance of S. Yu. Witte are preserved in the archives.

An important supplement to K. I. Globachev's memoirs are those written by his wife Sofia Nikolaevna Globacheva (*née* Popova), entitled "Prelude to

Events that are now Happening in the World." This was a woman of strong character, devoted to her husband and children, who exerted all her strength and strove to stand her own ground during the difficult time of the revolution, the Civil War, and emigration. Never losing hope, she undertook desperate measures to free her husband who had been arrested by the Provisional Government. She succeeded in getting meetings with Minister A. F. Kerensky and P. N. Pereverzev, who was in charge of such matters. She continued her struggle when her arrested husband was in the hands of the Cheka.[1]

Introduction to My Memoirs

General Globachev

I must state that I had absolutely no intention of setting forth a history of the Russian Revolution in making these memoirs available to the public, nor to examine in any broad terms the reasons behind this pernicious event. This is too complex a task at the present time and will be the lot of a future dispassionate historian. I only wanted to present this information, which with other material might serve in the drafting of such a history.

As someone who was close to senior government officials, and by the nature of my work having direct contact with various sectors of the population, I was able to communicate with various people, and to observe and note that which might escape the attention of an ordinary citizen or a person of little experience in internal political affairs. Many minor items have slipped from my memory because years have passed since the time that these events took place, but everything that deals with the characteristics of political figures and the character and meaning of events themselves have remained fresh in my memory. I greatly regret that there is much for which I cannot offer documented evidence, because all records of the Security Bureau, as well as my personal belongings, were either burned, pillaged, or fell into the hands of the new revolutionary authorities during the early days of the riots.

Over a two-year period I was witness to the preparation of the riots against the sovereign power, unstoppable by anyone, bringing Russia to unprecedented shock and destruction. I use the word "riot" and not "revolution" because the Russian populace had not yet "ripened" for revolution and because the masses, in general, did not participate in the overthrow. In fact, what is essential to the very essence of revolution is an idea. If we look at history, we will see that revolutions take place under the influence of some sort of idea taking hold of the breadth of the populace. For the most part, these ideas are patriotic-nationalistic. Was there an idea among the leadership of the Russian Revolution? There was, if we can call ambition and self-interest of the leaders—whose sole purpose was to grab power, at whatever cost—an idea.

Russia was engaged in a colossal war. It would seem that for its successful conclusion it would have been necessary to exert all of its strength, forgetting all of one's personal interests and bringing everything in sacrifice to the fatherland, remembering that, before all else, it was necessary to win the war, and only afterward to be occupied with domestic matters. Meanwhile what did the cream of the crop of our intelligentsia do? With the very first military misfortune, it tried to undermine the people's faith in sovereign authority and the government. Not only that, but it tried to lower the prestige of the bearer of sovereign authority in the eyes of the masses, accusing him from a platform of People's Representatives, now of government betrayal, now of immoral dissolution. The State Duma—the representative organ of the nation—became an agitating tribunal revolutionizing the nation. These People's Representatives, to whom all of Russia listened, decided without considering the consequences to incite the masses on the eve of the turning point of military fortunes on the front, exclusively for the purpose of satisfying their own ambitions. Was there a patriotic idea here? On the contrary, the essence of all the activities of these people was betrayal of the government. History has no examples of a similar betrayal. All of the activity of the Socialists and Bolsheviks that followed in the dismantling of Russia was only the logical aftermath of the betrayal by those traitors who planned the overthrow, and the last of these is less to blame than the first. They were right in their own way; they wanted to transform the government and the social order in Russia according to their program, which was the ultimate goal of their many years of work and dreams, cherished by every kind of socialist. This was the realization of their ideology.

The Russian intelligentsia should have learned from other governments that were involved in the war, where notwithstanding their difficult ordeals and class struggles, they closed ranks behind their governments and forgot their domestic feuds, and all personal interests were sacrificed for the common good where everything was risked to achieve one cherished goal—defeat of the enemy. Everybody worked in the name of a national idea. In Russia they worked to the advantage of the enemy, trying as much as possible to pull down the army and tear down the powerful monarchy. If the Central Powers presented a united front against Russia, they had an ally among the leaders of the intelligentsia who constituted a united domestic front to besiege our army's rear. The work of this internal enemy was carried out methodically over a two-year period, taking advantage of every misfortune, every mistake, and every event or occurrence at this time.

Special organizations were created that were supposedly subsidiary governmental agencies whose purpose was the successful conduct of the war, but in reality their intentions were solely to eat away at the government and army from inside. Even in establishments in the capital, they tried to foment discontent and opposition to the established order. Everything was used: false rumors, libel in the newspapers, the tough economic times, influence on the working masses, underground revolutionary movements, discord among government officials, personal intrigues, and other tactics. In short, everything was set in motion to create a revolutionary atmosphere so that there would not be a single defender of the old order once the banner of the revolutionary center was raised. The government, in its weakness, unwittingly played into the hands of its adversary, unable to bring forth a single individual from among its own who could at least be talented and firm in political action and capable of stopping this evil matter. So, the awful Russian revolution began, and its nightmarish consequences continue to this day, and nobody knows when this will end.

The Russian people often rebelled during Russia's thousand-year history, in each case egged on by traitors who deceived them. Let us recall "The Time of Troubles" and "The Streltsy Uprising," which were brought about by Boyar sedition, "the Stenka Razin insurrection," "Pugachev's Rebellion," and the Decembrist revolt. In all these instances, traitors to Russia deceived the masses. Relatively recently, in 1902, during the agrarian disturbances in Ukraine, agents of revolutionary committees incited peasants against landowners by spreading false rumors of a supposed royal decree that allowed peasants to take the land and property from landowners—and the peasants believed this. This serves to demonstrate that the Russian people were capable of insurrection, but not revolution. It was the same in the 1917 revolution; the people were deceived by the alleged oncoming famine; they shouted, "Give us bread," but nobody cried out "down with Nicholas" or "down with the Tsar." Did Rodzianko or Alekseev inform the Tsar of this? I do not know, but I think not. In addition, if the Tsar had abdicated and someone had been found who was capable of suppressing the February nightmare, nobody would have called it a revolution, but simply an insurrection of the Petrograd garrison.

We could more easily call the events of 1905, after the unfortunate war with Japan, a revolution rather than an uprising. This revolution was caused by extremists who used displeasure with the war's misfortunes as the foundation of a national idea that the monarchy had lost its prestige as a great power. In the defense of national interests, a new power needed to emerge—a national power capable of restoring Russia's former greatness and giving the country a new order that would provide a robust national life instead of an incompetent outmoded monarchy. Thus, the revolution of 1905 moved and grew under the banners that were founded on national patriotism.

I will not stick to a chronological order in my memoirs, but I will pause on those events, occurrences, and individuals that stand out as phases in the preparation of the February uprising of 1917, the prior two years, and the subsequent development of the Russian Revolution.

2

The Globachevs' Early Years

Vladimir G. Marinich

Konstantin Ivanovich Globachev was born on April 24, 1870. The world was an active place. Alexander II, the Tsar Emperor of Russia, was in his fifteenth year of reign, had initiated major reforms in Russia, and several years earlier had sold Alaska to the United States. Elsewhere, Bismarck had unified the German states into one empire, and Cavour and Garibaldi had unified Italy. Across the Atlantic, Ulysses S. Grant was President of the United States, and the country was in its fifth year of the Reconstruction Era following the Civil War. Konstantin was born in the Ekaterinoslav Province of Russia, where his family had recently been awarded hereditary nobility.

Globachev's father, Ivan Ivanovich Globachev, was born in the Ekaterinoslav Province in 1835. The major city of that province was Ekaterinoslav, now known as Dnepropetrovsk; then as now it was a major industrial and transportation center on the Dnieper River. Ivan Ivanovich's career included several years in the army, from which he resigned with the rank of Staff Captain, before entering into a career in police work as a local police superintendent of the Fourth Precinct of the Sokolskii District of the Grodno Province. By 1860 he had become the Chief of Police of the province, a rank equivalent to that of a lieutenant colonel, and who reported directly to the provincial governor.[1]

In 1869 Ivan Ivanovich was given a significant award. His family name was entered into the registry of hereditary nobility. This type of award did not bestow property or title to the recipient, but it did raise the family socially and helped to open doors of education and job positions to the family. Ivan Ivanovich died in 1876 at the age of forty-one as a result of an infection that developed in his foot. Konstantin was six years old when his father died and, throughout his life, Konstantin disliked the scent of hyacinths because it reminded him of his father's funeral.

5

FIGURE 2.1. Konstantin Globachev, about ten years old. Marinich collection.

Konstantin had two brothers, Nicholas and Vladimir. Vladimir was the oldest of the three. Nicholas was next, and Konstantin was the youngest. Their mother remarried a man whose last name was Axenov, who had two or three sons by a previous marriage. One of these sons was named Leonid, and he became a physician.

Konstantin attended secondary school at the Polotz Cadet Corps and then the First Military Academy of Paul. He graduated in 1890 and was commissioned as a junior lieutenant in the Keksholm Life Guards Regiment, which was stationed in Warsaw. Warsaw was a major city, and since the eastern part of Poland was part of the Russian Empire, Russian regiments were stationed throughout. Globachev's higher education continued in the General Staff Academy of Nicholas in St. Petersburg, after which he returned to his regiment. His two brothers were also officers in the Keksholm Regiment, and all three were known throughout the regiment as Vladimir "the happy Globachev" (веселый Глобачев), Nicholas, "the talkative Globachev" (болтливый Глобачев), and Konstantin "the handsome Globachev" (красивый Глобачев). The two older brothers continued in military careers. Vladimir became a colonel and a Politz-

FIGURE 2.2. Globachev as a Junior Lieutenant. Marinich collection.

FIGURE 2.3. Nikolai Korneleevich Popov. Marinich collection.

meister (police chief) of a district in Petrograd. He died in Finland after the Revolution. Nicholas attained the rank of major general and was commander of the Novogeorgievsk Fortress during World War I. He was arrested in Russia after World War II and died in Siberia.

It was during his regimental tour of duty in Warsaw that Konstantin met and married Sofia Nikolaevna Popova. Sofia Nikolaevna Popova was born in Warsaw in 1875. She was the daughter of Nikolai Korneleevich Popov, who was a Councilor of State for Peasant Affairs (Destvitelnyi Statskii Sovetnik).

Sofia's parents may have died when she and her siblings were not yet adults. Sofia's daughter Lydia stated that a guardian raised Sofia and her brothers and sisters. Sofia had three brothers and two sisters. The brothers were Michael, Nicholas, and Vladimir, and the sisters were Olga and Maria. They all received a good education. Sofia became fluent in French, German, and

FIGURE 2.4. Sofia, circa 1898. Marinich collection.

FIGURE 2.5. The newlywed Globachevs, 1898. Marinich collection.

Polish, in addition to her first language, Russian. She was also an excellent piano player. Sofia and Globachev met in Warsaw and were married there on January 9, 1898. He was twenty-seven years old, and she was twenty-two. They had three children: Sergei, who was born around 1900 and died around 1902 or 1903 from typhoid fever; Lydia, who was born October 21, 1901, and Nicholas, born in 1903.

Sofia's brother, Nicholas, was a colonel and regimental commander of the Brest Infantry Regiment during World War I, and had seen action in the Russo-Japanese War. Following the 1917 Revolution, Nicholas and his family became separated, and he wound up either in Latvia or Lithuania. The night before he was to be reunited with his wife and daughters, Tamara and Alla, he died of a heart attack.

Sofia's brother Michael was in the army and served most of his career in the east, possibly near the Chinese border. He was married to a German

FIGURE 2.6. Globachev as Staff Captain. Marinich collection.

woman by the name of Anna, and they had a son, Boris, and three daughters, Olga, Tatiana, and Vera, the youngest. The third brother, Vladimir, was an artillery officer stationed in Riga during the war. He and his wife, known as "Aunt Musia," had three children: Olga, Nina, and Alexander. According to Konstantin's daughter, Vladimir died of a heart attack during the Revolution when he was about thirty-six years old.

In her memoirs, Sofia states that one of her brothers (she does not mention his name, but it must have been Michael) was captured and shot by the Bolsheviks during the Civil War.

In 1903 Globachev transferred out of the regiment and into the Special Corps of Gendarmes with the rank of captain, and was appointed adjutant of the Peterhof Provincial Gendarme Administration. In 1904 he was transferred to Bialystok (Poland) as chief of the Security Bureau. His wife, Sofia, wrote that Bialystok had an active revolutionary movement, including instances of government officials being assassinated. She wrote, "I could not guarantee from one day to the next that my husband would not be murdered by revolutionaries."

In 1905 Globachev was appointed head of the Lodz Gendarme Administration, and in 1906 he was promoted to the rank of lieutenant colonel.

3
———

Our Years in Poland

SOFIA GLOBACHEVA

Globachev was assigned to Bialystok as the war between Russia and Japan began in 1904. The war ended the following year with President Theodore Roosevelt mediating a peace agreement between the two warring countries. For his efforts, Roosevelt would get the Nobel Peace Prize in 1906.

I will begin with the year 1904, when my husband was assigned to the city of Bialystok, in Poland, where a large part of the population was Jewish. When the revolutionaries appeared on the scene, which expressed itself in the constant killing of officials, the government established a small security bureau in Bialystok and put my husband in charge. He was still a very young man, having finished the General Staff Academy, and only a year before he had transferred from the Keksholm Life Guard regiment, where he was everyone's favorite, officers as well as soldiers.

He was now part of the Ministry of the Interior, and it was with our arrival in Bialystok that my life became anxiety-ridden and tormented, since not a day went by that I could not be sure that my husband might not be killed by the revolutionaries. Several of the many killings in Bialystok involved not only officials, but also common soldiers; these somehow are especially etched in my memory. I remember how, for no reason, an orderly who was coming home from the bazaar was killed by a revolutionary who had sneaked up behind him. I remember how a company of soldiers was returning to their barracks from lessons, and they were singing. All of a sudden, there was a burst of revolver fire and a bomb was thrown by a group of young Jews. Several soldiers were wounded, and the company of soldiers returned fire. The city fell silent. Searches began of the houses where the revolutionaries who did the shooting were hiding. The gunfire was continuous, both from the soldiers

11

FIGURE 3.1. A commercial street in Byalystok. Wikimedia Commons.

and the revolutionaries, shooting from windows. In Bialystok, many houses, especially those in the Jewish neighborhood, had windows in the front and back, so bullets also hit innocent passers-by and people sitting in front of their homes, even people far from the shooting itself.

Because of this, several old people, women and children, two military clerks, and several innocent residents were killed. Whether the soldiers' or the revolutionaries' bullets killed them was not known, but the revolutionaries immediately took advantage of these accidental killings by shouting that the government was killing old people, women, and children.

My husband was at the scene together with other officials. I couldn't stay calmly at home, and so along with one of my friends I took a streetcar that ran along the main street to find out exactly what was happening. Jewish shopkeepers who knew me personally came up to the streetcar and insisted that I return home before a stray bullet killed me. I had to acquiesce and go through those awful hours at home until my husband returned. The burial of the innocent victims of the shooting was a frightening sight. Thus began a whole series of killings of officials by shootings and bombings, ending with a pogrom caused by the revolutionary provocateurs who stated, "The worse; the better."

It was my good fortune that by this time we were no longer in Bialystok. All of the officials who were there, including military, were sentenced to death by the revolutionaries, who started to send their terrorists to those cities where these people were located, and all were killed, although at different times. My husband later received word that they came to the city of Lodz, where my husband had been transferred, with the intention of killing him, but discovering from their own sources that during the time of the Pogrom he had already been in Lodz, they abandoned this idea for the time being.

We were in Bialystok only one year. Before our departure I experienced a terrible night, but it ended all right and even with a little humor. My husband received word that an important terrorist had arrived in Bialystok to prepare bombs. Since carrying out the arrest of this terrorist was very dangerous, my husband himself, with police personnel designated for this, went to supervise this arrest, which was above and beyond his area of responsibility. Having entered this terrorist's apartment, the police threw themselves headlong at him and seized the already-made bomb from him, which he held in his hands to throw at his attackers, and of course, killing himself in the process.

I couldn't close my eyes all night, knowing the kind of danger that my husband was heading for. Toward morning I was very exhausted from emotion and worry, and I dozed off for a minute. I awoke in terror, still drowsy because I heard some kind of crying. To my great joy I saw my husband alive and unharmed standing beside my bed in his overcoat. He took a squealing puppy, only a few days old, from out of his sleeve. Apparently, as he was returning home, he heard some sort of squealing and saw a puppy shivering from the cold. He put the puppy into the sleeve of his coat to warm it and brought it home. This rescued puppy turned into a most beautiful dog.

From Bialystok my husband was assigned as Chief of the Gendarme Administration in Lodz, where mass strikes and killings had begun at that time. Not a day went by that someone wasn't killed. When our nanny was taking our children for their walk, I strictly ordered her not to leave immediately after my husband or his staff and to keep away from any oncoming government officials at whom bombs might be thrown from around a corner. No government officials went outside without being surrounded on all four sides by soldiers with rifles, but despite these precautions many were killed, and not only the chiefs, but also those of lower rank. One of my husband's aides perished in a horrible manner. This man left his house at the same time every day and, surrounded by his soldiers, went to work.

The revolutionaries had been informed of his schedule and his route and waited for them. When he and his soldiers came to the street corner they suddenly heard a distracting shot from the rear, and when they all turned around, young revolutionaries sprang out from both corners of the street in

FIGURE 3.2. Petrovskii Avenue in Lodz. Postcard.

front of them and dropped them all where they stood and then fired ten more bullets into the fallen, already-dead officer. This sort of terror lasted for quite a while. The Jewish owner of a large factory came to negotiate with the strikers. They seized him, tied him up, beat him, and tortured him for three days, giving him nothing to eat or drink. It was only after this incident that the residents of the city cried out in panic and begged for strong rule. It was then that General Kaznakov was appointed to replace the previous temporary governor general, a weak and indecisive man.

Kaznakov arrested the perpetrators and turned them over to the military field court, which sentenced ten people to the firing squad. Among those sentenced was a woman who was the chief instigator. Those condemned did not believe the sentence. Sitting in prison they mocked the Catholic priest, who had come to prepare them for the court-ruled death sentence, saying, "They wouldn't dare." However, when they were brought to the woods to the place of execution and they saw ten dug-out graves, they started to shout, cry, and beg for mercy. After this, the strikes ended and killings occurred only infrequently.[1]

The revolutionaries constantly spread all sort of absurd rumors to stir up the public. One time a rumor was spread that a pogrom was being planned. A Jewish shopkeeper living in a house next to ours came to me with a request to allow him, his wife, and six children to take shelter in our kitchen in the event of a pogrom. I tried to prove to him that the authorities would tolerate no pogrom and that he could be absolutely unworried, but he didn't calm down until such time as I promised him that in the event of a pogrom, which of course would never happen, he could locate himself and his entire family in our apartment, in the servants' quarters. The fact that the Jew sought asylum in our apartment clearly shows that the residents did not believe that the authorities organized them, as the revolutionaries kept shouting.

This is the environment we lived in, surrounded by soldiers with rifles whenever we left the house, but somehow we got used to this and didn't even notice it. Friends who came to visit us from Warsaw were amazed at how we could tolerate such a stressful life, but apparently people get used to even the very worst and, however strange it may seem, the four years spent in Lodz remained as the very best of my memories, notwithstanding all that we had to

FIGURE 3.3. Lieutenant Colonel Globachev. Marinich collection.

experience there. I think this was because the residents and the factory workers, who were for the most part Jews, as well as the civil and military authorities who were quartered there treated us with great sympathy and good will. I cannot neglect to mention the then–city president of Lodz, a Pole, who was the head of the town council of Pinsk (in Poland, the head of the city council was called the city president). This was a man of exceptional honesty and deeply loyal to the Tsar and to Russia. Whenever he or someone else present spoke of the royal family, he faithfully stood up and remained standing respectfully for as long as the speech lasted.

The city of Lodz, with a population of half a million, represented the largest industrial city in Poland. Approaching the city, one could see from several kilometers away a huge cloud of thick, black smoke permeating the city, and old-time residents assured us that perhaps because of this smoke in Lodz the city never had any epidemics—even when all of Poland was ravaged by cholera, Lodz escaped it. Spending the summer in such a smoke-filled city was impossible, and anyone with children tried to get away somewhere. In this context, Spala represented a wonderful place. This was the summer residence of the Tsar, where he often came with his family to rest and to do some hunting. The palace stood in a huge pine and oak forest. In the forest one could find herds of deer, wild boar, and pheasant. Mangers were built throughout the forest containing hay for the deer. There were also high platforms from which boar were shot during the Tsar's hunts.

The palace stood near the access road that went through the whole forest. This was a not–too-large two-story building with only a few modestly furnished rooms. The main decoration in the rooms and entry was the walls that were adorned floor to ceiling with deer antlers of all sizes and huge boars' tusks of the deer and boars that were killed by the Tsar, Grand Dukes, and dignitaries from abroad who were guests of the Tsar in Spala. Beneath each pair of horns was a silver plaque with the name of the hunter and the date of the kill; similar plaques were beneath the boars' tusks. Some of the antlers were so big and wide that it seemed impossible that such a tree could grow out of a deer's head and that they could so easily carry such a weight.

Surrounding the palace were additions that housed the retinue and servants accompanying the royal family and stables and barracks for the resident squadron of Dragoons. Within half a kilometer of the palace lived a small landowner, a Pole, who built several cottages on a hill in the forest, which he rented out. So each summer I went with the children, along with our old German nanny and a servant, to one of these cottages. Russians living in Lodz also occupied the other cottages. And if it were not for my constant worry about my husband, who stayed back in the unstable city of Lodz, a nicer and more calming place would be hard to find. There were children from one to five years old who made friends with each other and played happily under the supervision of my old nanny. We adults did not stay with them but greatly diverted ourselves with such games as Lapta (akin to American Baseball), bowling, and the like. I frequently rode my bicycle along trails, deep into the woods. Often I had to stop when I heard the thumping sound of many hoofs and a huge herd of deer would rush past me—a breathtaking and captivating sight.

A few minutes' walk from the cottages, a fairly wide river, the Drventsa, flowed; it was a tributary of the Vistula, where twice a day adults as well as children went to bathe. Sometimes, two or three deer would gaze at us bathers, in amazement, from the opposite bank of the river. On moonlit nights we adults would go to the river to bathe, and our singing would carry far down the river. Often, at night, wild boars would come to the cottages, leaving the ground dug up all around as a souvenir of their visit.

I remember one episode following our last stay at the cottage in Spala, which nearly cost me my life. There was a squadron of dragoons stationed at the palace as part of the Tsar's security, and the officers became acquainted with us vacationers. Discovering that I loved horseback riding, they promised to bring me a horse so we could go riding together. A day before our scheduled ride they trained the horse to be ridden with a ladies' saddle (side saddle), hanging a sack on the side. I was in a riding habit when the horse was brought

FIGURE 3.4. Sofia Nikolaevna Globacheva, circa 1910. Marinich collection.

to me, and the orderly, having foolishly led her near a deep ravine, sat me on her. Before I could get hold of the pommel, the horse, frightened by my riding habit, started bucking, rearing and stomping her rear legs. No one opted to go near her, and after three or four bucks, she threw me. I found myself beneath her front hoofs, with which she was hovering over my head, trying instinctively not to step on me. Fortunately, she didn't fall together with me into the ravine—that would have been the end of me.

Just as I started to fall, the vacationing children who had come to watch me ride began to laugh loudly. Seeing that the horse had reared and that I had fallen off and was lying on the ground, the children must have thought that I wanted to show them some circus trick. Everyone gave a sigh of relief when I got out from under the horse. I was young and foolish, and in spite of the protests and pleading of the other vacationers, my pride required me to get back on the horse. I did tell the orderly to cover the horse's eyes and walk her down a ways for a few steps. As soon as the horse's eyes were opened, she shot off. I was scared, but little by little my horse calmed down. Since the officers rode slowly in the back and there were no other horses close behind me, everything worked out well.

The most noteworthy individual on the dacha was a Jew by the name of Yankel, who with his uncle, a venerable and honest old man, rented a small house at the foot of a sand hill, where there were dachas, and he opened a shop there. Yankel was a pale, thin youth of about eighteen who was affable, and we all treated him very well, forgiving him all his little deceptions when it came time to pay the bill. In this respect, his uncle's constant lectures on honesty had little effect on him. One had to be amazed at Yankel's endurance and patience. He opened his shop at five in the morning and returned to his nearby residence at ten or eleven at night. Our maid would often forget to buy this or that, having gone to the store in the morning, and then we would be calling Yankel all day long to deliver what was forgotten, and this poor fellow with his friendly face would run up and down the sandy hill in the heat, carrying out the duties of the maid. For his friendliness and tirelessness, we vacationers forgave him when he, having talked us all into buying more chickens and ducks in the already overfilled chicken coop, he rode over on his cart at night and stole them all and sold them to us all over again. As a result of this, the next summer, the landowner didn't want to lease the shop to Yankel. He gave it to a certain Pole, who opened the shop at nine in the morning and went home at two in the afternoon. The maids rioted, and we vacationers declared to the landowner that if he didn't rent Yankel the store next summer, none of us would come to these dachas, and Yankel once more appeared on our horizon.

After four years in Lodz my husband was appointed chief of the Security Bureau (Okhrana) in Warsaw. The temporary governor general, General

Kaznakov, was also leaving for St. Petersburg, to get his next assignment. The city of Lodz organized a joint send-off for the Governor General and my husband, with all of society participating. This lasted for two weeks at one or another city representative's homes. My husband enjoyed great affection and respect among the Christian, as well as the Jewish, population of the city because of his honesty, sense of fairness, and accessibility.

On the eve of the Governor General's departure from Lodz, my husband got word that the revolutionaries had decided not to allow General Kaznakov to leave Lodz alive. They intended to blow up the palace of the factory owner where the Governor General was staying and where he had his office, or to toss a bomb at him as he was leaving. My husband ordered a search to be made of their entire house and cellars, but nothing suspicious was found.

The next morning, my husband left for Warsaw to assume his duties, and I went to escort the Kaznakovs, with whom we were very friendly. As they were seating themselves in the carriage that had arrived, they began to say goodbye to me, but I announced that I would accompany them to the railroad station. It amazed me that they exchanged a glance between themselves, but they said nothing, and we arrived safely at the station, where the whole town had come out to say goodbye. It was only two weeks later, when I was already in Warsaw having breakfast with my husband and the Kaznakovs at the Bristol Inn, that I learned why the Kaznakovs had exchanged glances when I announced that I was going to escort them. Madam Kaznakova took me aside and said to me that she would never forget that I, the mother of two children, knowing that her husband's assassination was being planned, sat with them in the same carriage. In this manner, without suspecting it, I became a heroine.

I was happy to live in Warsaw once again, a city that I knew very well. It was here that I had completed the Alexander-Marinsky Institute and where I had been married. After all, I had lived in Poland almost from birth, and those Poles whom I knew since childhood, both adults and children, with whom we were friendly, treated us very well and amicably, notwithstanding the fact that we were Russians.

Because of this, I have to relate one episode that amazed me. Two years ago I was at the home of a Russian family in New York. I met an intelligent, middle-aged Polish engineer there who, not knowing that I had lived in Poland, began relating how Poland had been under the yoke of Russian domination. He said that the Russians forbade speaking Polish, and for children to be able to learn Polish it was necessary to gather in cellars and drape the windows so that the light of candles would not be seen from the streets. This, he said, was oppression.

Having listened to all this, I asked him whether he had been to Warsaw, and discovering that he had been there from birth and lived there until his

FIGURE 3.5. A major avenue in Warsaw. Warsawtour.pl.

arrival in America, I told him that it seemed very strange to me to hear all this. I said that I had lived in Poland and studied at the Institute and could state that in our Russian Institute of the Empress Maria Feodorovna, located in Warsaw at No. 8 Veiski Street, there were many Polish, Catholic girls, daughters of well-to-do parents, and Polish widows of nobility who attended, and almost all these girls were either on a free account or were supported at the expense of Her Majesty. One third of each class consisted of Polish girls. We Russian girls often were outraged that almost all of them were being educated for free, whereas Russian parents, bureaucrats, and military had to pay for their daughters.

The Institute had three churches: Orthodox, Catholic, and Lutheran. A Russian priest, a Catholic priest, and a Lutheran Pastor taught Bible study twice a week, and each conducted class in his own language. A Mullah also came to instruct the Muslims, of whom there were few. The Catholic priest and the Lutheran Pastor held services in their churches. All Polish holidays were celebrated on a par with Russian holidays, and there were no lessons on those days. Twice a week we had an instructor teaching Polish, as I recall his name was Pan Grzmbowski. The Russian girls would leave the class, and only the Polish girls would remain. I often sneakily remained in the class, and because of this I learned to read and write Polish. Before the start of lessons, two monitors, one Orthodox, the other Catholic, always came to the center of the classroom. They read prayers in Russian and Polish respectively before lessons started and also before lunch. I remember once when, as a joke, I and a Polish girl friend decided to exchange identities. I read the prayer in Polish and she in Russian. The teacher did not notice this until we finished the prayer, at which time she reprimanded us for our inappropriate prank. During Easter, the graduating class did not go home, as was customary, but during the Catholic holy days, we Russians all went to the Catholic church for Mass, and for Russian Easter the Catholic girls all came to our church. Afterward they joined us in the Easter celebratory supper. During Catholic feast days all the Russian officials were present for services at the Catholic cathedral. When the Catholic Archbishop from Vilnius came to Warsaw, and the procession, with all of its images and banners, came down the road, the Governor General and all of the officials marched along. The servants in Russian homes, both male and female, were for the most part Polish. They spoke their own language, and their masters would address them in Polish. How was this oppression?

4

Nizhni Novgorod and Sevastopol

Sofia Globacheva

We spent three years in Warsaw, and in view of the fact that the year 1913 represented the celebration of the 300th anniversary of the Romanov Dynasty, primarily in Nizhni Novgorod, my husband was assigned there as Chief of the Gendarme Administration of the provincial government. [For a fuller account of the reasons for Globachev's transfer, see Appendix C.]

I did not like Nizhni Novgorod. Although it was the main city on the Volga, it was sleepy and boring. The view of the Volga, however, was remarkably

FIGURE 4.1. Colonel Globachev and staff of the Nizhni Novgorod Gendarme Administration. Marinich collection.

beautiful, with loaded barges and huge, grandiose, richly appointed passenger ships scurrying about all the time.

The city came to life during the Fair, which was held on the opposite side of the Volga and seemed to be something from a fairy tale, especially at night when it was awash with lights. Merchants and industrialists gathered here from all over Russia, and deals worth millions were concluded. All the nationalities of Russia brought their finest merchandise and crafts, and there was nothing you couldn't get there. Your eyes would wander all over trying to take it all in; life and merriment was in full swing. Theatres, the most luxurious restaurants, and various forms of entertainment opened during this trade fair.

The Volga River presented a grandiose spectacle during its ice flow. The ice cracked with such a loud noise, as though someone was shooting a cannon, and when it began to move, the ice floe would rise to form high hills that crashed into each other. During the time of such ice flow, communication between the two riverbanks was interrupted. Since the railroad was on the other side of the Volga, the side where the fair was held, passengers who arrived by train had to wait until the ice flow passed—there was no bridge.

One time I was going to Moscow, and as I was leaving, the Volga River was still frozen solid. Returning after several days, having received a telegram that the children had gotten sick, I approached the Volga River and was

FIGURE 4.2. A major avenue in Nizhni Novgorod. englishrussia.com.

FIGURE 4.3. Nizhni Novgorod straddling the Volga. From W. Chapin Huntington, *The Homesick Million* (Boston: The Stratford Company, 1933).

horrified to see that the ice had begun to break. The other passengers in the same train headed off to hotels, since one could not tell how long the ice would flow—sometimes it would take two or three days, and at times a whole week. I was very worried about the children and began to talk boat owners into taking me across to the other bank, that is, to Lower Novgorod. No one would agree to do this, advising me to wait until the ice flow passed and not assume the risk, but my worry was greater than my fear, and I succeeded in convincing a trio of daring boatmen to make the crossing for ten rubles. They sat me in a fairly small boat and got in after me. There, where the water was clear of ice and new ice was fairly far away, we floated, and where the ice still covered the water in a thick layer, the boatmen got out and pulled the boat with me in it onto the ice and dragged it on the ice until we saw water free of ice, and in this manner we made our way to the other shore in two hours. People standing on the shore watched our crossing with horror, although at the time it seemed to me to be nothing very frightening.

The Volga was very dangerous during the periods of the ice flow. Once, I went down to the Volga to order a sturgeon and, upon returning, I stopped a fairly far distance from the river, to look at the ice flow. Suddenly, I heard a fisherman shouting at me to hurry and move further away because an entire huge block of ice was floating in my direction. The cry was so striking that I ran back just in time. I was amazed by the power of this block of ice, which, in a minute sliced off, as with a knife, a huge chunk of the shoreline and both

FIGURE 4.4. Visit to Nizhni Novgorod by Tsar Nicholas and family. Royal Russia.

it and a small house that stood on it floated away. If I had not run away, I would have been carried off as well.

In 1913 Nizhni Novgorod was preparing for a visit by the Tsar's family. Nine ladies were selected from the Nizhni Novgorod society to be presented to Her Majesty, and I was among them. All of the ladies wore white dresses and white hats. I recall one episode during our being presented: Her Majesty's lady-in-waiting, Countess Narishkina, wrote down all of our surnames in the order in which we were to be presented. On the day we were to be presented, one of the ladies took ill and was unable to attend. When it came time for Countess Narishkina to present us, having forgotten to cross out the absent lady's name from the list, she presented each of us by the wrong name. The Director of Government Properties was very upset and disappointed that his wife had been presented to Her Majesty under the wrong name. I calmed him, assuring him that it made no difference by which names we were presented. Her Majesty would not have remembered a single one; she would have had to remember much too much. As we were presented to Her Majesty, we executed a deep curtsy and kissed her hand. The Grand Duchesses were lined in a row with the eldest first and the youngest last. We shook hands with them, and they smiled pleasantly, obviously amused by this whole procedure. The Tsarevich was not there. Her Majesty approached each of us and asked several questions. I could not detect any accent in her Russian speech, about which so many had been critical.

When the Royal Family was leaving, the royal ship was followed immediately by the Tsar's retinue, and half an hour after their departure another ship left in the evening for a brief entertainment cruise with the representative deputies from the Volga cities, industrialists, ship owners, and others. I was on that ship; my husband did not go, because, during those days, he was very exhausted. Everyone was joyous, happily disposed and shared their impressions. The ship was flooded with lights, champagne flowed like rivers, there was

FIGURE 4.5. The Tsar's riverboat. Royal Russia.

huge sturgeon, bowls of caviar, the best fruit from different lands, and other expensive delicacies that were placed on tables in abundance. Our ship was going in the same direction as the Royal ship. When we passed the Sormovski factory, known for its revolutionary leanings, the factory workers, thinking that ours was the Royal ship, lit up sparkling multicolored lights, furiously shouted "Hurrah," and the factory orchestra played "God Save the Tsar" until our ship disappeared from view. There was something astounding in this enthusiastic expression of the workers.

Globachev's tenure as head of the Gendarme Administration in Nizhni Novgorod was only about a year but, as mentioned, 1913 was very active for him, and was significant in several ways. The preparation for the Tsar's tour with his family and the rest of his entire retinue required a lot of work, as did the responsibilities of running a security operation. Things were going well for him in general, but his year in Nizhni Novgorod was not without incident.

Lieutenant Colonel Alexander Pavlovich Martynov was head of the Moscow Okhrana in 1913. He had been appointed to that position in 1912 on the recommendation of the Director of the Department of Police, Stepan Beletskii. In August 1913, Martynov went to Nizhni Novgorod to investigate Globachev's administration because of a report that Martynov received about the questionable activities of one of Globachev's agents. Martynov's report to his superiors in St. Petersburg was apparently very critical of Globachev.[1] *Beletskii, who was Martynov's superior, responded to Martynov's report in November with a seven-page memo to the latter. In his response, Beletskii quoted Martynov's attack on Globachev—"In this entire matter there is a fundamental absence of any control over secret agents . . ." He further recommended that Globachev initiate more effective procedures to deal with agents.*[2] *Beletskii then assessed Globachev's record and concluded that the policies and procedures that Martynov had recommended were in fact in place prior to Martynov's investigation. The Director of Police further criticized Martynov's methods, motivation, and attitude, saying that this unjustified investigation was bad for the department and for Martynov's career.*

On December 13, the Assistant Minister of the Interior, General Dzhunkovskii, who was Beletskii's superior in St. Petersburg, wrote to Martynov and reprimanded him very severely, accusing him of arrogance in attacking a more senior officer who had greater experience than he, being too hasty to judge, and being misleading. Dzunkovskii's final sentence in his communiqué to Martynov expressed his "extreme displeasure in this matter."[3]

Within a year of his appointment to Nizhni Novgorod, Globachev was transferred to be the Head of the Sevastopol Gendarme Administration. His appointment was effective February 1914, but it was another month or so before he actually took charge in Sevastopol. The city was a major commercial and naval port on the Crimean peninsula. Globachev got there just before World War I began.

Sometime after the Romanov celebrations, my husband was assigned to the city of Sevastopol. When World War I broke out, however, he was in St. Petersburg on official business, and rioting had broken out. He was amazed by the instantaneous change in attitude when the Tsar's declaration of war was read to the public. All of the students, all of the workers, who had participated earlier in anti-government demonstrations, overturning a trolley, smashing store windows, and so on, changed in the blink of an eye, national flags appeared from somewhere, and the crowds, enthusiastically singing the hymn "God Save the Tsar," moved about St. Petersburg until late at night.

During the war we were already located in Sevastopol. The Emperor came there to inspect the fortifications and for a while resided in Yalta, where my husband had to make frequent visits because that area was under his jurisdiction. During this time my husband was invited twice to the royal breakfast of only twelve people aboard the "Standart," the Emperor's yacht. The Emperor spoke at length and posed questions, and my husband was amazed by his memory and wonderful education.

FIGURE 4.6. A view of Sevastopol from the sea. Marinich collection.

By August the war had begun, and Sevastopol, being a major port city, would be involved. Two German warships, the battle cruiser Goeben and the light cruiser Breslau, had been patrolling the Mediterranean Sea, and at the outbreak of the war they bombarded ports in Algeria. Chased by British ships, the German cruisers made their way to Constantinople and were transferred to the Ottoman Empire, although still under German command. "On the 28th and 29th of September the German warships under the Turkish flag shelled Odessa, Sevastopol, and Novorossisk."[4]

FIGURE 4.7. The German Battleship Goeben in Constantinople. Wikimedia Commons.

The arrival of the "Goeben," the Turkish warship, in Sevastopol created a terrible impression on me. At dawn my husband was summoned to a military conference by the admiral, who was the fleet commander. Information had been received that the "Goeben" had sailed in the direction of Sevastopol. No sooner had my husband returned home than the most frightening cannonade began; many homes were damaged, two or three ordnance batteries were razed, and those soldiers near the weapons were torn to shreds—what remained was only tatters of clothing and boots. We were afraid that the house where we were living could collapse, as it was located right opposite the bay across which the "Goeben" was firing at ships that were there, which is why we went out onto the street and did not return to our house until the "Goeben" was chased away by Russian shells. After the "Goeben's" departure, a rumor spread throughout the city, upsetting the populace as well as the seamen, that it had hit a minefield and "danced there" as the expression went, for several minutes. The mine officer, however, did not push the button to explode it, thinking it was the transport that was expected from Yalta that accidentally hit the mines.

We were still in Sevastopol when we met the 1915 New Year. About thirty people had been invited to our home to celebrate the New Year. Precisely at midnight, as we were congratulating each other, my husband received a telegram appointing him head of the Okhrana in Petrograd. All of the guests congratulated him on this appointment, but I felt some sort of heaviness on my soul. I didn't want to go to Petrograd, having a premonition of all that we would have to live through there, and I expressed this. The guests tried to convince me that I had no right to try to talk my husband out of this, thereby harming his position, and that in general an appointment cannot be refused. So, we sat until five o'clock in the morning engaged in this conversation. In the evening my husband left for Petrograd. He was escorted by many, and although I still felt very bad from the day before, I went to the train station. Upon returning home, I immediately lay down, and in the morning I was already unconscious: I had developed a very serious case of typhoid fever. A telegram was sent to my husband, who had just arrived in Petrograd, and he, presenting himself to the Minister of the Interior, requested permission to return to Sevastopol. The Minister responded very sympathetically and said that my husband should stay with me until I was fully recovered.

5

Petrograd

Sofia Globacheva

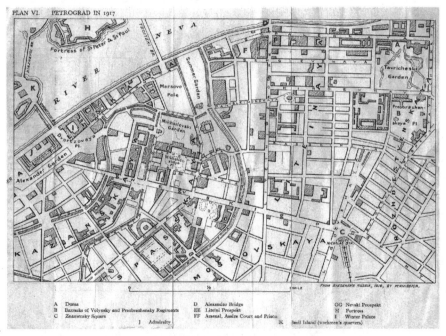

MAP 1. Map of Petrograd. Copied from *Fall of the Russian Monarchy* by Bernard Pares (New York: Alfred A. Knopf, 1939). Map is from Baedeker's *Russia*, 1914.

With our move to Petrograd our life became a real nightmare, with all the emotional upheaval caused by the failure of the war and the growing internal revolutionary mood among the intelligentsia. This was not the case at the front, and officers, arriving on leave, tried to return as quickly as possible from this somber mood of rumors and gossip. Underground organizations were almost inactive thanks to the always-timely measures taken by my husband. On the other hand, the State Duma and intelligentsia tried with all their might, intoxicated on foolish rumors and gossip, to undermine the people's faith and respect for the Tsar's family and authority. The main trump card in their hands for all of this was Rasputin. Society didn't realize that they themselves created Rasputin's power, attributing to him a great, but nonexistent influence over the Tsar's family. If the Tsar did not agree to send him away from Petrograd, this was understandable. If one takes into consideration that only Rasputin, using the power of suggestion, stopped the Tsarevich's bleeding on several occasions, and the Tsaritsa, who adored her son, feared that with Rasputin out of Petrograd the Tsarevich could bleed to death.

I never had occasion to see Rasputin. My husband saw him only once, when at the insistence of the Minister of the Interior he had to go to him to

FIGURE 5.1. Gregory Efimovich Rasputin. Wikimedia Commons.

personally reconcile Rasputin's complaints to Vyrubova regarding the constant presence of security people assigned to him after an attempt on his life by a vengeful peasant woman. These people accompanied Rasputin everywhere he went, even to the Yar (a restaurant with gypsies), where he often went to get drunk, as well as to the baths. In this way, my husband knew his every step. However, the day Rasputin was murdered he tricked the security detail, saying that he was not going anywhere, just going to sleep, and sent them home. Later he drove away with Yussoupov (son of the Moscow Governor General) who came for him for a night of carousing, which ended with his death.

My husband told me that when he arrived at Rasputin's apartment, the latter came out to meet him completely drunk. Clicking his heels, he hugged my husband, led him into the dining room and was continually babbling some incomprehensible nonsense. My husband stayed there for half an hour, and as he was getting ready to leave, Rasputin's daughter entered to inform him that Vyrubova, a lady-in-waiting of the Empress, had arrived. My husband was shocked by the extraordinarily strong will of this person. A moment before he was staggering and couldn't put two words together and, suddenly, with the arrival of Vyrubova, he sobered up immediately, beginning a conversation on religious themes in a serious and steady manner. My husband never saw him alive again, only dead, as my husband was present when they found him, dragged from an ice hole. However many absurd rumors there were, I can present the following fact: one day I had gone to the Marinsky Theatre, and I invited into our loge our friends, a telecommunications engineer and his wife. When the opera was over, we left and, instead of our automobile, an old, small, hand-cranked car pulled up, and sitting behind the wheel was a police chauffeur who always went with Rasputin to Tsarskoe Selo. He reported that since our automobile, which had brought me to the theatre, broke down on the way home, he was ordered to come for me in this vehicle. I was embarrassed to invite my friends into such a vehicle, but we could do nothing else, so we all got in and went. On the way we began to talk about Rasputin, the topic of the day, and my acquaintance asked me whether it was true, as per the circulating rumors, that there is a specially armored automobile for Rasputin, inside which are machine guns on either side. I smiled and replied that if he considers this car in which we are sitting armored, and if he sees machine guns somewhere, then the rumors are accurate. This was the only auto sent to Rasputin and, at that, only when he went to Tsarskoe Selo, so that he wouldn't have to take a train, where some woman might again make an attempt on his life. During my husband's entire tour of duty in Petrograd, Rasputin never went to the palace; he met the Empress only in Vyrubova's apartment when she came there with the Grand Duchesses, and sometimes the Tsar would come there. Since the Empress was of a mystical nature, Rasputin's assurances that as long as he was alive nothing bad would happen to the Tsar's family could have influenced her a great deal, and therefore measures were taken for Rasputin's security. Rasputin's prediction really did come true.

After Rasputin's murder, which I will not expand upon since many people know about it and much has been written about it, the intelligentsia that dominated the State Duma (parliament) did everything to cause the revolution to break out. The last two years in Petrograd were alarming and terrifying. My husband, his subordinate officers, and all others who served worked day and night, not even resting on holidays, neither at Christmas nor on Easter. My husband got up at nine in the morning and would go to his office by ten. At that time the officers and other personnel arrived. At two o'clock I would send a servant to ask my husband to come for lunch, but he rarely did because he could not get things done in peace because the Chairman of the Council of Ministers or the Minister of the Interior would want to see him, or there was an emergency and he would have to go to the Department of Police or to the City Prefect. He would come home around seven in the evening, and sometimes he was able to lie down for an hour before supper, after which he went back to his office to read reports and give orders for the next day. It was the same every day until five in the morning. I sometimes had the opportunity to invite his officers for some late-evening tea. They all complained bitterly that they were working so hard for no results because the powers that be did not pay attention to my husband's daily reports in which he pointed to the inevitability of a terrible revolution unless immediate necessary steps were taken. However, they were apparently more involved in their own intrigues with one another so that they could hold on to their positions, and they distorted my husband's reports. My husband was witness to this because after his January 9, 1917, report on the strikes, major disturbances, and speeches, Minister Protopopov phoned Tsarskoe Selo and, in front of my husband, gave a very rosy report that everything was peaceful and that there was no need for worry. My husband often insisted that it was essential that he make his reports personally to the Tsar. Protopopov agreed and promised to arrange this, but apparently out of fear that the Tsar would get a clear and honest picture of everything that was happening, the arrangements never occurred.

My husband constantly told Interior Minister Protopopov and Chairman of the Council of Ministers Sturmer of the necessity, given the developing situation, to issue a constitution and not wait for it to be torn from them. My husband did not know whether they told this to the Tsar, but he thought that they did not. My husband was able to influence Protopopov to abolish the Pale of Settlement for Jews; the order had been signed, and the Chairman of the Council of Ministers decided to have it published on Easter, but the

FIGURE 5.2. Major General Globachev, circa 1916. Marinich collection.

revolution intervened. During Protopopov's term as Interior Minister, my husband brought up the issue of the Petrograd garrison's unreliability. My husband presented all the data on the organization and mood of the garrison. As a result, a report was developed for the highest authority, and the Tsar agreed to exchange several reserve units of the Petrograd garrison with a cavalry guard corps that was at the front. This decision was not acted on because the Tsar got a telegram from the corps commander with an urgent request to leave the corps at the front, and that both officers and soldiers pleaded for this. So, Petrograd remained without veteran soldiers and had to depend on the unreliable garrison.

My husband used to say that Interior Minister Protopopov was very superstitious, and he himself told my husband that he was corresponding with a famous London occultist, whom he met on his last trip when he was still a delegate of the State Duma. Protopopov got some predictions from this occultist about days in January and February 1917 that would be good days and bad days for him. Protopopov asked my husband to write these dates down for information purposes. Really, how strange it may seem that all the days the occultist predicted, both good and bad, were bad for Protopopov—indeed, they were awful. February 27 was the last day of the monarchy and the end of Protopopov's career.

6

The Organization of the Okhrana

General Globachev

The Petrograd Security Bureau. Its organization. The secret service. Carrying out of searches. The office. External surveillance. The Security Command. The Central detective detachment. Registration Department. The chief of the bureau. The mission of the Security Bureau. The revolutionary and workers' movement. The public mood.

I was appointed Chief of the Petrograd Security Bureau in January 1915. The official name was the "Bureau for public security, safety, and order in Petrograd." With six hundred employees, this was the largest political investigative agency in Russia, and was organized as follows: (1) the Security Bureau itself, (2) the Security Command, (3) the Central Detachment, and (4) the Registration Bureau.

The Security Bureau was organized into the secret service unit, investigative unit, external surveillance, and the office and archive. The secret service unit was the basis of all the political inquiry, as this is where all spontaneous information acquired from our secret agent sources was centralized. The functions were distributed among experienced gendarme officers and clerical staff who were tasked with each part of secret agents' reports. Thus, there were several officers in charge of reports on the activities of the Social Democrat Bolshevik Party, several for the S. D. Mensheviks, several for Socialist Revolutionaries and national socialists, several for social movements, several for anarchist groups, and a special officer for general workers' movements. These individual officers had their own secret collaborators who served as sources of intelligence; they had personal meetings with them at clandestine apartments and handled these collaborators, protected them from failure, and ensured that the intelligence they received was accurate and not possible provocation. The intelligence obtained, particularly for each organization, was verified by external surveillance and cross-referenced with the secret service. It was then further processed to guarantee the identity and addresses of the people and determine their contacts and relationships. Once intelligence was developed and verified, its accuracy and authenticity could be determined as fully established. When the organization in question was sufficiently investigated it was liquidated, and all materials removed during a search were delivered to the Security Bureau—namely to the secret service unit, where they were filed. Materials that could subsequently be used in criminal testimony were separated from the rest. The systematized materials—records of searched and arrested individuals and even reports of secret agents on the matter at hand—were transferred to the investigative unit.

It was the job of the investigative unit to question witnesses and those who were arrested, to produce evidentiary materials, examine them, get further clarification and, if necessary, to conduct searches and arrests. After that, the entire matter was handed over to the examining magistrate of the provincial gendarme administration or to the military, depending on the direction the case took—that is, whether the matter fell under page 1035 of the Regulations on Criminal Legal Procedures, or under administrative jurisdiction. All inquiries were conducted, by law, under time restrictions, and those arrested were transferred in custody by competent staff, along with all collected data.

The police, sometimes (in more serious cases) with Security Bureau officials present, conducted searches themselves, always in the presence of witnesses; all confiscated materials were listed in the protocols and then were sealed and delivered from the local police precinct to the Security Bureau.

In order to identify individuals and their addresses quickly, every police precinct in the capital had a special police supervisor who did this work and who was responsible to telephone the Security Bureau twice a day to relay even the smallest incidents in his precinct and to report urgent and serious situations immediately.

All routine correspondence, telegraph communication, accounting and finance matters, etcetera were the responsibility of the Security Bureau office and under the supervision of a chief clerk.

This office had the archive and card file index, which constituted a major part of the office's responsibility because this index categorized by reference number and page information all people who had ever come to the Bureau's attention. Over the years, the index was a very reliable record; an inquiry into a particular individual took fewer than five minutes. If any person had compromised himself in the past in any way, it was possible to get the most thorough information on him. Information on persons who had not crossed the Petrograd Security Bureau's attention could also be accessed easily, with the

FIGURE 6.1. An office within the Special Corps of Gendarmes in Petrograd, approximately 1913 to 1915. *Russian Journal*: Rodina, Number 2, February 2008, Moscow.

help of police supervisors or by telephone inquiry to the regional investigative agencies anywhere in the Russian Empire.

The external surveillance bureau consisted of one hundred civilian observers or detectives, two supervisory officials, two of their deputies, and a small office for arrangements, summaries, and other meetings. The qualifications for detectives included prior military service—primarily noncommissioned officers who were literate, mature, and of good moral character. The detectives were organized into two groups for the effective carrying-out of their work, and they reported to their respective surveillance supervisors. Each group had its surveillance task and a number of surveillance posts. Some detectives conducted their surveillance as cabbies in horse cabs—the Security Bureau had several carriage horses and harnesses. The detective detachment was very important because it was they who verified the secret agents' intelligence information and supplemented it in the investigation, activities, and connections of organizations under surveillance. All current surveillance was recorded in daily logs and was reported to the head of the Security Bureau on a daily basis by group supervisors.

The Security Bureau's office routine and supervision was the responsibility of an assistant to the chief of the Security Bureau. An officer, two police supervisors, a duty officer, and around-the-clock workers and detectives ran the operation of the Bureau.

The Security Command consisted of three hundred security workers and two officers and was under the responsibility of a second assistant to the head of the Security Bureau. The Command occupied its own building at 26 Morskoi Street, where it conducted classes for employees on their responsibilities. The mission of the Command was as follows: His Majesty's security along his routes in the capital, security of the Imperial theaters, security of the Imperial family, and security of highly placed individuals as needed. Individuals accepted into the Security Command were selected on the basis of their reputation in their military careers as noncommissioned officers and for being literate and mature.

The Central Detective Detachment consisted of seventy-five surveillance agents or detectives under the command of a special officer who reported to the Chief of the Security Bureau. The detachment was made up of specially selected and experienced detectives who were assigned to investigate the more serious organizations, both in and outside of the capital. Some of them occasionally were assigned to one of the provincial investigative agencies for a more careful and thorough workup of some matter. In addition, the ranks of the detachment were also assigned to top-secret surveillance tasks and security, and to maintain surveillance over the routes taken by the Imperial entourage. This central detachment received all the resources needed to carry out its task, such as disguises, costumes, and materials and equipment belonging to street merchants, newspaper vendors, and so on and so forth. Some of the agents were people with higher education, and some were ladies and everyday women.

The Registration Bureau had about thirty (the number fluctuated) police surveillance supervisors and an officer in charge of the bureau who reported to the Chief of the Security Bureau. This bureau's job was to maintain surveillance and to keep records on politically suspicious people arriving in the capital and staying in hotels, furnished houses, and rooms. For this purpose the entire city was divided into districts that had several police precincts authorized to have a special police-surveillance supervisor. The latter had his own agents who were placed as hotel employees, managers, porters, and janitors. Thus, it was possible not only to collect data on the identity of a suspicious person but also to thoroughly inspect his or her belongings without them suspecting anything. In addition, the registration department verified in detail the authenticity and legality of the suspects' documents by making telegraph inquiries of places they had been. These efforts were very productive and gave the Security Bureau extremely valuable information on people coming into the capital. Staff members of the registration department, and often the head of the department, were temporarily assigned to a province well in advance of the Tsar's travel to record data on the local population through which the Tsar would travel and to assist the local investigative agencies.

The Chief of the Security Bureau personally directed all departments of the Security Bureau and regulated the order of their work. The heads of the department, officers in charge of agents, and staff in charge of external surveillance made daily reports to the Chief of the Security Bureau, either personally or by telephone, and were assigned further tasks and received directions from him. There was not a single detail of the daily life of the capital that was supposed to get past the Chief.

There was a mindset in society that the power of the Chief of the Security Bureau, especially in Petrograd, was boundless. This view was entirely wrong. All the authority and responsibilities of the Chief of the Security Bureau were strictly regulated and, in the area of prevention and foiling of crimes against the state, his power was extremely limited: first, by law, and second in every possible way that individuals to whom he reported were able to use their powers of influence. This latter circumstance positively tied the Chief of the Security Bureau's hands from fully applying lawful means in fighting the revolutionary movement. Of course the initiative to liquidate criminal organizations and individuals was in his hands, but the execution of the liquidation required, at least, the approval of the Assistant Minister of the Interior, or even of the Minister himself. This approval was easily given when the matter concerned underground organizations, workers groups, or unimportant individuals, but it was an entirely different matter if, among those designated to be arrested, were individuals who held a government position or significant social status. Such circumstances could cause all kinds of friction, delays, demands for irrefutable evidence of guilt from the start, the person's connections, the inviolability of a member of the State Duma, and so on. Notwithstanding that the matter involved government security, it could be set aside or given a categorical "Veto." If the Chief of the Security Bureau accomplished liquidation because of an exceptional emergency, but without a prior report, first he would be reprimanded and, second, if among those arrested were people in one of the categories mentioned above, he was released very shortly by order of higher authority. Naturally, during a state of affairs in which the revolutionary and insurgent mood was growing, workers' groups and their periphery were mainly responsible, but the leaders of the intelligentsia slipped by and continued to be involved in their criminal affairs.

Even during the war, the Security Bureau operated under strict law, and confirmation from the highest authority. Any individual who was detained and charged was held in custody no more than two weeks during the time of security conditions, and no longer than a month under war conditions. Then he was either released for lack of evidence or else transferred into the statutory criminal judicial process for further investigation and then directed to the appropriate court—that is, to a judicial investigator or to the Chief of the Provincial Gendarme Administration. Under extraordinary conditions, those arrested were detained at the Security Bureau for a day or two, but under far better conditions than in the more common jails; afterward they were transferred to city jails or houses of detention. Thus, the Chief of the Security Bureau was not the accuser nor the judge and could not keep a person detained indefinitely, as many people thought, but he simply arrested active revolutionaries to hand them over to be held accountable under the law, and even this had to be done only after considerable investigation.

The Security Bureau, with all its departments, reported officially to the Petrograd City Prefect, but the latter was not really involved in the Bureau's activities. The Security Bureau's direction came from either the Department of Police or, more often, the Assistant Minister of the Interior responsible for political matters, or sometimes from the Minister himself. The Security Bureau's mission was very broad, including active struggles against the revolutionary movement, compiling information on the mood of various strata of society, surveillance of the workers' movements, maintaining statistics on daily occurrences, overseeing population registration, and providing security for the royal family and highly placed personnel. Moreover, the Security Bureau was also assigned special secret tasks that were not directly related to its enumerated responsibilities and that depended on the needs of the Department of Police, Interior Ministry, members of the Imperial family, and sometimes the military.

All the intelligence collected by the Security Bureau was put into a report submitted to the Department of Police, Assistant Minister of the Interior, the Minister, the City Prefect, Commander–in–Chief of the Petrograd Military District, and the Palace Commandant. Thus, all these officials were kept apprised of the political situation and mood of the current moment. From the excerpts of the reports that are cited by Blok in his article in Volume IV of the "Archive of the Russian Revolution," it is possible to get some sense of the reports. It can be concluded from these excerpts that there was no matter that was not realistically reported by the Security Bureau in which the inevitability of the oncoming catastrophe was not clear.

In addition to written reports, the Chief of the Security Bureau gave oral reports to the Director of the Department of Police, City Prefect, and Assistant Minister of the Interior, and in emergency cases to the Minister and Commander in Chief.

The Security Bureau was, as were other political investigative agencies throughout the Empire, perfectly well organized in terms of the technical machinery for its active struggle against the revolutionary movement, but it was completely powerless to fight against the growing revolutionary mood of the sulking intelligentsia. For that, different governmental measures were needed outside of the Security Bureau. Under these conditions, the Security Bureau was only able to scrape together information, recommendations, and wishes that were persistently passed over in silence.

The Security Bureau's struggle against the underground revolutionary movement was conducted very productively and successfully, and it can be said with certainty that the functioning of the secret associations and organizations in Russia were never so weak and paralyzed as at the moment of revolution.

The following revolutionary organizations were in operation during the last two years before the revolution: Socialist Revolutionary parties, the Russian Social Democratic Party of Bolsheviks and Mensheviks, and various anarchist groups. The first group dragged out a miserable existence until 1916, when it became defunct. The S.D. Bolshevik Party, the most active organization, was brought to complete inactivity with the succession of liquidations, but it still had influence in the workers' environment and fought for its own survival. The S.D. Menshevik Party mainly took a lawful approach; that is, they involved themselves in professional unions, cultural educational societies, the Central War Industry Committee, and other organizations. Their entry into the latter group increased their influence with the workers' circles of Petrograd considerably. Anarchist groups sprang up from time to time, their numbers increasing at the approach of the revolution. These groups were wholly liquidated, and almost all members were incarcerated and awaiting trial. The revolution liberated all the incarcerated anarchists and their associated criminal elements, which explains the growth of the anarchist movement during the time of the Provisional Government; it brings to mind the black automobiles, Durnovo's dacha, and the Moscow barrier.

Right after the revolution, when members of the former imperial government and I were in custody at the Ministerial Pavilion of the State Duma, individuals who had been arrested for belonging to various political organizations and had been freed from being incarcerated by the new revolutionary order visited us and expressed their surprise at how successful the revolution was. They said it was a real surprise for them and that they could not take credit for it. But, really, what power did they possess now as a result of the revolution? All those who were talented and energetic were either in emigration, exile, or spread out in prisons. It was only after the revolution that they all rushed into the capital, afraid to be too late, so to speak, to divide up the social pie. Of the more visibly active Bolsheviks, for example, who were in Russia and who would later be part of Lenin's administration, were Podvoiskii, who had served in the city government but was arrested in 1916, and Alexander Chliapnikov, who returned to Russia from abroad not long before the revolution and settled in Petrograd under a forged passport and was designated for detention at some undetermined time.

The efforts of the underground organizations rested on the worker masses of Petrograd. The number of workers in the capital during the war, and especially in 1917, had grown considerably compared to prior to the war because almost all the major and minor enterprises that had expanded considerably were working on defense. The general number of workers in Petrograd had grown to 300,000. The mood of the working masses fluctuated depending on our successes or losses in the war, and was just as sensitive as the moods of all the other elements of society to our foreign successes. By the beginning of 1915, fertile ground was already being established consistently for revolutionary propaganda, but because underground organizations were not strong enough to be in complete leadership of the working class, their agitation was directed mainly to improve their material condition with the intent of moving to purely political demands. The country's economic situation, experiencing a crisis of unprecedented measure because of the war, was conducive to such agitation. The years 1915 and 1916 stand out because of the progressive struggle between workers and employers through economic strikes. Mills and factories, however, struck separately; some ended their strikes while others began. Some strikes involved an entire enterprise, with the number of strikers sometimes reaching 200,000. But the strikes never became general strikes. Strikes almost always ended in the workers' favor; that is, wages went up. There were some political strikes that lasted only a day, but they were not particularly successful and did not take hold among the working masses. These strikes were usually timed to coincide with an anniversary of various political events, such as January 9, in remembrance of the 1905 revolution, or April 4, in remembrance of the Lena events.

After the Zimerwald and Kiental socialist conferences in 1915, defeatist slogans began to pop up among the Petrograd working masses, influenced by the agitation that resulted from these conferences. All the Social Democrat Bolsheviks and some Socialist Revolutionaries under Kerensky's leadership joined this defeatist movement. Although all the worker groups joined the defeatist movement under the slogan "war on war," they nevertheless neither stopped nor sabotaged defense work. In general, the obstinacy of striking was disadvantageous because those who were liable for call up could be sent to the front.

Overall, the mood of the working masses cannot be said to be antagonistic to the existing order. If there were defeatists among them, most still believed sincerely in victory. They did not fear being sent to the front, because they had a sense of duty to the homeland and to brothers-in-arms.

The material condition of the Petrograd workers was very satisfactory, as even though the cost of living was rising, wages were also rising and were paid on time. It can be said that in their material condition, the Petrograd workers were in much better shape than other elements of the population of the capital. For example, government employees were paid much less than the workers were. With the increase in the cost of living, the lower-level government employees absolutely went hungry, and even if they received occasional raises, the raises usually lagged behind the necessities of life. This was partly the reason for the creation of a whole class of embittered bureaucratic proletariats.

The population of Petrograd before the war was barely one million, but it increased to three million (including its suburbs) by the end of 1916, which, of course, created higher prices and very difficult living conditions (scarcity of apartments, produce, heating, transportation, and more). All the personal interests of this population of three million were naturally concentrated on the course of the war and on the country's internal economy and political situation. The population reacted quickly to every change at the front, to everything that was talked about among the people in the market place, in the State Dumas, the State Council, in print, what was going on at Court, and within government. Every piece of news and rumor was distorted and considered by all persons according to their viewpoint and wishes. Society was generally being fed all kinds of nonsense and propaganda in which the truth was intentionally distorted.

Nearly every foreign and domestic misfortune was explained as being caused by treachery or treason and blamed on the Tsar, his Court, and his ministers. The State Duma set the tone for all this and took advantage of the government at this difficult time to revolutionize the people. It was not a representative organization that had an obligation to lift patriotic feelings and to unite everybody in support of the Tsar and government. On the contrary, it was the center of opposition that took advantage of the country's stressful moment to incite revolution among all classes against the existing order. When the "progressive bloc" was formed among members of the State Duma and the State Council, it became clear that an internal war had been declared against the Russian government and the throne. Not only Petrograd, but the entire country, listened to these national representatives, thinking that there was at the same time a war against a foreign enemy as well as a domestic war in the form of the monarch and his government. It can safely be said that by the end of 1916, the prevailing mood was that nobody in the government camp would stand up and defend it in the event of a decisive attack.

The press, responsible for reporting the public mood as it really was, instead created a mood of opposition and moved the masses toward revolution. Even such semiofficial newspapers as the "New Times" took the side of "popular" public opinion in promoting the struggle against the government . . . and what can one say about the other newspapers that were in the hands of people of the left wing? Military censorship removed parts of printed materials that had already been composed, filling newspapers with gaps (white spaces), which made the news agencies even more popular with the public because they took the gaps to indicate that the agencies were fighting for justice and truth.

Here, then, are the conditions under which the Security Bureau in Petrograd operated. The public, government agencies, the ministers themselves, military leaders, representative agencies, and even those surrounding the Sovereign were unsympathetic to the struggle against the revolutionary movement. Some consciously, and others unconsciously, pushed Russia to the precipice.

7

The Role of the Central War Industry Committee

GENERAL GLOBACHEV

The Central War Industry Committee. A. I. Guchkov. The official mission of the CWIC. The political significance of the CWIC. The later group of the CWIC. Elections to the group. Connections with the working masses. Liquidation of the workers' group of the CWIC. The significance of the CWIC after the February upheaval.

The Central War Industry Committee (CWIC) was founded through the initiative of A. I. Guchkov as an agency responsible for providing large-scale help in getting supplies and military equipment to our army. This was the official mission of the committee, and its execution was to be borne by industries that would help the government during the heaviest trials of this European war of unprecedented scale. But the hidden goals of this organization were revealed, and they were far from noble or patriotic. This committee was conceived by Guchkov, his comrade Konovalov, and some other individuals who represented mostly opposition and anti-government parties, who naturally viewed this committee as having purely political goals.

The committee showed those legal possibilities where it could be fully protected to conduct its destructive work in shattering the foundation of government and, to a certain extent, create one of the revolutionary centers and cultivate its political aims with its agents in society and in the army. Its methods for this were very simple: in advertising its activities in supplying the army, the committee at the same time deprecated, slandered, and compromised the efforts of the identical government agencies. They did this to create the impression in society that the only source of supplies was the public organization,

FIGURE 7.1. Alexander Ivanovich Guchkov. Wikimedia Commons.

the CWIC. In short, if there were no committee, the army would be left without cannons, without arms, and without ammunition—that is, without all that was the major reason for our defeats in early 1915. As an example, to advertise its productive activities, the CWIC opened a factory in Siberia for the manufacture of containers that would be used at the front. These cases were supplied to almost all factories in Russia that were in defense work. In this way, almost all the military supplies that arrived at the front were in containers marked with the initials CWIC, which gave the false impression of the extraordinary productivity of this public organization, making it look as if it was just about the only useful one in supplying the army. When statistical information was collected in 1916 about the manufacturing productivity of military supplies for the army by state factories, private enterprises, and the CWIC, it turned out that the major amount of military supplies were produced by government orders to state factories, less to private enterprises, and only 0.4% to the CWIC. Here then was the truth about the productivity of this celebrated public organization.

But let us turn to the main goal of the CWIC, about which people did not speak aloud—the political goal. In this area, the leaders exerted startling energy. The Central Committee and all its provincial bureaus, as I already said, were filled with individuals who were opposed to the government and the throne, starting with the chairman Guchkov and right down to the outlying districts. All of the official sessions were political conferences and meetings rather than business-oriented meetings. The committee's agents and even the chairman constantly traveled to the front to slowly build up a mood of opposition among the command staff, and Guchkov himself took on as his responsibility the frontline commanders and the army commanders. He also tried to become popular among the line officers. At the receptions of the officer gatherings, he tried to get the younger officers interested in him by being approachable and well mannered, and by giving speeches in which he shaded the meaning of his own services; at the same time, he criticized all the decrees of the government. As an example, in one of the regiments in Riga, Guchkov announced at an officers' gathering that it was only thanks to his petition that a directive from the highest authority was issued by the war department about speeding up the promotion of officers to the next rank when they went to the front. This caused such a torrent of excitement, that when he left he was carried out on the officers' shoulders.

Working in full contact with another such opposition organization, the Union of Zemstvos and Towns, the CWIC slowly but steadily conducted its destructive work, eating away at the military's confidence in the Tsar's leadership, in a successful end to the war, and in the greatness and strength of the thousand-year foundation of the Russian monarchy.

The very purpose of the CWIC gave it the opportunity to have its agents maintain complete ties with the army in order to carry out its destructive influence on the army, and this organization had no difficulty doing it. This means that, as needed, the CWIC could count on the readiness of the command staff not to oppose it—rather, they guaranteed to support it.

Nevertheless, it was necessary to secure another, no less important, element in preparing for a revolution: the workers. Thus Guchkov proposed to the committee to include workers' representatives as equals to manufacturers' representatives in the committee. Of course, the committee accepted this proposal because from a political perspective it held great promise for future developments. The workers elected to the committee established ties with the working classes immediately, thus giving this organization the support of that social class which, being influenced by agitation, had an anti-government outlook. The workers themselves supported this proposal, especially those who were S.D. Mensheviks, as this proposal was in keeping with their party tactics of employing all legal means.

The election of the workers' group to the CWIC was to be held on August 30, 1915, in the town of Solianov, and was organized as follows: every one thousand workers sent one elector to the meeting, which added up to two hundred delegates/electors. Naturally, most were from parties—

S.D. Mensheviks, S.D. Bolsheviks, Socialist Revolutionaries—and only a small percent were nonaffiliated. The delegates, having convened at noon, met until deep into the night and were unable to come to any positive results, because about half of them, namely the Bolsheviks, being defeatists, stubbornly refused to join a bourgeois institution that supported the war because they were boycotting the war under the influence of the Zimmerwald and Kiental Conference. The meeting ended, accomplishing nothing, and the election was not held. Guchkov was very distressed with the results and did not give up under any circumstances to establish ties with the working masses. He began to convince the worker Gvozdev, the former chairman of the August 30 meeting, to request a new meeting, and subsequently the newspapers carried an open letter from Gvozdev inviting the Petrograd workers to participate anew in the elections. This second meeting was held on September 30 in the same place. This time, about half the delegates—Bolsheviks—left the meeting dramatically in the same hour that the meeting was convened. They gave the same reason as the last time for refusing to participate. The meeting nevertheless took place with those who were left (about a hundred delegates); from this number, ten representatives were elected to the workers group of the CWIC, with Gvozdev as the chairman, and six elected to the Petrograd district committee. All the elected representatives were S.D. Mensheviks except one or two Socialist Revolutionaries.

From the very beginning of its existence, the workers' group was involved strictly in political work. It had its own separate office, its own separate meetings, its own clerical staff, and complete connection with mills and factories. In a small way, this was the soviet of workers' deputies. In the general meetings of the CWIC, the workers' group was little interested in questions of supply, but pushed for priority for exclusively political matters.

It was in 1915, after the first defeats in the war, that the State Duma, as I already said, began to revolutionize the country, and in 1916 it organized a definite revolutionary center, with the silent blessing of its president, Rodzianko. There were private nightly meetings of a small group, with Kerensky and Miliukov in charge, already orchestrating the mood in the capital, and across all of Russia. This center leaned on powerful groups and organizations at the time, such as the Progressive Bloc, Union of Zemstvos and Towns, and the CWIC. This last organization tied the revolutionary center with the working masses through the workers' group. This gave them the opportunity to lead these masses in its initiatives and instructions.

By the beginning of 1917, the role of all of the center's components became so clearly known to the Security Bureau that it became urgently necessary, if not to liquidate the center, at least to paralyze its activities, even if only to isolate it from its supporting base. A lot of work and effort was expended in getting the former Minister of the Interior, Protopopov, to agree to liquidate the workers' group of the CWIC, and finally, on January 27, the entire group and its chairman Gvozdev were arrested. The materials found during the search confirmed all the previous evidence of the criminal activities of those arrested. They were brought to justice and indicted for their crimes, as stipulated in page 102 of the New Criminal Code.

The arrest of the workers' group had a stunning effect on the CWIC, especially on Guchkov, who, as they say, had his feet knocked out from under him. The connecting link was removed, and the tie between the center and the workers' groups was destroyed. Guchkov could not stand this. He was always very careful in his plans, but at this moment he lost his self-control, and in attempting to intercede with the Commander of the Petrograd Military District to free those arrested, he risked an open call to the Petrograd workers to protest what they called the unlawful arrest of elected people. A CWIC directive about this was circulated to mills and factories and was signed by its chairman A. I. Guchkov.

Now it seemed that the next legal action by the government would be the arrest of Guchkov himself. Unfortunately, this was not carried out, nor were other things that I had brought up to Protopopov a long time ago. The most important means of protecting the government from the oncoming revolution was to dissolve the State Duma completely, and to liquidate the revolutionary center and leadership of the CWIC, the Union of Zemstovos and Towns, and the Progressive Bloc. These measures would definitely have wrecked the possibility of a revolution. The successful military counterattack in spring 1917, which was certain to happen, would improve and change society's mood.

It is difficult to believe that the government tolerated and funded all these so-called public organizations. Indeed, even at a time when the administrative and executive branches were well organized and on top of the situation, there were no government officials capable of saving Russia—not even by exceptional heroic acts.

The best confirmation that the CWIC was a political organization whose goal was to prepare revolution and had little concern with the country's defense is demonstrated by the fact that after the February Revolution, the CWIC lost all meaning in terms of being an organization working for defense as well as being a political organization. Its role had been played out by February 27, and neither the Provisional Government, nor the workers, nor the army, were interested in it any longer.

8

Alexander Kerensky

GENERAL GLOBACHEV

A. F. Kerensky. Kerensky joining the State Duma. Kerensky's underground activities. The Miasoedov affair. Kerensky's tour of the provinces. Ties with workers' groups. Military detachments. Kerensky's efforts with the labor group in the Duma. Kerensky's defeatism. Government measures. Kerensky's efforts in society. Attitude toward the war.

I was not personally acquainted with Kerensky, but because of my position in the last two years before the revolution I was fully acquainted with his political activities. I will not go into details of Kerensky's biography or personality; too much has already been talked about and written about this. Rather, I will deal with the role he played in preparing for revolution.

Kerensky was a lawyer by profession, but was quite commonplace and did not stand out among Russian lawyers. It can even be said that he was bad, as he was called a "three-ruble lawyer." In political ideology, he belonged to the Socialist Revolutionary Party, and as such he carried a lot of weight because of his agitating talent, his good oratorical skills in meetings, his sharp judgment, and in general his ability to influence less politically conscious minds. This is why the Socialist Revolutionary Party called him from Saratov, where he had become a leader of the Trudoviks, to be elected to the State Duma by the Socialist Revolutionary Party. Thus, to give him the needed, even fictitious, qualifications, a small house was purchased for him as his personal property for one hundred rubles.

Kerensky had no personal material resources of his own. He and his wife and two children lived in Petrograd at Peska on Odessa Street on the three hundred rubles monthly salary that he received as a member of the State Duma, which allowed him to live better than modestly.

FIGURE 8.1. Alexander Fedorovich Kerensky. ideeaconfronto.blogspot.com.

All of Kerensky's speeches in the State Duma were sharp in form and empty of substance; they were never business related. But they appealed to the Trudoviks and to the Socialist Revolutionary Party that supported them. He belonged to the extreme left opposition in the State Duma and he worked with the opposition-oriented center, especially after A. D. Protopopov became an official in the administration. Strictly speaking, he really had nothing to do in open meetings of the State Duma, for criticisms of the government had already passed him. Most of Kerensky's efforts were behind the scenes. The first test of his power was the treason incident of Colonel Miasoedov, on which I will concentrate later. The Miasoedov matter arose in February 1915 when our defeats began at the front. This matter, as we shall see later, was shady and complicated, which played right into the revolutionaries' hands. It allowed all kinds of dirt to be thrown at the government, which created a sensation. Kerensky hastily wrote an open letter to the Chairman of the State Duma, Rodzianko. Although it was not openly printed anywhere, it included a sharp condemnation and blame of the administration's and command staff's betrayal of the government. The letter consisted of several pages, was printed in the thousands, and was clandestinely distributed in Petrograd and the provinces—which was the whole point, since there was not a grain of truth in it. Nevertheless, it was successful, especially among students and workers.

After this, in spring 1915, Kerensky toured Russia along the Volga, visited Kharkov, Kiev, and other cities, where he gave biased lectures with the aim of explaining our military misfortunes and to raise a mood of opposition in peoples' minds.

On his return to Petrograd, Kerensky began to seek closer ties with workers' groups that tended to be more S.R.-oriented, which he tried to build into a solid opposition. A workers' committee of the Socialist Revolutionary Party was formed, with Kerensky as the leader. Furthermore, Kerensky proposed to the committee the creation of an armed organization to carry out various terrorist acts. Kerensky took it upon himself to supply members of this unit with arms, for which the workers raised and gave him seven hundred rubles. However, this enterprise failed for the following reason: Kerensky was in need of money, so he spent part of the money on himself. He did not purchase the weapons, and after repeated demands to return the money, he returned at most three hundred rubles of the original sum. Following this, the committee expressed its distrust and severed all ties with him. Having parted company with the workers, Kerensky began working exclusively with the Trudovik faction of the State Duma at their secret meetings.

The Trudovik faction had a special, prearranged apartment for their private meetings. This apartment, on the corner of Suvorov Prospekt and 9 Rozhdestvenskii Street, was rented by one of their members, who also lived there. The meetings were almost daily and were of a conspiratorial character, and the moving spirit of these meetings was Kerensky. Surveillance of everything that went on in this apartment was so well organized by the Security Bureau that the government knew what was said there with textual accuracy. These meetings took stock of the public mood, the temper of the troops, both at the rear and at the front, the characteristics and reliability of the command staff, the mood of the Court, the chance of revolution, the basis for an uprising of the Petrograd garrison, and so on. In January 1917, Kerensky already believed firmly in the success of a revolution and preached its pressing urgency. He stated, "We need a revolution, even if it means defeat at the front." For him, spring 1917 was the only possible moment to overthrow what was for him the hated government order, even if this threatened to be the greatest shock for the country and the entire government.

At the same time that he was working with like-minded colleagues, he was also preaching in the evening sessions of the State Duma in the same spirit where a revolutionary center was developing, and even though he was of a different political slant, the desire to take power united the Kadets and Socialists. That is why Kerensky went with them arm in arm, not demanding too much for his like-minded party colleagues, and limiting himself strictly to becoming personally involved in the future Provisional Government.

One can easily ask the question: where was the administration that was aware of Kerensky's and his comrades-in-arms' efforts to prepare for revolution? It was silent. It packed all the evidence of the oncoming catastrophe and archived it, and confined itself to graciously consenting to the liquidation of the periphery—that is, the workers' committees and underground socialist organizations that, as I already stated, were completely paralyzed and inactive at that time. The authorities' hands were tied by fear of being held responsible for arresting revolutionary leaders who had immunity in the eyes of society. This fear of the indignation of society prevailed over the inevitable danger that threatened the downfall of the government.

It would have been necessary to arrest Kerensky back in 1915 for his patently anti-government activities, and it could have been guaranteed that any materials found on him would have been enough to bring him to justice. Yet, in spite of my persistent reports, the Assistant Minister of the Interior at the time, S. P. Beletskii, refused to give his approval for the reasons mentioned above.

As I stated before, Kerensky had no personal financial means. But by 1916 he was supposedly preparing to subsidize a printing operation for the Socialist Revolutionary Party in Moscow in the sum of 15,000 rubles. The question arises: where could he have gotten this money? After all, the workers had broken with him, and at that time there were no organized elements of the S.R. party in Petrograd. Their remnants had already been liquidated in 1915. This means that they could not raise these funds. This situation and the indirect ties with pro-German individuals, as this had been established through the Security Bureau's surveillance, led to the conclusion that Kerensky was conducting his work with German money. This conclusion is borne out by Kerensky's own words that the revolution had to be accomplished in the spring of 1917, even if it meant Russia's defeat. The sum total of all these data made the Security Bureau conclude that Kerensky was involved with German espionage, about which the Security Bureau had a memorandum, although it was not on a form and nor was it signed. I think that this memorandum after the revolution first fell into the hands of Burtsev, who at that time was investigating the record keeping of the Security Bureau. Otherwise, how do we explain his special interest in Kerensky's ties with the Germans long after the downfall of the Provisional Government? Further surveillance of Kerensky's activities could have confirmed the Security Bureau's conclusions, but unfortunately the February Revolution intervened, and the agencies of the new government did not bring up this issue, even with the existence of circumstantial evidence, because Kerensky immediately assumed a dominating position in the Provisional Government, and this would have to be taken into consideration.

In general, Kerensky at that time needed to be scrutinized for his defeatism, for his sympathy for the Zimmerwald and Kiental theses, for the nature of his activities, and for the speeches that he made at meetings of the Trudovik faction, where boycotting the war ran through the group. Even if he had not clearly proclaimed the slogan that was adopted by the defeatists, "war on war," he still condemned the war. Of course, after it was his fortune to become the War Minister, Commander in Chief, and Chairman of the Council of Ministers, he began to sing a different song and became one of the most pro-war members of the Provisional Government.

9

The Politics of the Miasoedov Affair

General Globachev

The Miasoedov affair. His service in the Special Corps of Gendarmes. Miasoedov's reasons for leaving this service. Second Lieutenant Kolakovskii and his testimony. Investigation of the Miasoedov matter. His ties with Germans, General Sukhomlinov, and others. What the investigation turned up. Society's attitude to this affair. Miasoedov's trial. Errors raised in the entire investigation. How the revolutionary goals used this affair.

During the war Colonel Miasoedov was the chief of the counter-intelligence unit on the staff of the 10th Army of the northwest front; he was appointed to this position through the patronage of the War Minister, General Sukhomlinov. Miasoedov did not have a good reputation in military circles. His military service was mostly in the ranks of the Special Corps of Gendarmes, and a big part of that was as chief of the border bureau of the St. Petersburg-Warsaw railway police administration stationed at Verzhbolov. He was a very clever individual; he formed some excellent ties with local German border authorities and did them many small favors in return for favors from them. Thanks to his position, he established some necessary personal connections with highly placed officials on both sides of the border, Russia and Germany. Undoubtedly, this is when he formed a close acquaintance with Sukhomlinov and his family, who often traveled abroad and who got his special attention. The Germans were quite respectful to him, and even Kaiser Wilhelm himself invited him more than one time to go hunting in East Prussia.

Around 1908 or 1909, I don't remember well, Miasoedov had to leave his job, having been dismissed from the Special Corps of Gendarmes because, in spite of his service responsibilities, he took part in transporting contraband. Now dismissed, Miasoedov became involved in commercial activities. Thanks

FIGURE 9.1. Colonel Sergei Nikolaevich Miasoedov. radikal.ru.

to his former ties with Germans, he joined a maritime transport association as a member of the board, the majority of the directors being German nationals.

In 1911 Miasoedov returned to military service by order of War Minister Sukhomlinov and was assigned as a staff officer to the General Staff. At that time his quarrel and unsuccessful duel with B. A. Surovin caused a sensation.

With the start of the war, Miasoedov personally requested to be assigned to the 10th Army staff, where he first was a staff officer in communications and later chief of the counter-intelligence bureau.

At the end of January 1915, Sub-lieutenant Kolakovskii arrived in Petrograd from German captivity and went to the General Staff, where he made the following deposition: having been taken prisoner in 1914 during the battle of Soldau, but desiring to return to Russia, Kolakovskii offered his services to the Germans as a spy for Germany. His offer was accepted, and after a long training period, as best I remember, he finished a special intelligence school and was sent back to Russia through Sweden. Moreover, he was given, as he himself said, a general assignment to serve Germany; instructions and details of his assignment would be given to him by Colonel Miasoedov, to whom he was to report at the Russian front. This account was very strange because he was sent back to Russia without having been provided by the Germans with any secret rendezvous or passwords—nothing to give Miasoedov, if he was in fact a spy, confirmation that Kolakovskii was truly sent by the German general staff.

This was the entire substance of Kolakovskii's declaration, and it seems the General Staff thought little of it, as the Staff gave no orders on the matter for an entire month. Meanwhile Kolakovskii was proclaiming from the house-tops the unmasking he had done and that the military authorities were doing nothing about it. Word of this got to the Assistant Minister of the Interior at that time, V. F. Dzhunkovskii, who directed me to investigate Kolakovskii and to question him in detail. Kolakovskii did not provide anything new in the interrogation. His account repeated what he had stated the first time to the General Staff. The Security Bureau sent the record of Kolakovskii's interrogation to the counter-intelligence bureau of the General Staff as being in their area of responsibility. Strictly speaking, this is when the Miasoedov affair began—everyone in Petrograd knew about it and talked about Miasoedov, pro and con.

The General Staff turned the matter over to the commanders at the front. Miasoedov was arrested, and an investigation began that lasted quite a long time. The only materials that the investigation collected on this matter were correspondence between Miasoedov and people who were associated with him in commercial activities before the war, his relationship with General Sukhomlinov, and ladies who corresponded with him, such as Magerovskaia, Stolbina, and others. They were all also arrested and charged with being tied to Colonel Miasoedov and receiving some items of war booty that was looted in East Prussia.

The investigation came up with nothing to establish Miasoedov's guilt in military espionage—only the one unsubstantiated declaration of Kolakovskii. However, public opinion was so aroused by this affair that nothing was left to do but to subject Miasoedov to court martial. All the leftist elements played on this, blaming Miasoedov, the War Minister, and the command structure, almost for being complicit in treason.

Of course, I was not in the know about what went on in the court, but I know from reliable sources that the only thing proven about Miasoedov was the looting, for which many who were in military operations in East Prussia could be incriminated. As far as spying for Germany, there was no proof. Nevertheless, the Miasoedov Affair caused such a sensation that the High Command had to affirm the court's sentence to satisfy the public mood, and so Miasoedov was sacrificed and executed.

The High Command committed a colossal error at the very beginning of this affair. Immediately upon getting Kolakovskii's first account, it was neces-sary to establish the truth of his deposition by sending Kolakovskii to Mia-soedov. The goal was to find out how Miasoedov would react to this envoy of the German general staff, what mission and instructions he would give to Kolakovskii, and, added to all that, to establish the tightest surveillance on Miasoedov. If Miasoedov was a spy, this was the only way that his guilt could be determined. These were the ABCs of the matter, yet no such things were done. There was so much that was unclear and shady in Kolakovskii's account that when the military assigned him to a reserve unit in Penza after his disclosures, the Department of Police kept him under secret surveillance for a long time. It is doubtful that the German general staff was so naive as to trust Kolakovskii's sincerity, which is why they did not give him a secret rendezvous or detailed mission, but simply directed him to contact Miasoedov, recalling his good relationship with German border officials before the war. Perhaps in that regard there would be the off chance that, in talking to Kolakovskii, Miasoedov might actually enter into dealing with the German general staff and thus become a valued agent who was at the Russian front in the capacity of chief of counter-intelligence. The Germans were risking little with Kolakovskii, but if their scheme worked, the risks were fully justified.

10

Rasputin

GENERAL GLOBACHEV

Gregory Efimovich Rasputin, his real name being Novykh. My acquaintance with him. Rasputin's family and his entourage. His relationship to women and men. Debauchery and drunkenness. His relationship to authorities. Appointments, contracts, supplies, etc. Simanovich's role. Meetings at Tsarskoe Selo. Relationship to the royal family and to the Court. Rasputin's political significance. Rasputin's security. Rasputin's murder and the investigation of his murder.

My official duties caused me to cross paths with Rasputin, as all external surveillance over him for the last two years of his life crossed my desk. I became acquainted with him in 1915 when he was at the height of his influence. In general, he made a fairly pleasant impression on me. His appearance was rather rough and serious. His movements tended to be jerky. He had a soft, pleasant voice, and his speech was that of a common peasant, but a smart one. The only thing that was not pleasant about him was that when he spoke to someone, he did not look them in the eye. His deep-set, gray eyes darted back and forth across the room. He did not impress me as a person endowed with a special gift of prophesies, as some people claimed. There was no doubt that this was a man with a strong will who was able to subordinate others to his will, but still he seemed to me to be an ordinary, but smart, peasant. Rasputin had no formal education whatsoever. His early learning of grammar, dogma, and church doctrine, which he liked to show off, had been developed during his lengthy pilgrimages and wanderings, before he became a firm presence at court.

Rasputin lived in a modest apartment at No. 64 Gorohovaia Street with his family, which included his wife, two daughters, and a son. The furnishings in the apartment were middle class, maybe even lower class. Poor people would gather in front of his door every morning, and he would hand out a ruble, or two, or three to each person. His family lived modestly, but I do not think that they wanted for anything. On any given day, people visited him from all walks of life and all areas of officialdom and society. Some people were simply sympathetic to Rasputin, others sought his patronage, and still others hoped that by being near him they could stuff their pockets financially. The list of people who visited Rasputin for one reason or another was long. In addition, there were the habitués—that is, his friends whose composition changed depending on Rasputin's mood of the moment.

Most of his friends were women, lady admirers who believed in him as in a saint. Many of them were on close intimate terms with him, while others were still striving for that honor. The belief in Rasputin's saintliness was so strong that women kissed his hands, took food from his dirty hands, and willingly tolerated his insults and rudeness, considering themselves to be especially fortunate. Rasputin was always affectionate and tender with new women, whom he referred to as still unsaved, but he was especially rude to those with whom he was already intimate. I do not think that he favored one woman over another; he did not demonstrate any true love for any one of his lovers. His attraction to women was simply lust and depravity. Often when he was bored with his volunteer harem, he made use of common street prostitutes. Among those women with whom he did not have a close relationship, he tried to seduce them with affection and his ability to appeal to their soul by creating an aura of his saintliness in their eyes and a blind belief in him.

The men in Rasputin's entourage can be put into two categories: those who did not hide their closeness to him and visited him openly and spent time with him intimately involved in his life, so to speak; and those who hid their relationship with him and denied they had anything to do with him, but all the while benefiting from his influence in personal, political, and financial matters.

The first category of people included his secretary, Simanovich, Bishop Isidore, his daughter's fiancé, Lieutenant Pakhadze, the owner of the Villa Rode Restaurant, and others. These people were constant visitors to 64 Gorohovaia Street, as if they were members of the family.

The second category consisted of highly placed individuals, some in high office, others seeking appointments, favors, reception at court, the termination of lawsuits against them, and more. Rasputin's meetings with these people were held on neutral territory, sometimes in Dr. Badmaev's apartment, Golovina's apartment, Reshetnikov's apartment, Chervinskoi's apartment (arranged by Interior Minister A. N. Khvostov specially for such meetings), and also in automobiles. Some of those who met with him were A. N. Khvostov, Sturmer, Beletskii, Protopopov, Dobrovol'skii, the banker Rubinshtein, and the banker Manus. And there were many others.

In addition to his attraction to women, Rasputin had a passion for drinking and debauchery. This was exploited by his entourage, who seduced

FIGURE 10.1. Rasputin (left), Bishop Iliodor (center), Priest Germogen (right). Wiki-media Commons.

him with these things almost daily. These drinking bouts were organized at 64 Gorohovaia Street, and at restaurants, most of them out of town. Rasputin particularly liked to frequent the Villa Rode Restaurant where, thanks to his close relationship with the owner, the revelry lasted well into the night and ended at five or six in the morning at the Gypsy restaurant Novaia Derevnia. They generally drank until they lost their senses, and all this was accompanied by frenzied dancing and depraved activities with loose women. One had to be amazed by Rasputin's strong constitution. After these orgies ended in the morning, he went to a bathhouse, and, after not sleeping more than two hours, was refreshed and ready to start anew.

Rasputin did not booze with society ladies and tried to hide his usual behavior from them, especially from those with whom he did not have a close relationship. One time I had to go to Rasputin's apartment on official business (his personal security). He invited me into his study, which was a small dirty room furnished with a cheap writing desk with an inkwell on it, an armchair, and a sofa upholstered in leatherette that was quite worn out. Rasputin was completely drunk, which manifested in his dancing about, talking gibberish, and constant embraces and kisses. He gave the impression of a person totally out of control. I was ready to leave so that I could come back another time when he would be in a more normal state, when the front doorbell rang, and one of Rasputin's daughters came to say, "It is Annushka"—that is, Anna Alexandrovna Vyrubova. Rasputin quickly transformed so that one would not recognize him; his drunkenness disappeared, he jumped up, assumed a normal behavior, and rushed to greet his visitor. He invited me into the dining room to have tea, and I found quite a group: Vyrubova, Bishop Isidore, several ladies, and his family. The tea party lasted half an hour and all this time Rasputin conducted himself completely normally and entirely correct in his relationship with Vyrubova, and he debated Bishop Isidore on a theological subject. After Vyrubova left, Rasputin regressed into a drunken state, or so he seemed. This relationship with Vyrubova can be explained by Vyrubova's deep belief in Rasputin's saintliness. She was like a phonograph record of Rasputin's thoughts that she communicated to the Empress; thus Vyrubova's view of Rasputin was very important to him. His relationship with Vyrubova's sister, Alexandra Alexandrovna Pistolkurs, was entirely different. His normal behavior was not inhibited with her, given their longtime acquaintance.

Rasputin's drinking bouts were sometimes accompanied by scandalous behavior; that is, things got to the point of fights, as Rasputin's excesses could go beyond familiarity and impertinence. Two or three times he was beaten up when he was in a familiar setting but came into contact with strangers. Rasputin kept such incidents secret and never complained to anyone. On two occasions I had to pay the fines assessed against him by the municipal court for reckless driving (the automobile belonged to the Security Bureau; Rasputin used it for his trips to town and to Tsarskoe Selo). As they say, Rasputin had the "morals of an alley cat" and was "cowardly as a rabbit." On one occasion, he was invited to dinner at the home of the sculptor Aronson on the Petrograd side, and Rasputin made a crude remark to one of the ladies present. The lady's husband was also present, and in her defense he was intent on beating up Rasputin. Rasputin got so scared that he ran out of the apartment without his hat, jumped into the first carriage that came by, and, fearing pursuit, spurred on the driver with punches to get him back home to Gorohovaia.

FIGURE 10.2. Rasputin entertaining ladies and gentlemen of Petrograd society. The Empress' Lady-in-Waiting, Anna Vyrubova, is fifth from the left. Wikimedia Commons.

Rasputin really did not know how to discriminate among people. He separated people into two categories: "ours and not ours," or friends and enemies. It was very easy to get into the first group—one needed only to be recommended by one of Rasputin's friends. As a result, many individuals became "ours" who were not only unfavorably disposed to him but were also provocateurs who profited from their relationship with him and at the same time were willing to slander him and do him dirt. It was not just common folk who transgressed like this, but government ministers too. Among those in the clique of "ours" were dignitaries, bankers, speculators, officers, clergy, ladies of society, prostitutes, and many more. This entire group sought to be close to Rasputin for personal gain, knowing of his influence on the Empress and Tsar. Officials attempted to strengthen their positions; bankers and speculators filled their pockets through Rasputin's influence by getting contracts and making deals; officers sought promotions; ladies made efforts on behalf of their husbands; and members of the clergy tried to get better parishes and dioceses. I cannot name all the appointments and deals that Rasputin arranged, but some stick in my memory.

For example, the following people were beholden to Rasputin for their appointments: the Minister of the Interior Alexei Nikolaevich Khvostov, his deputy Stepan Petrovich Beletskii, Minister of the Interior Sturmer, Minister of the Interior Protopopov, Head of the Holy Synod Raev, Justice Minister Dobrovol'skii, Metropolitan Pitirim, Bishop Varnava, Commander in Chief of the southwestern front General Ruzskii, and others. It was not difficult for me to determine who would be designated for which position, as Rasputin was not only under the protection of my subordinates but also under their surveillance, and not a single clandestine meeting of his with people seeking a high position evaded my subordinates' watch. These meetings and negotiations sometimes lasted months, and were not always crowned with success. After an unsuccessful command of the western front, General Ruzskii was relieved of command and then, with Rasputin's influence, was appointed commander of the southern front. Regardless of this, revolutionary groups saw him as one of their own, so after the February Revolution, his stock with the Provisional Government rose—until the nature of his prior appointments became known and were grounds for his dismissal.

Rasputin's bankers Manus and Rubinshtein handled major deals and contracts. Both of them organized dinners and drinking parties for Rasputin. Rasputin got a cut of all the deals; sometimes he was content with what he got, but at times he argued and demanded more. The money went for the upkeep of his home and for charities. After his death a court investigation found 3,000 rubles in his home.

Rasputin often assisted individuals convicted of crimes by attempting to get them pardoned or have their sentences reduced. By the way, the former Minister of War, General Sukhomlinov, who was held in the Peter and Paul Fortress while he was being investigated, was released thanks to his wife's efforts and pleas to Rasputin. There were even instances of convicted individuals who were freed by royal decree.

A significant role was played by Rasputin's private secretary and friend, the Jew Simanovich, who had replaced a certain Dobrovol'skii, whom Rasputin suspected of appropriating some money due to Rasputin for some deal. Simanovich had been a jewel merchant on the sly, and was also a gambler at cards. He was called a casino "swindler," but I do not think that was so, since he played an honest game and lost often enough. Simanovich was not educated and spoke Russian poorly, but he was not at all stupid and was quick on the uptake. Notwithstanding his personal economic well-being that put him close to Rasputin, he was bound to Rasputin and protected his interests. In addition to his personal interests, he worked on the Jewish cause to abolish the Pale of Settlement and guarantee them equal rights, and he probably succeeded, as Minister of the Interior Protopopov and Justice Minister Dobrovol'skii were inclined to promote this reform soon afterward. I will say even more: Dobrovol'skii told me personally (after the revolution) that a law on equal rights for Jews was ready and in all probability would have been announced on Easter 1917. According to Simanovich, after the death of Rasputin, over 50,000 rubles were raised by Jews to aid Rasputin's children—since, as I have mentioned, he had only 3,000 rubles.

The only person from court who frequented Rasputin's apartment was the lady-in-waiting Anna Alexandrovna Vyrubova, who was a constant conduit between him and the palace. They did not have intimate relations, despite the gossip one heard after the revolution. The inquiry conducted by the Provisional Government fully affirmed that. Meetings between Rasputin and the Tsar and Tsaritsa were held at Vyrubova's dacha at Tsarskoe Selo. Rasputin did not go to the palace at all in the last two years. In the beginning, he would go to the palace by train, but later he was assigned one of the Okhrana Bureau's automobiles—a measure taken to ensure his personal safety. The Tsaritsa always came to the meetings either with the heir to the throne or with one of her daughters; sometimes the Tsar also came along. The meetings were one or two times a week and lasted between half an hour and an hour. Upon returning from Tsarskoe Selo, it was almost like clockwork that Rasputin and some of his companions would go to have drinking parties at some suburban restaurant or other. His behavior with the Royal Family was always correct, even at those times when he was really binging, and he never allowed himself to speak disrespectfully of the Royal Family in front of either friends or strangers. Thus, all the stories about how Rasputin addressed the Tsar by his first name, or bragged of his relationship or his influence, are complete fabrications, the aim of which was to discredit the royal family in the eyes of the masses.

Rasputin's influence on the Empress is explainable solely by the faith that she had in his prayers for the protection of the precious health of her son, the heir to the throne, and she came to this conviction when on several occasions Rasputin not only relieved her son's suffering but also, in her eyes, performed miracles. In addition, by getting close to Rasputin's family, she believed that she became closer to the Russian people, whose representative was this simple peasant, Rasputin. This was the full meaning of the Tsar's and Tsaritsa's persistent defense of their relationship with Rasputin, notwithstanding the repeated attempts by some individuals who were sincerely devoted to the Tsar and tried to convince him to send Rasputin away, since he was a trump card in the hands of some groups who were inclined to revolution.

Rasputin did not promote himself as some kind of major favorite; he was a simple and smart peasant who found himself in a situation that he could exploit. However, the entourage that surrounded him made him a serious evil that compromised the dignity and aura of the Tsar's power in the eyes of the people. It is possible that Rasputin's life was more valuable to revolutionaries than to the Tsar's family, and no revolutionary would risk an attempt on his life, knowing that such a premature act would inflict great damage to the revolutionary cause. Rasputin could only be killed, as indeed happened, by members of the right wing, or even by those close to the throne. The participants in Rasputin's murder—such as Yusupov, a relative of the royal family, and Purishkevich, a member of the right wing of the State Duma—contributed greatly to the revolution by giving society the confidence to oppose the throne, and these were not just the extremists, but also those close to the Royal family and loyal to the monarchy.

After the unsuccessful assassination attempt on Rasputin by Guseva in 1913 (in the Tobolsk region), the Minister of the Interior ordered continuous personal security for Rasputin, which lasted right up to Rasputin's death. This security was assigned to the Petrograd Okhrana Bureau and included two agents—bodyguards, if one may use that term—and two or three alternating agents who maintained surveillance outside Rasputin's apartment. In addition, an automobile with an Okhrana Bureau chauffer was assigned to Rasputin in 1915 to take him to Tsarskoe Selo and for his use about the city. Thanks to this, Rasputin's every move was known, and the identities of everyone he visited and who visited him were recorded. Rasputin went mostly to Tsarskoe Selo, to the Alexander Vitvinitskii Monastery, to visit Metropolitan Pitirim, to visit Dr. Badmaev at No. 14 Liteiny, and to his summer dacha on Chernyi Creek in Villa Rode—and also to Novoye Derevnia to visit Gypsies.

Rasputin understood full well that his security guards were also maintaining surveillance on his every mood, and this did not always sit well with him, especially in those instances when he was trying to promote the cause of someone for some position. At those times he usually complained to Vyrubova that people were following him right on his heels. This put the head of the Okhrana Bureau in a difficult position; the Minister of the Interior insisted on giving Rasputin security protection and surveillance over him, but from Tsarskoe Selo came the request not to annoy or watch over him. Thus it became necessary for the head of the Okhrana Bureau to negotiate with Rasputin on the matter of his security and to reach a mutual understanding.

Rasputin often released his bodyguards early, saying he would not be going out anymore that day. So it was on the tragic night of December 16, 1916. At 10 p.m., he told his bodyguards that he was not going out and that he was going to bed, though he certainly knew that Prince Yusupov would be coming to get him at midnight. This was obvious when there was a ring at the back door, and Rasputin asked, "Is that you, my little one?" (which is what Rasputin called Yusupov), and he put on his fur coat and boots and left with Yusupov. One could have guessed that if Rasputin would be murdered that it would be because he could be easily trapped by being enticed with wine and women.

The circumstances of Rasputin's murder, as they were detailed in the inquiry, were as follows: Yusupov came for Rasputin at midnight on December 16, 1916, as I have mentioned, and they both left the apartment and got into the automobile that Yusupov came in to pick up Rasputin. Yusupov's acquaintance, who chauffeured the auto, was part of the conspiracy. On that day Yusupov was planning a housewarming evening party to celebrate the remodeling of his apartments in his palace at No. 104 Moika. There was a house next to his palace that he also owned, No. 102, which he rented out privately. This building's façade did not face the street directly but had a courtyard in the front with an iron fence and a gate that led out onto the Moika. An iron door opened onto the courtyard from Yusupov's study. I will not discuss how the murder was committed, but here is how the investigation was carried out immediately afterward, on the morning of December 17.

At five o'clock in the morning, a police supervisor of a local precinct arrived at the office of the City Prefect with a policeman who was on duty on the Moika near Yusupov's house, and he reported the following: at 3:30 in the morning, as he was walking along the Moika in the direction of the Potseluev Bridge, he heard a gunshot from the direction of Yusupov's house. When he got to the fence of No. 102 and saw the young Prince Yusupov and his orderly looking for something in the snow, he became interested and asked whether the gunshot came from there. He was told, "No," and he proceeded back toward the Potseluev Bridge. After a short time the very same orderly ran up to the policeman and said that the Prince asked him to come back, which the policeman did. Upon entering through the main entrance into the Prince's study, he saw the Prince and another person he did not recognize. Both were very excited, as if from drinking, thought the policeman. The stranger asked him, "Do you know me?" The policeman said he did not, and was told, "I am Purishkevich, a member of the State Duma. Rasputin was just killed; if you love your Tsar and Russia, you will keep quiet." After this, the policeman left and informed his police supervisor immediately.

An inquiry established that on December 16 Yusupov had ordered his two servants (one of whom was his orderly) to prepare tea for 10 p.m. for six to eight people, after which they should not come into the interior rooms, but should remain in the vestibule of the main entrance. Of all the people who were invited that evening, only the Grand Duke Dimitri Pavlovich drove up to the main entrance from the Moika; the rest of the guests, among which were two ladies, came through the courtyard of the adjoining house. This is the courtyard where the wounded Rasputin was finished off, as evidenced by the puddles of blood in the snow. His corpse was wrapped in a piece of curtain and tied like a packet, covered by his own fur coat, and driven out in the automobile through the aforementioned courtyard.

At noon the next day, Yusupov arrived at the City Prefect's office and expressed his astonishment at the suspicion that Rasputin was murdered in his house, explaining that he had had an evening housewarming party, the guests had drank a lot, and the Grand Duke Dimitri Pavlovich had shot and killed a dog in the courtyard. The dog's body could be produced as proof. After that, Yusupov went to the Justice Minister with the same story, after which the Justice Minister gave orders that the inquiry that was begun by Justice Ministry personnel be stopped. But in light of Rasputin's disappearance, the police investigation continued, and the analysis of the blood collected in the courtyard established that it was human blood, not canine, even though Yusupov's orderly brought a dog's carcass to the police that same day. It was presumably killed by Grand Duke Dimitri Pavlovich. Given these new circumstances, the investigation was renewed, as it was clear that the dog was killed later. Nobody paid any more attention to this staged and childish alibi. The investigation established that Yusupov and Purishkevich murdered Rasputin.

Shortly thereafter, on December 19, personnel of the river police found Rasputin's body in a hole in the ice near the bridge that crossed the Neva between Krestovskii and Elaginii Islands. It was determined that the corpse was taken to the aforementioned bridge in the automobile and thrown into the ice hole, as indicated by blood on the bridge's rails and on the wooden dock. Also, one of Rasputin's boots was found in a crossbeam of the dock. After the body was identified and the corpse examined medically, the body of the departed was taken to a chapel on the outskirts of Moscow by a Red Cross automobile. There, Bishop Isidor performed a requiem service, after which the departed was taken to Tsarskoe Selo and buried under the foundation of the infirmary that was being built in A. A. Vyrubova's name.

Rasputin's killers likely had idealistic motives for committing this criminal act—to serve their homeland by freeing the throne from the influence of this "dark force"—but the result was extremely unfortunate and perhaps something they never anticipated. Rasputin was now seen as a martyr to his former admirers. His murder at the hands of Yusupov and Purishkevich, with the participation of the Grand Duke Dimitri Pavlovich, further undermined society's respect for the throne and put it into a double-bind. On the one hand, the law required that the murderers be punished; on the other hand, it was not possible to put the Grand Duke Dimitri Pavlovich, a member of the Royal house, on trial. The murderers did not gain popularity, but instead lost the respect of many. Rasputin's close relationship to the throne was a major evil, but an even greater evil was his murder under such circumstances.

11

Many Ministers

GENERAL GLOBACHEV

The Ministers of the Interior during the last two years of the monarchy. Relationship to domestic politics. Relationship to Rasputin. The political situation under which the ministers operated. N. A. Maklakov. The Union of Zemstvos and Cities. The reports of the Chief of the Okhrana Bureau. Assistant Minister V. F. Dzhunkovskii. Prince Shcherbatov. G. G. Molov.

In my two years of service in Petrograd I had direct contact with six Ministers of the Interior, and I must point out one characteristic that they all had: they understood little of the revolutionary movement in Russia and were little interested in it. Recalling that the Minister of the Interior had a deputy who was responsible for political matters, it would seem that they would have shown some interest in these issues. Each newly appointed Minister devoted all his efforts and energies to strengthening and holding on to his job, which created serious problems in light of all the influences and intrigues that were going on. Moreover, of major importance to the security of a Minister's job was his position in relationship to Rasputin—friendly, antagonistic, or indifferent. A Minister could not be neutral in this matter. He absolutely had to be in one of the categories of "ours or not ours," and even though Rasputin did not give much importance to this, the clique that surrounded him considered this of major importance, since it affected its personal interests. It was essential to the clique that the Minister should be one of their own, as then he could be counted on to promote their interests to their advantage.

Indeed, Minister Prince Shcherbatov and A. A. Khvostov lasted barely three months each in their jobs because they were indifferent to Rasputin. B. V. Sturmer was able to keep his job for a year and a half because he clung tightly to his friendship with Rasputin.

Before turning to the character of the Ministers' activities in the area of domestic politics, let us look at the political situation within which the Ministers had to operate. Everyone recalls the wave of patriotism that swept over Russia the moment that war was declared in July 1914, and how it increased during our military advances in eastern Galicia. There were some weak flashes of opposition and underground revolutionary activities that always enticed some part of the liberal intelligentsia and working class, but they were suppressed. All the thoughts and hopes of the population were for the speedy and victorious end of the war.

But the successful execution of the war changed. In early 1915, our army still held Galicia, but began to withdraw from the western and northwestern fronts. The withdrawals did not represent any major danger, but the home front that always reacts to any changes at the war front began to doubt how the war would end. This provided a ready and fertile basis for the unbalanced rambling of some who blamed the government for military misfortunes.

The opposition and revolutionary elements, which had been at a complete standstill because of the broad wave of patriotism that had swept over Russia at the start of the war, reared their heads anew and began their destructive work. The underground revolutionary movement, which depended on the working classes, constituted no great danger. It had always existed, even in greater number, but government agencies had the resources if not to eliminate it completely, at least to paralyze it systematically. What was much more serious and what could not be fought with the usual resources was society's growing mood of opposition. New policies were needed, as well as exceptional measures and a firm administration of government agencies, which unfortunately the heads of many departments did not demonstrate, especially in that area responsible for the administration of internal political issues: the Ministry of the Interior. In the two years that saw six ministers replace one another, not one showed enough will or talent to be able to paralyze and break up those forces that were consciously besieging the government and who were reducing Russia to ashes.

The first minister with whom I had contact as part of my responsibilities in Petrograd was Nicholas Alexeevich Maklakov. He was a person of extreme right-wing leanings politically, and it seems to me that if he had been even a bit of a government servant, if he had even some of the qualities of the late Stolypin, he could have at least stalled the anti-government opposition, as Stolypin had done, even if he could not paralyze it. Maklakov was a very superficial individual and not thoughtful enough—he made governmental decisions off the cuff. As an example, Maklakov can be blamed for approving the organization of the Union of Zemstvos and Cities.

This organization was brought to Maklakov's attention in the guise of having the Union take care of the sick and war wounded in the zemstvos and

Figure 11.1. Nicholas Alexeevich Maklakov. Wikimedia Commons.

cities. The goal seemed absolutely splendid, but was it thought out to approve the Union's plan as it was presented, without having any governmental supervision or control? First of all, there was already an identical government agency that was operational, namely the Red Cross. Second, what was it about the cities and the zemstvos of the provinces that should bring them into such a Union? In reality, all the cities were self-governing, and the Ministry of the Interior essentially united the zemstvos. Why was it necessary to create a government within a government?

By authorizing the Union, Maklakov created a large social-political organization within which all the anti-government elements joined and provided minimal help to the sick and wounded but gave maximum effort to the struggle against the government. This was a big mistake. It could have been possible to authorize such an organization for each province and city separately as subsidiaries of the Red Cross, but under no circumstances to organize it into such a powerful union that had the same administrative rights at the front and at the homefront as did the Red Cross. The Union cost the government huge sums of money, consciously opposed every governmental control, and played a role equally as vile as that of the Central War Industry Committee in the destruction of Russia. Both of these organizations were led by the Kadet Party and worked for the overthrow of the monarchy, both at the front and at the home front.

Both organizations worked hand in hand toward the same goal but with just one difference: the CWIC played itself out and vanished from the scene after the revolution, but the Union of Zemstvos and Cities tried to hold on to its political existence, for the most part by providing free meals and shelter to the members of the former Kadet Party. After the Bolshevik takeover, the Zemgor joined the White Movement in the south of Russia, and its various groups and cells continue to operate in various European countries even today.

The head of the Okhrana Bureau had a special appointment with Interior Minister Maklakov every Saturday to give him an oral report. This was in addition to the written reports, and I think was just a formality. Maklakov was not interested in these reports and would often cancel the meetings for one reason or another. Between February and June 1915, I gave him an oral report only twice. Maklakov limited his responses to my reports to comments such as, "Brilliant," "As it should be," "Continue in the same spirit," and the like. Moreover, he did not seem to have time to discuss jointly issues of the revolutionary movement with someone who was close to the issues, nor did he express his views or even offer general directions.

The Assistant Minister of the Interior under Maklakov who was responsible for the political division was General Vladimir Fedorovich Dzhunkovskii. He was appointed to this position in 1913, having been the Governor of Moscow, and he immediately developed a biased attitude toward the use of secret agents in the investigative organizations, considering all secret agents as provocateurs.

Dzhunkovskii was on the job for only two years, but he began to realize that you could not judge all agents from this point of view, and that the foundation for coping with the revolutionary movement was in having intelligence acquired by internal agents. But thanks to his views in 1913, Dzhunkovskii was able to get approval from the highest authority to issue a directive that prohibited the use of secret agents among the military and in secondary schools, and prohibited surveillance over political activities in the army and in secondary schools. It was self-evident that this directive untied the revolutionaries' hands in terms of their ability to propagandize and agitate among the youth and the army's rank and file. From that moment on, the investigative agencies were able to pick up intelligence only in passing and by chance, and what

FIGURE 11.2. Major General V. F. Nikol'skii, Chief of Staff Corps of Gendarmes (on left); General V.F. Dzhunkovskii, Deputy Minister of Interior (in center); V. A. Brune de St.-Hyppolite, Director of Department of Police. Approximately 1913. Marinich collection.

they learned was superficial. As an example, some intelligence that was picked up made it known that as early as 1916 the mood of the Petrograd garrison suggested danger, but in the absence of secret agents, this matter could not be investigated with any thoroughness. Thus it was not possible to take measures to liquidate this dangerous situation.

After Dzhunkovskii's dismissal, the new Assistant Minister, who understood the harm of the aforementioned directive, brought up the matter of its repeal, but as it turned out it was too late. The commission assigned to deal with this issue defeated it by a majority vote. The commission consisted of the chairman, Lieutenant General Leontiev, who was at that time the Quartermaster General of army headquarters, and two of his subordinates who were officers on the General Staff: Major General N. M. Potapov and Colonel Machul'skii (both of whom got prominent positions with the Bolsheviks after the October Revolution). The Vice Director of the Department of Police, E.

K. Smirnov, and I represented the Ministry of the Interior. Our two votes to repeal the directive had no power against the three votes from the army in favor of continuing it, and thus the matter was defeated.

Maklakov's and Dzhunkovskii's relationship with Rasputin was antagonistic, which was one of the reasons they were dismissed simultaneously. They say that Maklakov's replacement, Prince Shcherbatov, was appointed on the recommendation of the Grand Duke Nikolai Nikolaevich—Shcherbatov having been up to that time the Director of Government Horse Breeding. He was not familiar with the organization of the Interior Ministry and was inexperienced in political issues. His entire record was that he had been a member of the first State Duma and a leader of a right-wing party.

From the very start, Shcherbatov tried to curry favor with the public, but it came to nothing. Everybody remembers his speech in the Duma and his references to the writings of Korolenko. There were also amusing incidents of another kind. In the summer of 1915, the Tsar Emperor was in Petrograd at the Baltic and Admiralty construction works for the launching of the two dreadnaughts Ismail and Borodino. In order to favor public opinion, Shcherbatov refused the service of personal adjutants, which he was his due in his position, and on two occasions he wound up in ridiculous situations. On one such occasion he was not allowed onto the launching site because nobody knew him on sight, and there was nobody with him to identify him. The second time, after the conclusion of a ceremony and in the absence of a personal adjutant, and after the public had already gone, Shcherbatov was the last to leave, and it took him half an hour to find his automobile. After those two episodes, Shcherbatov began to use the services of personal adjutants.

The Political Bureau under Shcherbatov was under the supervision of his personal friend Ruschui Georgievich Molov, who was appointed Director of the Department of Police and Assistant Minister of the Interior. Although Molov had been a prosecutor of the Odessa Judicial Court, he was as incompetent in internal political matters as Shcherbatov was, so it was natural that he was not able to give him good advice in running the department or in political matters. After all, Shcherbatov got his reports only from Molov. As best that I could know, he did not even take reports from the City Prefect. He was very interested in Rasputin and his entourage. He ordered Molov to supply surveillance reports on Rasputin, but he did not enter into any contact with Rasputin and was never considered to be in Rasputin's category of "ours."

Shcherbatov lasted in his job for three months and brought neither harm nor good to it. I think he was dismissed due to pressure from Rasputin's people, as at that time Alexei Nikolaevich Khvostov, who had been a member of the Duma, was being promoted for the position of Minister of the Interior.

12

Khvostov, Komissarov, Kamenev

GENERAL GLOBACHEV

A. N. Khvostov. The way he was appointed. S. P. Beletskii. His relationship with Rasputin. Khvostov's assistants. Komissarov. Kamenev. Komissarov's role vis-à-vis Rasputin. B. Rzhevskii. Khvostov's scheme. Rzhevskii's arrest. His exposure. Beletskii's and Komissarov's falling out. Khvostov's dismissal.

Through Rasputin the right wing promoted A. N. Khvostov to be Minister of the Interior. It was said that Khvostov himself fought for this. Subsequently, Rasputin used to say that Khvostov asked his help and swore on an icon that he would protect Rasputin with all his might, and he showered Rasputin with gifts. I cannot judge the accuracy of this, but in any case Khvostov himself worked on Rasputin and through Beletskii to get this job.

In addition to Khvostov's appointment, Stepan Petrovich Beletskii was appointed Assistant Minister of the Interior in charge of the Political Bureau, replacing Molov, who was appointed Governor of Poltava.

Khvostov initially did not concern himself at all with the Political Bureau, but left it entirely to Beletskii. At first, the attitude toward Rasputin was one of good will, based on the principle that Rasputin was the personal business of Their Majesties into which the authorities should not meddle. Intelligence and reports about everything that was going on with Rasputin still had to be done as before, as personal reports for the Minister. But soon it turned out that such a neutral attitude in this matter became unthinkable. Rasputin demanded to be paid in promissory notes for appointments. Rasputin's requests, sent directly to Khvostov or through others, absolutely bombarded Khvostov. Khvostov realized this issue was not easy to deal with, and in his heart he knew that Rasputin was a danger to Russia. Moreover, Khvostov's pride suffered from the knowledge that he was in the clutches of a peasant,

FIGURE 12.1. Alexei Nikolaevich Khvostov. photoarchive.spb.ru.

Rasputin. Khvostov often received letters from Rasputin addressed, "to Minister Khvostov," and sometimes these were close to being orders. Having been put into this kind of a situation, it appears that Khvostov decided to rid himself of Rasputin's influence one way or another. Khvostov always seemed to me to have a criminal side, but he did not think through how to carry out his goal. Even when he was the Governor of Nizhni Novgorod, back in 1912, he chose people of questionable reputation and shady enterprise as his assistants. He continued in these ways as Minister. For secret operations he chose two individuals, one of whom was recommended by Beletskii, a gendarme general named Michael Stepanovich Komissarov. The other was a former minion in the Nizhni Novgorod province, a certain Captain Kamenev, who was promoted to the rank of colonel and transferred into the Special Corps of Gendarmes outside of any official process.

Komissarov was assigned the special task of establishing a relationship with Rasputin, and this he did quickly. Komissarov was a very smart and

FIGURE 12.2. Stepan Beletskii, Director of the Department of Police and subsequently Assistant Minister of the Interior. Marinich collection.

capable man, but he was unscrupulous when it came to his personal interests. He was also a big fan of intrigue and willing to enter into any relationship that served his interests. Because of his extraordinarily cynical outlook and lack of morality, he spoiled any assignment he was given.

With Komissarov's arrival on the scene and striking a relationship with Rasputin, Khvostov and Beletskii developed a definite plan. I think the plan was to lure Rasputin into a trap and kill him, and to explain his death as either an accident or to lay the blame on somebody else. There was no other way to explain Komissarov's behavior toward Rasputin, and apparently he had no other assignment from the Minister. His official assignment was to keep Rasputin from binging and to protect him from bad influences. In reality, however, as we shall see, Komissarov tried to get him to drink even more and to bring all kinds of scoundrels into his (Rasputin's) company. Komissarov would be at Rasputin's every day, and sometimes several times a day. He became acquainted with everyone who visited Rasputin, and he participated in the frequent drinking bouts. Komissarov gave daily reports to Khvostov and Beletskii. In addition to the official protection that Rasputin had, Komissarov organized his own group of people who were loyal to him. He was also given an automobile and a horse cab.

After the facts that follow, my eyes were completely opened to Komissarov's real role.

On one occasion he approached me with the Minister's approval with the request that I lend him my horse and a sleigh without a driver for the entire night. The reason he gave was that my horse was fast. The request was verified by telephoning Khvostov and, based on his confirmation, I fulfilled the request. I was very surprised when my horse was returned the next day all lathered, and the sleigh with a broken shaft. It became perfectly clear to me that if Rasputin was discovered killed or thrown through an ice hole, and if my carriage were found, all the blame would be on me. After this I talked my way out of all Komissarov's subsequent requests to borrow sleigh or horse by saying that my horse was sick and the sleigh was in repairs.

The relationship between Rasputin and Komissarov became strained eventually because of Komissarov's intemperance, rudeness, and the gossip that he himself spread about Rasputin. Komissarov would come to Rasputin's apartment and yell, curse, and use foul language in front of others, claiming that he was parting company with this peasant and so on. One time when he was a guest at Badmaev's dacha, while skinning a piece of smoked fish, he said, "This is how I will skin Grisha." This, as well as his telling of his experiments in poisoning cats as a test for poisoning Rasputin, became known to Rasputin, who broke things off with Komissarov completely. Rasputin was so terrorized that he did not know how to get away from Komissarov.

Khvostov saw that his desires were not fulfilled by Komissarov, nor did he accomplish anything. Khvostov thus devised another plan without involving Beletskii or Komissarov. When Khvostov was the Governor of Nizhni Novgorod, a newspaper reporter was there, a certain Boris Rzhevskii, who contributed to a right-wing newspaper and who had been Khvostov's devoted man. He was unbalanced, hysterical, and unprincipled. During the war Rzhevskii had some kind of menial job with the Red Cross. At the end of 1915 he showed up in Petrograd and naturally got in touch with Khvostov, who decided to use Rzhevskii, as he (Khvostov) had a plan firmly in mind to eliminate Rasputin. The plan was thought out and implemented in the following way: Rzhevskii received an advance in Swedish money (about 60,000 rubles) and was given top secret orders to go to Norway on a mission. Upon its completion, he was to return to Petrograd and report immediately to Khvostov. This mission was top secret; not even Beletskii was informed of it. The latter thought he should know about any political action by the Minister, since he was responsible for the Political Bureau. When Beletskii learned of Khvostov's independent enterprise, he decided to sabotage this plan, and Rzhevskii helped him, as he was unable to keep secrets, given his indiscretion and arrogance.

Upon his return to Russia, Rzhevskii got into a personal argument with a gendarme officer at the Beloostrov train station, and Rzhevskii hurriedly declared that he had been out of the country on a special assignment as the secretary of the Minister of the Interior. Nevertheless, he was thoroughly searched and returned to Petrograd under surveillance. Later it came out that the argument at the Beloostrov train station and the search were staged by order of Beletskii in order to uncover Khvostov's secret. The search produced material that indicated Rzhevskii's abuse of his responsibilities to the Red Cross. He had order forms for many items; pretending that the Red Cross needed them, which he sold to speculators for five hundred to six hundred rubles. Of course, all this was unrelated to what Beletskii was interested in, but he was very pleased and used the information to sensationalize the matter. A special officer from the staff of the Corps of Gendarmes was assigned to investigate Rzhevskii's abuses, but the latter was always at liberty during the investigation. When the inquiry was concluded, Beletskii gave me the file and asked me to become acquainted with it and to await his order to arrest Rzhevskii. Although the evidence clearly proved Rzhevskii's guilt, for some reason Beletskii was slow in having him arrested. Seemingly he was waiting for something, and it was not until two weeks later that he ordered Rzhevskii's arrest.

During a second search of Rzhevskii's apartment, among many letters, a parcel was found addressed to Alexei Nikolaevich Khvostov. The officer conducting the search opened the parcel, which contained a petition from Rzhevskii that stated in the event of his arrest everything should be done to release him. Rzhevskii had a foreboding that he would be arrested. The fact of his arrest did not seem particularly unusual, but it later led to serious consequences for Beletskii and Khvostov, and cost them their jobs. Up to this time they had had a close friendship, but they now had a complete falling out and became irreconcilable enemies.

At four in the morning on the day following Rzhevskii's arrest, Khvostov sent his adjutant Kamenev, who ordered me to meet him immediately on a business matter. His first question addressed to me was, "Where is the parcel that was found at Rzhevskii's that was addressed to me?" When I presented the opened parcel to him, Khvostov asked me nervously, "Who dared to open a parcel addressed to me?" To my response that the officer conducting the search opened the parcel, Khvostov became very agitated and stated that this officer should be fired. Despite my explanation that the officer had acted correctly and that in conducting the search he acted within the law in opening all correspondence found during a search, even if such correspondence were addressed to the Tsar, Khvostov did not calm down. When he finally read the contents, he was relieved and said, "Well, there is nothing here." It became clear to me that Khvostov was expecting something very unpleasant in the letter that could become known to others.

The entire matter really came down to this: Khvostov had sent Rzhevskii to Kristiano to see Iliodar Trufanov, a sworn enemy of Rasputin, with the intention of bribing him and, with the help of his fanatic follower from Tsaritsyn, to murder Rasputin and blame it on religious enmity. I cannot judge whether Rzhevskii made a deal with Iliodar or not, but the plan failed because Khvostov was betrayed by Beletskii, on the one hand, who took Rasputin's side and thought that by causing Khvostov's fall he would get his job. On the other hand, at the very last minute Rzhevskii disclosed the whole plan. It turns out that Rzhevskii figured out that he was caught in this intrigue and could wind up personally suffering for it, so he prepared two letters in the event of his arrest—one was to Khvostov asking for his release, and the other was addressed to A. A. Vyrubova in which he disclosed the entire plan against Rasputin. He gave this letter to an engineer friend of his with the request that it be delivered. The latter did this, but being unable to deliver it to Vyrubova, he gave the letter to General Belaiev, the War Minister.

Thus, everything became known to the Empress, who asked the recently appointed chairman of the Council of Ministers, Sturmer, to conduct an inquiry and report back to her. The inquiring commission appointed by Sturmer consisted of I. Ia. Gurland and Manusevich-Manuilov. I led the formal part, but did not deal with accusations against Interior Minister Khvostov, who was my immediate supervisor. Khvostov explained everything very simply. He had sent Rzhevskii to Kristiano to buy all the books published by Iliodar that were titled "The Holy Devil," which compromised the Royal Family because of its association with Gregory Rasputin.

While Sturmer was conducting the inquiry, Khvostov decided to distance himself from Beletskii by dumping on him all the blame and accusing him of intrigues to the Tsar. After the report to His Majesty, Beletskii was appointed Governor General of Irkutsk, and General Komissarov, his friend, was appointed City Prefect of Rostov. Beletskii was extremely dismayed. He claimed that Khvostov had deceived him, but that he would get even in time. Beletskii did not go to Irkutsk but arranged to join the Senate, and Komissarov was able to maintain good relations with Beletskii and Khvostov right to the end. The latter gave him 25,000 rubles, outside of my procedures, and a gold cigarette case. His appointment to Rostov was in part due to Rasputin, who asked the Empress to appoint Komissarov somewhere far from Petrograd, but with a promotion—that was how much Rasputin feared him. Komissarov was so cynical, that after Beletskii and Khvostov were removed from their offices, he was not at all embarrassed to declare, "Finally both fools were removed."

After having gotten rid of Beletskii, Khvostov told me that he would supervise the Political Bureau himself and that I should give him daily reports. My first report lasted not less than two hours, because it was necessary to present a lecture on the revolutionary movement in Russia, explaining the programs and tactics of each political party. It must be said, though, that Khvostov understood it all very quickly. He laid out a new program for me regarding Rasputin's security from evil influences, and then he ordered the searches and arrests of some individuals associated with Rasputin, who were released very quickly. The materials that were found during their searches pointed to their personal interests in maintaining close ties to Rasputin in terms of speculation, contracts, and supplies.

After Beletskii's dismissal, Khvostov lasted in his job not more than a month, and upon his dismissal he did not receive another appointment. Although he was a very smart man, in the six months that he was Interior Minister, Khvostov contributed nothing beneficial to Russia. He was preoccupied exclusively with personal intrigues and made some very unfortunate appointments. An example of this is the scandalous history with Beletskii and Rasputin, where he employed the services of Komissarov and Rzhevskii. By the way, the latter served in the Moscow Cheka in 1918 and personally shot counter-revolutionaries, and then joined the White Movement in Odessa in 1919, using the name Boris Raevskii. He was murdered by his own agents who served in the criminal investigation bureau of the Odessa City Prefect.

Khvostov's deputy, Stepan Petrovich Beletskii, was a very intelligent and efficient man who understood the political situation in Russia perfectly well. If it had been fated for him to become the Interior Minister, he would have been well placed, but the shame of it all was that he cast the net of intrigue widely and got caught in it. As with Khvostov, much of this was due to the fact that he sometimes used individuals who were completely unprincipled, and who betrayed him. In his political views he was very right wing and wholeheartedly dedicated to the Tsar.

13

Sturmer

GENERAL GLOBACHEV

Sturmer. The Minister's Day. Sturmer's closest deputies. Sturmer's attitude toward political and governmental issues. Sturmer's indecisiveness in important matters. Sturmer's pettiness. General Klimovich. Attitude toward Rasputin. The appointment of Foreign Minister (sic) A. A. Khvostov.

Sturmer was already the Chairman of the Council of Ministers when he was appointed to replace Khvostov as Interior Minister, thus he combined both roles in himself. Even before his appointment as Chairman of the Council of Ministers, when he was a member of State Council, Sturmer made every effort to get this job. He worked for this through Rasputin and his friend Metropolitan Pitirim for several months. Sturmer, like Khvostov, gave his assurances that he would protect Rasputin, and he must be given credit for holding true to his promise.

Sturmer was not a government man, although he had had major administrative experience in the past. In addition, he was old, incompetent, stubborn, and unable to fathom the most basic issues; in other words, he was not only unfit to be Interior Minister, but even played a passive role as Chairman of the Council of Ministers.

He got up very early, at six in the morning, and occupied himself in opening letters addressed personally to him as Minister, which was something that his secretary was supposed to do. A special large desk was put into his office for this, and every morning Sturmer was literally inundated with letters. Soon enough he became tired of this task, and the desk was removed from his office. Owing to a full day of tedious meetings and receptions with employees as well as with private parties, Sturmer was thoroughly useless by seven in

FIGURE 13.1. Boris Vladimirovich Sturmer. Wikimedia Commons.

the evening, and if he held a conference after that time he absolutely did not understand what was going on and kept dozing off.

His unofficial assistants were Ilia Iakolevich Gurland and Ivan Ivanovich Manasevich-Manuilov. The former was a very intelligent man whose advice was always good. The latter, smart but crafty, was an unprincipled adventurer, and an intriguer. Manuilov referred to himself as Sturmer's personal secretary, even though he had no such official position. God knows what bonded them; they say that they had some kind of dealings in the past. Manuilov hung around Sturmer's apartment and in the reception area, and Sturmer claimed to everyone that he had nothing in common with Manuilov and hardly even knew him. His old friend, Count Borkh, who lived next to the Minister at Fontanka No. 18, held the position of personal secretary and was also responsible for Sturmer's domestic matters.

Sturmer was not interested at all in either the political situation or the mood of Russian society, but he was extraordinarily interested in Rasputin and in court circles. How Sturmer attended to issues of major governmental importance is seen in the example below.

A serious problem came up in the early summer of 1916 of providing relief to Petrograd because of the extreme increase in the population as a result of the war. This was a very serious problem: first, in economic terms, and second, politically. The considerable increase in the population was due to the concentration of refugees from territories that had been occupied by the enemy, the increase in the reserve forces, hospitals, clinics, and even prisoners of war. All this caused major complications in terms of relief due to the rise in prices, living accommodations, and politically, as there was intelligence on propaganda among the reserves, in clinics, and in weaker military commands. In a word, the issue was so clear that it had to be dealt with one way or another. Sturmer called for a meeting in his office to which I was also invited. Various ideas were discussed on how to relieve Petrograd; I was asked to speak out. I outlined the political situation of the moment and approached the issue from the perspective of the government's security. I insisted on the need to remove all reserve troops and unnecessary medical units from Petrograd, showing and proving with hard data their complete unreliability. Given that each reserve battalion consisted of 9,000 to 12,000 troops that would be subject to evacuation from Petrograd to the provinces, this would represent a big enough number to resolve the problem of provisions and living accommodations. On the other hand, it would produce peace and security in the capital in a political sense. General Tumanov, who was the commander of the troops of the Petrograd Military District, stated that this was impossible; even such an approximate count for evacuation would cost the government nine million rubles. I could only remark to this that for the security of the country these measures were necessary, even if the government had to pay, not nine million, but hundreds of millions.

The meeting ended with no resolution; Sturmer did not come to any conclusion, and the matter remained an open issue. Thus, even up to the very revolution, the question of supplying Petrograd never came up again.

Sturmer was a petty and malicious old man. As an example, if he wanted to rid himself of anyone for one reason or another, he never took responsibility for the decision, but made it look like he was not involved. This can be illustrated by a little known fact. I do not know the reason, but Sturmer considered the journalist Kliachko as his personal enemy. One time Sturmer invited me to his office and said, "I have information that Kliachko is involved in military espionage for Germany; I ask you to arrest him and exile him from Petrograd." I asked him what this information was, as I had no such information in my official possession, and Sturmer replied that it was now my responsibility, and his request must be carried out. After two weeks of surveillance of Kliachko, a search was conducted. Neither surveillance nor search came up with anything, so Kliachko remained free. Sturmer remained dissatisfied and still insisted that Kliachko be exiled. I reported to Sturmer that I turned the entire matter over to military counter-intelligence, since this concerned their responsibility, and Sturmer agreed. Military counter-intelligence arrested Kliachko but did not know what to do with him because they had no evidence against him. I do not know what happened, but soon thereafter Sturmer gave me the following order: "Write to the military authorities not to deport Kliachko and to end the matter." I responded that I had already written that Kliachko was suspected of espionage and that I could not now write that I was mistaken, so it would be better if Sturmer wrote this letter himself. He agreed and said that he would discuss the matter with Prince Tumanov personally. Indeed, Kliachko was released quickly, and the matter was ended. Sometime later, Sturmer was upset over something and said to me, "But they could not exile Kliachko."

Sturmer was afraid of his own subordinates; he did not trust them, and at the same time did not use his authority to get rid of them. Such was his strange relationship with the Director of the Police Department, General Klimovich, who had been appointed to this position by Sturmer's predecessor, Khvostov. From the very start, Klimovich lashed out against Sturmer in every which way. Klimovich's tactlessness reached the point that even in receptions at his

FIGURE 13.2. General Evgenii Konstantinovich Klimovich. paradoxplaza.com.

headquarters, regardless if it was in front of a governor or a junior officer, he blamed Sturmer and called him stupid and dull. He criticized Sturmer's every order, discrediting him whenever and wherever he could. When Klimovich went on leave to the Caucasus, he started such a campaign against Sturmer that it finally came to the latter's attention. A different minister would have fired such a Director of the Police Department immediately. Sturmer's patience was finally exhausted, and he did fire Klimovich, but he also worked for his appointment as senator.

Sturmer's attitude toward Rasputin was very benevolent. None of the other ministers protected Rasputin as jealously as did Sturmer, who understood the stability of his position as being exclusively due to Rasputin's patronage. Sturmer was interested in every detail of Rasputin's daily activities, demanding to see the daily surveillance logs on him and becoming upset over every bit of minutiae. Once, Sturmer became terribly upset, having read in the log that when Rasputin was at the Kazan Cathedral, some beggar pilgrim recognized Rasputin in the crowd and said loudly, "This murderer should be strangled." Sturmer saw this as a direct threat on Rasputin's life, so he summoned me urgently, and I had to try really hard to calm him and assure him that there was no threat to Rasputin from this beggar woman.

There was another incident. It was on a Sunday between four and six in the afternoon, when I was making some necessary official visits. During my absence, the minister phoned the Security Bureau Office three times with the demand that I appear at his office on an urgent matter. When I learned of this and arrived at his office, his first words to me were, "Do you know what happened yesterday at Tsarkoe Selo?" I answered that I did not know. Then, in an agitated manner, Sturmer said, "Strange that I know, but you, the head of the Security Bureau do not know." I answered that this was not unusual because he was the Minister and received information from all over Russia, whereas I was the head of the Security Bureau only for Petrograd. Tsarskoe Selo was outside my area and the responsibility of the head of Palace Security, General Spiridovich. Sturmer apologized and said the did not know that. He then explained that the day before, two drunk naval officers showed up at Vyrubova's dacha at Tsarskoe Selo and demanded Rasputin's address. He saw this as a possible threat to Rasputin's life. This was the reason for the haste and the important matter about which I was phoned three times. I calmed Sturmer and told him there was no threat to Rasputin in this drunken escapade. In case of any real necessity to get Rasputin's address, they would not have gotten it this way. In addition, almost everyone in Petrograd knew that Rasputin lived at 64 Gorohovaia Street.

Sturmer surrounded his meetings with Rasputin with great secrecy. Most of their meetings were either at the Alexander Nevskii Monastery at Metropolitan Pitirim's, or at the apartment of Count Borkh at No. 18 Fontanka.

Sturmer carefully watched whether Rasputin had any clandestine meetings with anybody who might be soliciting any kind of position, knowing from personal experience how candidates for ministerial positions operated. For some reason, Sturmer was especially fearful that Rasputin was seeing secretly and setting up Sergei Efimovich Kryzhanovskii to be a candidate for the job of Minister of the Interior. Sturmer lasted in his job for a little over a year, after which he was appointed Minister of Foreign Affairs, replacing Sazonov, who was appointed to the State Council. During his tenure Sturmer showed no initiative, will, or desire to relieve the difficult conditions that the country faced during this year of hard times, and more important, he was not able to show any effort to protect the besieged highest authority from the excesses of a notorious society that had overstepped its mark. Simply put, as Interior Minister, Sturmer was literally a blank space.

The appointment of Alexander Alexeevich Khvostov, who was until now the Justice Minister, as Sturmer's replacement made a good impression on everyone. But, at the same time, everyone thought Khvostov could not last

FIGURE 13.3. Alexander Alexeevich Khvostov. Wikimedia Commons.

long simply because, at the moment, there was no other real candidate for this job. Actually, Khvostov could not have held on to his job—first, because he had nothing in common with Rasputin or his circle, and second, he was not fit for the position because, having spent his entire career at the Justice Ministry, he had no administrative experience. He was mild, fair, and a true gentleman, but he saw everything in terms of the law and legality and was not subject to any influences. Khvostov lasted three months as Interior Minister, and in October 1916 was replaced by A. D. Protopopov.

14

Protopopov and the Eve of Revolution

GENERAL GLOBACHEV

Reasons for Protopopov's appointment. The State Duma's attitude to this. Protopopov's assistants. Opposition. Protopopov's relationship to the royal family. Relationship with Rasputin. Official relationships and reports. Vacillation and attitude toward society. Liquidation of workers' groups. The Central War Industry Committee. The eve of the revolution. The mood of the troops. The measures taken by Protopopov and Khabalov. Military conferences. Protopopov's vanity. Protopopov's superstitions and the end of his career.

Alexander Dmitrievich Protopopov's appointment had been in the works for a long time by Rasputin and his clique. Protopopov frequently met Rasputin at Dr. Badmaev's (a Buriat), whom he had known for a long time and whose patient he was. There were also frequent visitors: Paul Gregorievich Kurlov, a future close advisor to Protopopov, and Alexei Tikhonovich Vasiliev, the future Director of the Department of Police. Protopopov's candidacy was completely acceptable to the Tsar. Protopopov was a people's representative and deputy to the president of the State Duma. He had the highest references from the King of England, from when he had been to England sometime before as a member of a Russian delegation. Thus, it would seem that Protopopov's appointment would have pleased everyone. But things turned out completely differently. The State Duma and the Progressive Bloc saw Protopopov as a turncoat, and could not forgive him for that. From the very first day of Protopopov's new position, the State Duma got into a vicious conflict with him. At the same time, Protopopov began to make many serious mistakes, thanks to his lack of competence and his ignorance in administering major departments.

As the head of the Interior Ministry, Protopopov did not have service competence, administrative experience, nor aptitude, and he did not want to

FIGURE 14.1. Alexander Dmitrievich Protopopov. Wikimedia Commons.

learn anything. He took P. G. Kurlov as a close advisor and wanted to appoint him as Assistant Minister of the Interior, but he could not do this—Kurlov's reputation was in the way. He had been dismissed from such a position in 1911 after the assassination of P. A. Stolypin. So, Kurlov was something of an unofficial advisor, and his role was unclear. The Director of the Department of Police was an old capable police department veteran, but he had little authority under Protopopov and little influence on him to give him good advice on broad political issues. Protopopov was left to his own devices, not having good responsible deputies or advisors. It is thus not surprising that the chaos in Protopopov's head caused blunder after blunder in his relationship with the State Duma and its president Rodzianko.

From the first days he took over the Ministry, Protopopov was badgered in the State Duma, as was the entire administration. It became immediately clear that Protopopov's tenure in office and the concurrent existence of the State Duma made it inconceivable that there would not be serious problems in the future, perhaps leading to a catastrophe. I told this to the Director of the Department of Police as early as November 1916, to which he answered that a firm course of action would be taken and there was nothing to fear. I was pleased by his answer because nothing was worse than uncertainty and vacillation for agencies that had to execute policies. I even gave my opinion that, given the harsh intransigent position of the State Duma toward the administration, it would be opportune to dissolve the fourth State Duma until the convening of the fifth State Duma, which could be done by the end of the war.

The "firm course of action" of the Director of the Department of Police turned out to be only words. Protopopov's relationship with the State Duma, the State Council, and even with the Council of Ministers became intolerable. However, Protopopov would not resign; at the same time, he did absolutely nothing against the opposition, against the revolutionary mood of the State Duma, or against the social groups, in spite of my many repeated reports. It must be that Protopopov either did not understand or did not want to understand his own position; on the one hand, he saw himself as a representative of society, and on the other he saw himself as indispensable to the Tsar and to Russia, destined to lead them out of great difficulties. In January 1917, as menacing events were imminent, he asked me during one of my reports, "What should be done?" I said there was only one decision: "You must either resign or dissolve the State Duma, after which its revolutionary center must be liquidated." Protopopov answered, "At such a difficult time I cannot abandon my Tsar, and as far as dissolving the State Duma, it is not up to me, but to the Chairman of the Council of Ministers, Prince Golitsyn, who has the order in his pocket but has decided not to make it public." Indeed, Golitsyn did have such an order, and he made it public on February 27, but it was too late.

I think Protopopov truly believed that he was called to save Russia and supposed that it would just happen by itself because of his dedication and closeness to the Royal Family. He should be given credit for loving the Royal Family deeply, especially the Empress Alexandra Fedorovna, whom he always mentioned with enthusiasm. He considered all of his success and firmness in his position as due to his closeness to the Royal Family, to which he was endlessly grateful. He was apparently able to figure out how the Empress had become so attached to Rasputin. I think that after the latter's death, Protopopov replaced him, and profited by the Empress' same boundless trust in him as she had had in Rasputin. This is the only way that it can be explained, that regardless of the bitter conflict between the State Duma and the administration over Protopopov, that he was not replaced until the very end.

Protopopov had treated Rasputin with great respect. He often visited with him at Badmaev's, and sometimes even visited his apartment, entering through a back entrance. He was interested in Rasputin's life, but not to the extent of Khvostov or Sturmer, and he did not address the problems of maintaining or reinforcing surveillance over him. He was not particularly affected by Rasputin's murder; the only thing he was anxious about was recovering Rasputin's body because that was what the Empress wanted.

Protopopov was completely ignorant in official matters; he did not understand, did not want to understand, and got everything mixed up. He did not
have a regular schedule for my reports, but he often called me, or I would go
to see him about urgent matters without an appointment. Sometimes when
there were extremely urgent matters, I had to wait for two hours in the reception area because he was carrying on personal conversations with acquaintances
or people he knew casually, and this was during scheduled official times. In
conversation he was a kind and courteous individual, but he liked to behave
in an affected manner that did not seem befitting a Minister. He met people
with the air of a weary woman, always complaining of the burden he carried
because of his love for the Emperor and Russia. Of the reports that he received
he understood nothing and got everything confused. He was completely unable
to understand who were the Bolsheviks, Mensheviks, Socialist Revolutionaries,
and so on. On more than one occasion he asked me to simply call them all
socialists—that way he could understand. At the beginning of 1917, he asked
me to brief his deputy Kukol'-Ianopol'skii, who must be given credit for quickly
grasping everything, notwithstanding that up to that time his duties had been
in an entirely different area.

After the January 9, 1917, liquidations I reported to Protopopov the
results of this liquidation and how the day of January 9 passed. Interestingly, it
was also the anniversary of the 1905 events. I reported that on this day about
200,000 workers went on strike in Petrograd and that the Security Bureau
liquidated three underground organizations, seizing three illegal printing presses
and a lot of illegal printed materials. Protopopov telephoned the Chairman of
the Council of Ministers, Prince Golitsyn, in my presence and reported that,
"January 9 went well. There were no strikes—just trifles. We arrested three
armed workers' detachments and seized a lot of material."

I became certain that Protopopov did not read the written reports of
the Security Bureau or of the Department of Police that were sent to the
Ministry on a daily basis. One time, in my presence, he called in his secretary
and ordered him to give him all of my reports and those of the Director of
the Department of Police for the past week. He wrote an inscription to the
Empress in English, personally sealed this mass of reports in a parcel, addressed
it to the Empress and ordered a courier to take it to Tsarskoe Selo immediately. If one takes into account that Protopopov could not repeat my report
accurately to Golitsyn, as I mentioned above, it is even more likely that he
did not give any reports to the Empress in person on the political situation
but simply left it to her to sort through all this written material. Whether the
Empress had the time or interest to read all that Protopopov sent her, I do
not know. Sometime later, in 1919, I was able to be convinced by what was
told to me by one of the Empress' ladies in waiting that Protopopov never

reported to the Empress on the seriousness of the political situation in Russia, and particularly in Petrograd, and that the Empress thought right up to the revolution that everything was fine.

Protopopov was unable to give decisive instructions, and when an urgent matter required this of him, he resorted to a collegial decision from his irresponsible advisors. So, when it became obvious that it was necessary to arrest the workers' group of the Central War Industry Committee, Protopopov was unable to sanction this, referring to how society would be unhappy about it (he did not want to accept that society no longer took him into account) and that the workers' group, being elected representatives, had legal immunity. When I demonstrated to him that he was wrong, he did not accept it and called for an emergency private conference to be chaired by Kurlov (an irresponsible individual). The conference decided to liquidate the workers' group, and Protopopov had to sanction the decision, but with a heavy heart.

When the workers' group of the CWIC was arrested, and when the investigation uncovered materials that clearly pointed to the serious preparation for revolt and the immunity that the leaders claimed—that is, as members of the State Duma—then the matter gathered momentum to liquidate the revolutionary center. However, Protopopov did not go along with this, no matter what arguments were presented to him. A complete list of the planned future Provisional Government came to light via agents of the Security Bureau. I presented this list to the Minister with a plea that this group also needed to be liquidated immediately, but Protopopov's only response was, "This is very important."

Toward the end, when the approaching catastrophe was close, Protopopov handed almost all decision making over to the Commander in Chief of the Petrograd Military District, General Khabalov. But Khabalov took no decisive measures, either, being fearful of "popular" society.

During Protopopov's tenure as Interior Minister I took the initiative to bring up the matter of the unreliability of the troops of the Petrograd garrison. I presented all the data on the makeup and mood of the garrison, repeating everything that I reported earlier to Sturmer. Consequently, a report was developed for the highest authority, and the Tsar agreed to replace some of the reserve troops of the Petrograd garrison with the Corps of Cavalry Guards transferred from the front. This decision, however, was not carried out as a result of the corps commander's request to leave the corps at the front. Thus, at the moment of the imminent workers' disturbances, Khabalov had to count on the unreliable garrison, which was ready to revolt at any minute.

It is true that Khabalov called a meeting prior to January 9 at the headquarters of the Petrograd Military District to discuss the degree of reliability of the garrison. The heads of all departments were present, all police chiefs,

and the City Prefect. I gave a report on the political situation of the moment
in relation to the events that were coming to a head. I concluded by stating
that if the military could guarantee the reliability and loyalty of the troops,
then the matter would turn out to be simply a typical workers' disorder that
could be put down quickly. When I turned to Lieutenant General Chebykin,
the commander of the reserves, with the question, "Can you vouch for your
troops?" He answered, "I can vouch for them completely, and even more, the
best of our crack troops from the training command will be assigned to put
down the disorders." The results of this meeting were reported to Protopopov
and Khabalov. Both were absolutely relieved. I was far from relieved.

As I have said, Protopopov understood nothing about running the Ministry, but he was very proud that such an important position in Russia was
given to him—it heightened his self-esteem. Not the least of his satisfaction
was that, in addition to being the Interior Minister, he was also the Commander in Chief of the Special Corps of Gendarmes. He even hurried to have
a Gendarme uniform tailored. It was funny to see Protopopov, a member of
the State Council, wearing spurs, trousers with general's stripes, an officer's coat
with red lining, and civilian epaulets. When he arrived at the State Duma in
this uniform, he was greeted with ridicule, after which he wore the uniform
only at home.

Protopopov relied exclusively on those agencies that were within his jurisdiction. After he had been in his position for about five months, he asked me
during one of my reports to explain the functions of the Department of Police
and its relationship to local gendarme agencies, which I did, schematically, on
a scrap of paper. I do not know why he did not ask this question of the Director of the Department of Police, Vasiliev, with whom he met on a daily basis.

Protopopov was superstitious. He corresponded with a famous London
occultist with whom he had become acquainted during his visit as a member of
the State Duma's delegation. Protopopov received predictions from the occultist
for January and February 1917 with indications of days that would be bad
and good for him personally. Protopopov asked me to write down these dates
for information purposes. I remember the predictions ending with February
14 and 27 highlighted as fateful days. Indeed, strange as it seems, these days
were fateful for Protopopov. February 14 was Miliukov's failed attempt to call
for a workers' uprising in Petrograd, and February 27 was the monarchy's last
day and the end of Protopopov's career.

15

Political Unrest—the Regiment Rebels

GENERAL GLOBACHEV

Plans of the revolutionary center and society's mood. Economic strikes. Political slogans and hunger. The government's rationing measures. The capital under military authority. The organization of military security in Petrograd. Rebellion in the Pavlovskii Regiment. Khabalov's optimism. February 27. The Soviet of Workers' and Soldiers' Deputies. Protopopov's behavior and optimism. Rebellion of the Volynskii Regiment. Kirpichnikov. Uprisings among other troops. Chaos in government institutions. The Security Bureau and a last conversation with Protopopov. Security troops join the rioters. Excesses and robberies. Gunfire on the streets. The situation at the end of the day on February 28. On the capital's streets. At Tsarskoe Selo. March 1. Pavlosk. Return to Petrograd. Machine gun fire. Brutality and excesses of the crowds. My arrest in the State Duma.

The Tsar Emperor's stay in Petrograd lasted a fairly long time. He left for the front only on February 22, after attending the church service at Tsarskoe Selo at the start of Lent. He stayed at Tsarskoe Selo for about a month. The leadership center of the Progressive Bloc decided to take advantage of this time to force the Tsar to present a responsible cabinet membership to the State Duma and thus limit the autocracy by reviewing the credentials of the ministers in advance. In spite of the repeated efforts of the President of the State Duma, Rodzianko, to compel the Tsar to do this, the latter decidedly refused to agree to this reform and left for military headquarters at Mogilev on February 22. When I met the former Justice Minister Dobrovol'skii after the revolution in one of the places where I was incarcerated, he told me that the order for a responsible ministry was signed by the Tsar and was in Dobrovol'skii's desk; it was to have been promulgated through the Senate at Easter. The Provisional

Government apparently knew this, but it was highly understandable why it failed to mention this.

The revolutionary center decided to take by force what they could have won otherwise by way of monarchical favor, but they did not count on that. The leaders were able to take the situation into account magnificently. The Russian army was holding its positions firmly for almost a year, and in the south in Bukovina the army was beginning to advance. All this time the country exerted all its might to supply the army and, in this regard, it surpassed itself, generating such stockpiles that would be enough to last for many years of a bitter war. The army was brought up to strength and enlarged. Everything was prepared for a common offensive for the spring of 1917 that had been planned and worked out by the allied command. The central powers would be crushed in this year. Thus, for a revolution in Russia there was a one-month window— that is, before April 1. Any further delay would ruin the revolution because of the military successes with which the favorable foundation for revolution would slip away. This is why the decision was made to take advantage of the first suitable moment after the Tsar's departure for headquarters and foment an uprising. I will not say that the plan for revolution was worked out in every detail, but the major phases and personnel were established. The game was played out very subtly. The military and court circles felt the approaching events, but they saw them simply as a palace coup in favor of the Grand Duke, Mikhail Alexandrovich, and an announcement of a constitutional monarchy. Even the leader of the K.D. Party, Miliukov, was convinced of this. This illusion was also accepted by many of the members of the Progressive Bloc. But the more radical elements under Kerensky's leadership had an entirely different view. They saw Russia after the monarchy only as a democratic republic. Neither they nor others were able to envision how things would turn out. There were some at that time who were prophetic, who understood that such a shock would result in a general collapse and anarchy, but nobody wanted to listen to them, considering them to be society's enemies. These were the sole surviving agencies, such as the Department of Police, Security Bureau, the Gendarme Administration, and some of the farsighted true Russian people who knew what would have to be dealt with in the future and what the destruction of the thousand-year monarchy would cost Russia.

Some isolated strikes began on February 23 in some factories and mills in the Vyborg side of Petrograd, and on the 24th the strikes grew, with the Putilov factory and manufacturing works joining from the Narva section. There were generally about 200,000 strikers. Such strikes had occurred in the past, and did not foreshadow anything dangerous for this time; but the CWIC that was involved with the mass of workers introduced political slogans and spread rumors about the approaching hunger and shortage of bread in the capital. It must be said that lines had begun to form in front of bakeries and bake houses to purchase bread. This did not happen because there was no bread or that bread was lacking, but because the population in Petrograd had greatly increased, and even though the number of bakeries grew, they did not provide enough hearths to bake a sufficient amount of bread. At the same time, the provisioning commission introduced a ration card system to regulate the distribution of bread. The supply of flour to provision Petrograd was sufficient. In addition, a sufficient amount of flour was trucked into Petrograd on a daily basis. So the rumors of impending hunger and absence of bread were provocations whose goal was to create great agitation and disturbance, and that indeed happened. Striking workers began to move to the center of the city in noisy crowds, demanding bread. What measures did the authorities take to put down these disturbances?

The commander of the Petrograd Military District, Lieutenant General Khabalov, was an excellent lecturer and pedagogue, having spent his entire career in a military education environment. He was neither a line officer nor a competent administrator; regardless of repeated advice and being in possession of complete, up-to-date information, he was unable to evaluate the situation and make the right decision, bearing in mind the unreliable reserve troops under him that were supposed to go the front, but that they absolutely did not want to do. Finally, he was not able, even by personal example, to attract the most steadfast troops to fulfill their duty and put down the disturbances.

On February 24, Khabalov took the capital into his own hands. Petrograd was divided into several sectors according to a preliminary worked-out plan. Each sector was under military command, but the police were removed from their assigned posts for some reason or other, and put under the sector commanders. Thus, the police, as of February 24, no longer served the city. The major streets and squares were set up with military posts, and communication between them and staff headquarters was by mounted patrols. Khabalov was at sector headquarters on Palace Square, and he directed all the defenses by telephone.

By removing the police, Khabalov decided to rely on the unreliable troops, on those factory-mill workers who had been activated two weeks earlier, and who had already been propagandized and did not want to be sent to the front. Of course some of the blame for this decision lies with the City Prefect, General Balk, who, apparently to relieve himself of all responsibility, had by February 24 handed over command of the city to military authority. In the meantime, he could have handled the disturbances and uprisings in a limited way, fulfilling his responsibilities to the end by use of foot and mounted police and the Petrograd gendarme division. In an extreme case, he could have invoked basic regulations of garrison responsibilities and requested assistance of some of the more steadfast cavalry units to put down the disturbances. The fate of Petrograd and that of Russia was given over to the unreliable Petrograd garrison that was under the influence of revolutionary elements that had infiltrated it. The garrison mutinied and, as it came to pass, brought shame and destruction to the country, which Kerensky later referred to as "the great Russian revolution."

The first signs of an uprising occurred on February 25. Soldiers of the Pavlovsk Life Guards regiment refused to obey their battalion commander and fatally wounded him on Koniushenoi Square. The ringleaders were arrested and turned over for court martial. Starting in the morning of February 26, crowds of workers moved from the outskirts to the center of the city, blocking the Nevskii Prospekt and Znamenskii Square, and moving toward the Tauride Palace, where the State Duma met. A demonstration erupted with red flags on Znamenskii Square that was stopped by the academy training command of the Volynsk Life Guards Regiment. The demonstrators were scattered by a salvo (eleven people were killed).

The mood of the troops during these days was one of vacillation. The infantry posts that were located on the main streets allowed the crowds of workers to come right up to them, engaged them in conversation, and let them pass through. The cavalry units allowed the workers to pet and feed their horses and chatted amiably with them. In a word, there was fraternization between the soldiers who were supposed to disperse the workers and the latter. Some military units had already gone over to the side of the demonstrators at this time. For example, a Cossack squadron on Znamenskii Square did not allow a mounted police detachment to disperse the crowd, and one of the Cossacks of this unit hacked to death a police officer who had tried to take a red flag away from a demonstrator.

All this was symptomatic and should have led General Khabalov to understand that his approach to maintain order was impossible.

At about six o'clock in the evening of February 26, I reported all this to General Khabalov, stressing that the troops were unreliable, to which he replied with irritation that he did not agree and that it was simply that some of the units being young soldiers were poorly instructed. With regard to the killing of the police officer, he responded, "I could never believe this." There and then I reported to him that I had intelligence that on the morning of February 27 there would be elections for the Soviet of Workers' Deputies at the factories and mills where workers would gather. Khabalov wanted to shut down all the factories and mills to prevent the elections, but I advised against that because the impression would be created that the authorities were keeping workers from returning to work, and the election of representatives to the Soviet of Workers' Deputies would take place anyway. Indeed, on the morning of February 27, rumors began to spread among the workers that the factories were shut down, and workers were not even trying to show up there. In addition, rumors were being spread of invitations by the State Duma to organize a Soviet of Workers' and Soldiers' Deputies, and this happened indeed, on the spur of the moment. The more energetic of the revolutionaries, who were hardly ever workers or soldiers, showed up at the State Duma and announced themselves as deputies from one or another industrial works or some military unit.

The Director of the Department of Police, Vasiliev, called me on the evening of February 26 to come to his apartment and forewarned me that the Minister of the Interior, who was there, wanted to see me. I found Protopopov and Vasiliev having coffee, as they had just finished supper. Sitting at the table, we of course talked about the instability of recent events. I reported on the activities of that day, of the excesses and of the mood of various units of the troops, and I attached great significance to all this. But, in looking at Protopopov, he seemed unconcerned; he seemed merely to have the heightened humor of someone after a good supper. From what Protopopov said, it became evident that he relied completely on Khabalov, and was convinced that all the disturbances would be put down. Protopopov spent the entire evening talking about his relationship with the Empress, and he recalled with considerable enthusiasm how she was such an intelligent and sensitive woman. As I left Vasiliev's, I could not understand why I was summoned at such a serious time; surely it could not have been to spend time having coffee.

By the morning of February 27, strikes spread throughout the capital's districts, and the strikes became one general strike. Crowds of workers began to move toward the State Duma; it became clear to anyone that this was the revolution's center. About noon, four regiments rebelled and went over to the workers: the Volynsk Life Guards, Preobrazhenskii Life Guards, Litovskii Life Guards, and Sappers. The barracks of all four of these regiments were in the district of the Tauride Palace and they became the first strongholds of the revolution.

The revolt began in the following way: the training command of the Volynsk Life Guards, having put down disturbances on Znamenskii Square the day before, was being formed in the morning in the courtyard of its barracks to be ready to put down any further disturbances. At this time, noncommissioned officer Kirpichnikov shot and killed staff Captain Mashkevich (sic), the commander of the training command. Not one of the officers present took command or punished the murderer. On the contrary, most of them, who were junior officers, fled, leaving command entirely to Kirpichnikov, who was proclaiming revolutionary slogans. The rebellious Volynsks headed for the Preobrazhenskii Barracks and almost used force to get them to join them (the first to join was the 4th Company of the Preobrazhenskii Regiment), and

Дни революцiи. Разгромлен. полиц. архивъ

FIGURE 15.1. Revolutionaries destroying police archives. Marinich collection.

later the same thing happened with the Litovskii Regiment and the Sappers. As soon as these units rebelled and went over to the workers, all the weapons in the barracks that were under the control of the regiments passed into the hands of the workers, whose first action was to rout the prisons, which were full of criminals and political prisoners, and to plunder the arsenal. Thus, an army of the most energetic rebels was formed, and things began to move even faster. Under the leadership of the liberated criminals, before anything else, government offices that housed data on criminals were destroyed. The district court was burned down; police precincts and criminal investigation departments were destroyed. For the time being, the Security Bureau was left alone. This is proof that the first leaders of the rebellious activities—or the "Great Russian Revolution"—were those released from prisons: the criminal elements. The troop units assigned to defend these institutions quickly went over to the rioters, and the destruction increased.

A half-company of the 3rd Strelkov Life Guards Regiment under the command of an ensign was sent to protect the regional Security Bureau Staff Headquarters. At three o'clock in the afternoon, I called in the commander of the half-company and asked him if he could vouch for his people. When he answered me that he could not, I ordered him to lead his half-company back to its barracks. I knew this half-company would bring me no advantage.

The work of the Security Bureau continued in a routine but reduced manner, providing information and reports on the course of events exclusively by telephone. Contact with police agencies and the Commander in Chief's staff ended. Although the telephone stations were still in the hands of the government, it was very difficult to get through, and with some agencies it was impossible. Contact was maintained with those organizations that had direct lines with the Security Bureau, such as the Winter Palace, City Prefecture, the Interior Minister, Tsarskoe Selo, and Security Bureau units that I kept informed of the course of events. Protopopov was at the Marinsky Palace at a meeting of the Council of Ministers, and I was still able to talk to him by telephone up to three o'clock. I reported to him one last time that the situation was hopeless; it was impossible to rely on the garrison, which was gradually going over to the insurgents.

The Commander in Chief, who had moved from the regional staff headquarters to the Admiralty and then to the Winter Palace, and who was informed of everything that was going on in Petrograd, finally understood that he could not count on the soldiers, since all those who were called up from the reserves to put down the insurgent troops were going over to their side. By the evening of February 27 he was left with only his own staff.

FIGURE 15.2. Dispersion of a demonstration in the streets of Petrograd as a result of machine gun fire. Wikimedia Commons.

Meanwhile, the uprising continued to grow: by five o'clock in the after-noon disorder had spread to the Petersburg [*sic*] side; looting of stores and apartments began; officers were disarmed on the streets; policemen were beaten and killed; and gendarme officers and junior officers were killed. In short, by five o'clock it was clear that authority no longer existed and the capital was in the hands of mobs.

At this time I gave the following orders regarding the Security Bureau: the Security Bureau building (on the corner of Mytninskii Embankment and Alexandrov Avenue) was to be surrounded by posted observers who would retreat as the crowd approached and report on the crowd's intentions, and all the while the work of the Bureau would continue. By five o'clock the various posts reported that an armed crowd of three thousand had destroyed the distill-ery on Alexandrov Avenue and was moving toward the Security Bureau, and so as not to endanger people to excesses or needless loss of life, I ordered all the staff present to leave immediately and go to their homes. Having done that, I locked all the entrances to the building and left with my closest subordinates.

There remained sentries on duty at the Stock Exchange Bridge and the Palace Bridge. They were already vacillating, which could be seen on the anx-ious faces of the soldiers and officers. Palace Square was quiet, but on Morskoi and Gorohovoi there was gunfire—some scant number of soldiers were lying scattered about, shooting at each other. From time to time an armored car drove by shooting at undetermined targets.

By six o'clock in the evening, I was in the Security Command Building (No. 26 Morskai, corner of Gorohovoi) and in telephone contact with Tsarkoe Selo (the Palace Command) and the Commander in Chief staff headquarters (the Winter Palace). My most important task was to report on the current flow of events in Petrograd to Lieutenant Colonel Terehov, who was the deputy of the Palace commandant, General Groten.

Around eight in the evening, security people began to gather in the Security Command. They were forced to abandon their posts of providing security to various highly placed personages and organizations. There were the wounded: one individual died of a head wound there and then. These people reported that many ministers were arrested in their homes and were taken somewhere. People from the Marinsky Palace reported that a meeting took place during the day between Rodzianko and the Grand Duke Mikhail Alex-androvich, who, as he was leaving, shook Rodzianko's hand warmly, exchanged some words, and left in an elated mood. From there, he went to the Winter Palace and asked Khabalov not to fire on the people, saying, "It is not befit-ting to kill people from the Tsar's palace."

The result of the last meeting of the Council of Ministers, as it became known later, was Prince Golitsyn's royal decree dissolving the State Duma and replacing Interior Minister Protopopov with Makarenko (who had been up to that time the head military prosecutor). It became clear to me from the reports of the Security Command staff that the government no longer existed.

Around ten in the evening, the gunfire fell silent and did not start up again until six the next morning. I spent the whole night at the telephone communicating with Tsarkoe Selo.

At six o'clock in the morning of February 28, gunfire started again, now with greater intensity. On the Morskoi, next to the Security Command Building, the telephone station (No. 24 Morskoi) defended by a company of the Petrograd Life Guards Regiment was taken by storm. This happened in less than half an hour, after which it became necessary to evacuate the Security Command Building because an armed crowd of workers and soldiers blocked the courtyard and rushed up a back entrance into the Command Building; there was time only to run out the main entrance onto Morskoi.

From that moment on, my official duties ended. All of my departments had been routed and were occupied by the insurgent mob. There was nothing further for me to do in Petrograd, so I decided that one of my subordinates and I would make our way to Tsarskoe Selo. I reasoned, correctly, that there, in the residence of the Tsar and Empress, the revolt would be repulsed. Also, perhaps loyal troops from the supreme Commander in Chief's headquarters had already been deployed to suppress the rebellion in Petrograd.

We both agreed with this decision and began to make our way along Gorohovoi to the Tsarskoe Selo railway station. It was almost impossible to get through; there was gunfire up and down the streets and across streets, and it was hard to figure out who was shooting at whom. I did not see any sentries guarding anything; I only saw groups of armed workers, soldiers, and sailors intermingling with all kinds of rabble; they were all firing, rushing about, but I do not think that they themselves knew what they were doing. Armored cars drove about noisily, and machine gun fire could be heard. I did not see any killed or wounded. We had to run with difficulty from one courtyard to another along Gorohovoi, and we were able only to get to the Catherine Canal. We could not get any further—it was impossible to get to Sennyi Square because it was blocked completely by armored cars, which were being driven into food stores. We had to turn sharply to the right and get onto Ismailov Avenue. This is what we saw there: almost the entire Ismailov Regiment came out of its barracks and gawked at the clouds of burning paper cinders floating in the air. The District Court was burning, and workers and rabble were coming out of the barracks armed with whatever: rifles, revolvers, sabers, broadswords, and even hunting rifles. It was difficult to walk down Ismailov Avenue because it was filled with crowds. We had to take a roundabout route, taking a sharp turn to the right toward the Obvodnyi Canal, and from there to the Warsaw

Railway Station. It was so hard to get through the city at that time that it took us almost four hours to get from Morskoi to the Warsaw Station. The area around the station was relatively quiet. The train to Gatchina had left at one in the afternoon after a check on the passengers by a hastily organized workers' committee. We got to the Alexandrov Station, and from there we got to Tsarskoe Selo by cab.

After everything we had seen and experienced in Petrograd, I was struck by the order and calm that reigned at Tsarskoe. His Majesty's escort guards were at their posts, the palace police continued to carry out their duties, and it seemed that the life of the town was proceeding normally. Even so, there was a sense of anxiety and anticipation of something inevitable coming; I saw this in the serious, gloomy faces of the staff.

In the absence of the temporary palace commandant, General Groten, I turned to the head of the palace police, Colonel Gerardi, and reported to him on the course of events in Petrograd. I asked if the defense of Tsarskoe Selo could be counted on, since in my opinion, the Petrograd insurgent mob would show up in Tsarskoe by evening. Gerardi told me that Tsarskoe Selo was absolutely safe—that a loyal garrison of up to five thousand would repulse the mob, that the Alexander Palace was encircled with machine guns, that Grand Duke Mikhail Alexandrovich was at Tsarskoe that day to ensure the Empress of complete security, that there was no threat or danger to her or the children, and that the palace was so secure that he was thinking of moving his family there. In addition, he persuaded the Empress to put off her trip to Mogilev with the children, after which the Tsar's train assigned to take Her Majesty was cancelled. In general, my discussions with Gerardi and others gave me the impression that they did not understand the essence of the developing events. In their opinion, everything was reduced simply to a palace coup in favor of Grand Duke Mikhail Alexandrovich. When I tried to refute this view on what was going on, it seemed to me that I was looked at with a certain smile, as if I did not know what they had all known for the longest time.

This happened between two and three in the afternoon. The Tsar's train was expected to arrive from Mogilev at midnight. At six o'clock I was at Gerardi's a second time, and found him in a very depressed state; he had lost his self-confidence. There was no longer any talk of defending Tsarskoe Selo; apparently everything was focused only on saving oneself and one's family, and I understood that here in Tsarskoe Selo, just as in Petrograd, it was not possible to count on any support in defense of the Tsar's throne. Indeed, by evening, revolutionary crowds from Petrograd were approaching, and gunfire began. No resistance was shown. The garrison at Tsarskoe quickly and consistently went over to the side of the insurgents, including Her Majesty's escort guard and palace police. The Empress, now aware of everything that had transpired in Petrograd, came out onto the balcony of the Alexander Palace and asked that there be no resistance at the palace so that there be no useless bloodshed.

What had happened in Petrograd now began in town: destruction of police stations, freeing incarcerated people from jails, robbing stores, and so on. The Tsar's train from Mogilev that was supposed to arrive at midnight did not arrive at two or at five in the morning. Rumors began to spread that the Tsar had been arrested and would not arrive at Tsarskoe. In light of there being no reason to stay in Tsarskoe, and even being dangerous to do so, my assistant, Lieutenant Colonel Prutenskii, and I made off on foot for Pavlovsk, where on the morning of March 1 it was as quiet as it had been at Tsarskoe the day before. However, from noon on similar disturbances began, mainly with store break-ins. A rumor spread that speculators fleeing Petrograd were hiding in the outskirts of the capital and that there was an order to detain them. This started a number of detentions and killing of innocent people.

My assistant and I found shelter in one of the dachas that were empty at this time of year, where we stayed until five o'clock. After that we decided to return to Petrograd. Going anywhere farther from Pavolovsk was unwise, because the revolutionary wave was rolling farther and farther, gradually seizing more and more neighborhoods of the province.

When we got back to Petrograd, we discovered that all former government officials and commanders had been arrested. The revolutionary committee occupying the State Duma was in charge of everything. All troops had gone over to the revolutionaries. The Soviet of Workers' and Soldiers' Deputies was formed under the chairmanship of Chkeidze and coordinated by the deputy chair Kerensky, who was also a member of the revolutionary committee. The only opposition to this authority came from the cadets of the Pavlovsk and Petrograd military academies, but they were quickly neutralized.

We had to go by foot from Tsarskoe Selo Railway Station to the apartment of an officer friend of mine on the Petrograd side, where we hoped to find temporary refuge, as no cabs or trolley cars were operating. The new authorities and some suspicious individuals used automobiles. Gunfire filled the streets, and I heard from somewhere the sound of machine gun fire, but I did not see who was being fired upon or who was doing the shooting. Nor did I see any dead or wounded, although the whistling of bullets could be distinctly heard. The gunfire on the Petrograd side was much stronger—this was the resisting cadets.

Even at that time I was very interested in knowing who was being fired upon in Petrograd, as there was almost no opposition, and particularly, who was firing the machineguns? For example, as I was passing by the St. Isaac Cathedral, I clearly heard machine gun fire, as if coming from one of the cupolas of the church. A few days later I recalled all this, and the reason for the machine gun fire became clear to me. A month before the revolution, the Security Bureau had received intelligence that three hundred machine guns, ready and packed for shipment to the front, had vanished. Even after a thorough search by the Security Bureau, the guns were not found. It was understandable that once the city was no longer maintained by the police, from February 24 on, that it became possible for the machine guns to be deployed with impunity to wherever was convenient, which had been done in case the troops did not go over to the side of the insurgent workers and had to be forced to do so.

Everybody still remembered 1905, when the troops were able to restore order, and the revolution was unsuccessful strictly because the troops remained loyal. Furthermore, as I have said, as the troops gradually joined the insurgent workers, mobs took possession of the troops' weapons, taking them from the barracks and arsenals, and this included machine guns. The placement of machine guns on rooftops, in attics, and belfries demonstrated that they had fallen into the hands of people who did not know how to use them. When it became clear that influencing the troops by force was not necessary, that the troops were coming over to the insurgents without being coerced, the placement of machine guns was dropped into the hands of fate. The machine guns were now being used by all kinds of criminals and hooligans to create as much disorder as possible. Except for the crackle of gunfire and noise, the machine guns could cause no harm, as they were being fired from positions at which they could not be effective.

Later, during the first days following the revolution, Kerensky and his closest associates tried to explain the machine gun fire by claiming that the machine guns had been placed earlier by orders of Khabalov, Protopopov, Balk, and me, and that it was supposedly the police who were firing them. However, this accusation could not stand up to any critique, and Kerensky had to dismiss this nonsense because he could not gather any evidence and, it seems, the data that were gathered showed that the workers were firing the machine guns from the start. It was necessary for Kerensky to spread this blame to inflame the anger of the masses against the old regime in general and against the police in particular.

The atrocities committed by the rioting mobs against the police, the Corps of Gendarmes, and even line officers in the February days are beyond description. This does not at all diminish the excesses that the Bolsheviks subsequently perpetrated.

I am talking only about Petrograd, and not referring to what everybody already knows about what was happening in Kronstadt. Policemen who hid in basements and attics were literally torn to pieces; some were crucified against walls, some were torn in half by having their legs tied to two automobiles, and some were hacked to death with sabers. In some cases, arrested policemen and gendarme never made it to where they were to be jailed but were shot on the Neva embankment, their bodies dropped into holes in the ice. Those of police ranks who were unable to change into civilian clothes and go into hiding were mercilessly killed. One police officer was tied to a couch and burned alive. The superintendent of the Novodervensk Precinct, who had just had a serious appendectomy operation, was dragged from his bed and thrown into the street, where he died immediately. A crowd broke into the Provincial Gendarme Administration and viciously beat Lieutenant General Volkov, breaking his leg, after which they dragged him to Kerensky at the State Duma. Seeing the wounded and disfigured Volkov, Kerensky assured him that he would have complete safety, but he did not keep him in the Duma and did not send him to a hospital, which he could have done. Instead he ordered that he be transported to a temporary jail, where that very night the drunken head of the guards shot him. Line officers, especially of higher rank, were arrested in the streets and beaten. I personally saw Adjutant General Baranov brutally beaten while he was being arrested on the street and taken to the State Duma with his head bandaged.

Unknown groups of people wandered about the city at this time, conducting general searches, accompanied by crowds, robbing and killing, supposedly under the guise of warrants granted by counter-revolutionaries. Some apartments were robbed clean, and the stolen possessions, which included furniture, were openly loaded onto carts in front of everyone and taken away. Government facilities and private homes and apartments were subject to complete devastation. For example, Count Frederik's personal home was looted and burned down.

There is a great number of such examples. At the time, Kerensky called all this "the wrath of the people."

By the evening of March 1, it was absolutely clear that the former authority did not exist, that the old regime had ended. There was only the slight hope of how the High Command and army might react to the events that had come to pass. Even this hope was of little comfort, as rumor was already spreading about the Tsar's abdication and that army commanders at the front were submitting to the new order. Bulletins and orders of the Provisional Revolutionary Committee signed by Rodzianko began to appear. Incidentally, an order by Rodzianko stated that everyone having military rank must register at the State Duma.

In such a situation, in light of an absence of refuge in Petrograd, and in order to avoid being the victim of the brutal excesses of the raging mobs, I decided to go personally to the State Duma. I asked an officer acquaintance of mine to take me there as if he had arrested me. It was hard to get into the Duma. It was late, and crowds of drunken soldiers and workers surrounded it. I got inside the building with some difficulty, and it was only thanks to identifying myself by rank and profession to a student who was at a control desk that he handed me over to a member of the State Duma, Papadjanov, who was responsible for the control and disposition of those arrested. The latter had me wait for at least two hours and finally had me sent under escort to the Ministerial Pavilion, where I was settled in as under arrest of the revolutionary order.

After experiencing the last three days, and having been in the streets of Petrograd, at Tsarskoe Selo, and Pavlovsk, and seeing the conduct of the old regime in terms of its opposition to the destructive forces that had been eating away at our government system over the past two years, I was convinced that the old order simply capitulated and showed no opposition to the insurgency. No one could stand in defense of the old order. Not a single authoritative individual could have averted the catastrophe by personal example, or by strength of conviction, or by showing enough energy. A simple rebellion of the Petrograd Garrison brought down the thousand-year monarchy. Did the Russian people participate in this in some general way? No, they did not. But then, the entire leadership of the intelligentsia class, not excluding some government agencies, willingly or unwillingly participated in the conspiracy. The people were entirely passive, and the worst of the criminal elements, taking advantage of the moment, gave in to their most cruel and brutal instincts.

Further, beyond the capital, the revolution progressed entirely painlessly. The provinces simply joined the new order, considering the matter over and done with.

Thus, no persons and no places opposed the insurgents. The only exception was during the first two days, on February 27 and 28, when some inconsequential skirmishes occurred between the rebelling troops and those who remained loyal. So there is no point in talking about some kind of martyrs for the revolution that Kerensky respectfully buried on Mars Field. I am deeply convinced that the two hundred people counted as martyrs included the accidental deaths of careless passersby or those killed by their own people. I am certain that among the counted martyrs were vagrant Chinese who died in hospitals, and even two Security Bureau detectives who were killed. Now they could all be called "martyrs for the revolution." Kerensky needed martyrs, come what may, so that he could intensify the "great bloodless Russian revolution," and so martyrs they became.

16

Globachev's Track Record

A Description and Commentary of Globachev's Tenure and Track Record as Head of the Petrograd Okhrana

ZINAIDA I. PEREGUDOVA, JONATHAN DALY,
AND VLADIMIR G. MARINICH

And so Globachev's tenure as Chief of the Petrograd Okhrana, and his career, came to an end, as did the careers and even lives of many of the other Tsarist government officials. Now the issue for Globachev was survival. But what might have been in the offing had the revolution not happened? Had he done enough? Could his security command have stopped or delayed what did come about? The commentary of Peregudova and Daly, from their introduction to the Russian edition of Globachev's memoirs follows, as the comments of Globachev's contemporaries, which attest to Globachev's activities and to those of others at that time.

"Of course, a major part of the blame for the inability to take the necessary measures lies with the government, and especially with the last emperor of Russia. Could it be said, however, that a more severe and demanding an official in charge of the Okhrana in Petrograd in February 1917 could have averted what fate had in store for that month?

"In the words of Alexander A. Blok, 'The reports of the Okhrana in 1916 give the best characterization of the public mood; they are filled with alarm, but their voice could not be heard by the dying regime.'[1] Based on reports of the Department of Police that have survived, and on Globachev's memoirs, in the summer of 1916 the latter called upon the commander of the Petrograd Military District, General N. E. Tumanov, to remove the army reserve units from the capital because of the unreliability and propagandizing activities. However, Tumanov refused to do this. In the fall of 1916 Globachev repeatedly warned of the growing hostility of the public against the political system, particularly against the royal family. The political police, however, were not able to convince its superiors of this extraordinary moment and the need to take decisive and effective measures.

"By the beginning of September the active discontent of the masses increased sharply. Complaints were heard from everywhere about overt violations, the worthlessness of the government, and the worsening of the material situation—hunger, unequal distribution of foodstuffs and other essential items, and the sharp increase in inflation. 'The foodstuff crisis, writes Globachev, is the sole and significant reason for the public's bitterness and discontent.' He continues, 'At the present time we have definite and accurate information that allows us to conclude categorically that this entire movement has an economic basis and is not tied to any purely political program. It will take only this movement to express itself in some specific act (a pogrom, a major strike, a massive confrontation between the public and the police, etc.) at which time it would become purely political.' Globachev's reports at the end of November repeated these apprehensions. It would seem that even though the results of earlier repressive measures against the Social Democratic organization left it in an 'awful condition,' and the SRs were absolutely 'broken up,' Globachev insisted on further arrests of the 'organizing body' (Mensheviks) on September 13 and the terrorist anarchist organization on September 17. Bolsheviks were arrested from December 9th to the 19th and on the night of January 1, 1917. As Globachev reported the next day to A. T. Vasiliev, the Director of the Department of Police, the steering committee of the Bolshevik faction of the Social Democratic Party remained intact and presumably was attempting to initiate demonstrations on January 9, the anniversary of Bloody Sunday. Three days later, on January 5, Globachev submitted a report based on intelligence from a secret agent. 'The mood in the capital is one of extreme uneasiness. The wildest rumors are circulating about the government's intentions to initiate various reactionary measures, and the intentions of groups hostile to the government and the public possibly starting revolutionary activities and excesses. Everybody is waiting for some exceptional act from one side or the other. Just as serious and as alarming is that people are waiting for a revolutionary spark or something in the near future—a palace coup—a precursor of which, as many thought, was the murder of Rasputin.' Globachev adds that the current political moment is reminiscent of the eve of 1905.

"From January 1 to the 17th the Okhrana conducted searches and arrests every day of the leaders of the Bolshevik Party, the Menshevik steering committee, and at the end of the month the working group of the Central War Industry Committee. With each passing day the reports grew more alarming. The day before January 9th, Globachev reported 'on the mood of the revolutionary underground' by party, and drew the conclusion that 'the number of recent liquidations have significantly weakened the underground, and at the present time, according to the reports of agents, it is possible that on January 9th there may be some uncoordinated attempts to organize meetings, but all this will be unorganized; however, we are watching the propagandizing of the proletariat.'

"The reports of the Okhrana become more comprehensive and address the mood that is rampant in all elements of Russian society. In an extensive memorandum from January 19th that the Department of Police received from an informant, it states that 'the postponement of the meeting of the State Duma up to now has become the center of opinions across all the various segments of the capital's society . . . the public (in the streets, in trolley cars, in theatres, in stores, etc.) criticizes the government's actions in the most intolerable and harshest of tones . . . The Duma is overpopulated with politicians who are not competent to do real work; all kinds of "home front heroes," dubious ambitious members of the councils of towns, Zemstvos, Central War Industry Committees, etc., etc., who are well aware of their impotence to help the government to set things right at home rather than cause destruction with their speeches . . . Their propaganda that was not stopped at the very beginning fell on the fertile ground of war exhaustion . . . it is possible that the dissolution of the State Duma will be the signal to spark the revolutionary ferment among the various elements of society and it will come to the government to fight, not against insignificant groups that break away from the majority of the Duma membership, but with all of Russia . . .' The memorandum continues with the mood of the army in that the anger of the people demands 'the bloody sacrifice of the bodies of ministers and generals, and even the families of politicians.' There is the beginning of loose talk of a dangerous tone that even touches on the sacred person of the Tsar Emperor.

"On January 26th Globachev writes to the Department of Police: 'As a supplement to my report of 19 January, Number 47, I am respectfully submitting the following to you. It is recent information from a secret agent known to me and deals with the mood and immediate intentions of the leaders of the progressive and opposition factions of the capital's society.'

"The report was very serious. It dealt with the situation in the State Duma and its groups, plans, goals, its relationship with the government, the Central War Industry Committee and its position, the mood of militant workers' groups, etc.

"This report of January 26th also addresses the mood and intentions of the liberal opposition and its thinking about which group might grasp power and how this authoritative group might 'share the bear's skin.' Everybody wanted to leave the right to be at the forefront of overturning the regime, and in paving the path to an 'enlightened future' with their corpses to some other group, not to themselves, but then to offer their services to the country as 'knowledgeable and competent builders of a new government.' What will happen and how all this will unfold is hard to tell at the present time, but in any case, the liberal opposition in society is without doubt correct about one thing: events of extraordinary importance that are fraught with exceptional consequences are 'on the horizon.'

"From all of the above-mentioned documents it is possible to conclude that the Okhrana was well informed of the situation in the capital. The composition of the officer staff of the Okhrana was very impressive, the officers received daily intelligence, analyzed it, and developed reviews and reports that were sent to the Department of Police.

"The arrests that were conducted in January confirmed the intelligence that the Okhrana had collected. The materials that were confiscated during searches of the workers' group of the Central War Industry Committee pointed to the group preparing demonstrations and support for the State Duma and in provoking the Duma to seize power. The demonstrations were planned for either the 10th or the 14th of February. Globachev's report of February 5 stated that they could be successful considering the resolute mood of the working masses. In reality, given the high inflation and the recurring unavailability of bread and meat in stores, 'we can expect large scale strikes, armed conflicts with the police and military, so that the bloody events will push the country to a revolutionary coup in favor of the bourgeois elements of society.'

"Globachev's reports of February 5 and 7 disturbed the Petrograd City Prefect, General A. P. Balk, who called for a meeting on what kind of measures to take to establish order and calm in the capital during February 10 to 14. Globachev was the first to speak at the meeting. He described the mood of the revolutionary organizations in Petrograd. Measures to counter potential disturbances were worked out at the meeting.

"On February 14th, 80,000 workers went on strike in Petrograd. It appears that Globachev did not order any arrests. He reported that crowds of about five hundred people were in the streets raising their voices, 'down with the war,' 'down with the police,' and 'beat up the robbers.' Bakeries that had gone through all they had closed their doors. The crowds demanded the resignation of Protopopov. There were rumors of imminent pogroms. Officers, especially of junior ranks, took part in the disturbances and ridiculed the police.

"The following week was colder, and it seems to have quieted things down. However, on February 21, when the Putilov factory, which normally employed tens of thousands of workers, was closed, the public mood became more belligerent. On February 23, people were in the streets celebrating International Women's Day. Within the crowds were many women, children, and students. It seemed to be a peaceful event, but the police were on guard and in several places they dispersed the crowd.

"February 23, 1917, saw the start of massive disturbances. 78,443 workers did not show up for work. The next day this number increased to 107,585, and on February 25, the figure was 201,248, although department records indicated 240,000 people.

"Petrograd's City Prefect, Balk, who was appointed in November 1916 by Protopopov, later claimed that Globachev was not in a position to explain the reasons for the popular disturbances of February 23. Balk states in his diary that 'neither the Department of Police nor the Okhrana could answer my question as to the motives for this occurrence. At the evening meeting, the Chief of the Okhrana, Major General Globachev, did not have information to explain that day's events.' Even though Globachev reported on the mood in Petrograd on a daily basis, and for months he sounded the alarm about impending disturbances, the events of February 23 seemed unexpected.

"Spiridovich in his book writes that Globachev constantly spoke of the inevitability of a revolution, yet he missed its start. Notwithstanding Spiridovich's respect for the Chief of the Petrograd Okhrana, he considered that Globachev was not able to take the proper measures. 'He was a realist who understood well the unfolding events, but he did not know how to deal with them.'[2]

"In an earlier report, Globachev warned A. P. Balk, S. S. Khabalov, the Petrograd Military District Command, and Protopopov that revolutionary activists were inciting demonstrators to make more decisive anti-government

FIGURE 16.1. Maj. Gen. Alexander Ivanovich Spiridovich. Wikimedia Commons.

protests the next day, and Globachev added that the troops in the city were unreliable. Khabalov gave orders to arrest the revolutionary leaders. Later, Globachev asserted that it could have been possible to end the disturbances by using the regular city police and the Gendarme Division. However, control of the situation slipped from the government's hands.

"Intelligence had found out that the Social Democrats were planning to disrupt the electric power plant, other essential utilities in the city, and to launch an armed uprising, and the anarchists were planning to blow up the Okhrana building and the regional Gendarme Administration facility. On February 25, Globachev recommended the immediate arrest of some two hundred revolutionary activists and of the regenerated workers' group of the War Industry Committee. That night the police detained one hundred members of revolutionary organizations, including five members of the Petrograd committee of Social Democrats.

"Although the Petrograd Okhrana actively continued its work, it got less support from the city police. On Sunday, February 26, the Okhrana received only six telephone reports from among all the city's police precincts. By contrast, Globachev received reports from five secret agents. On average there was usually one report per month from secret agents, so this is a large number of reports for one day. One of the agents, V. E. Shurkanov, waxed prophetic. He stated that if the troops remain loyal to the government, the revolutionary movement will be resolved, but if not, nothing will save the country from a revolutionary coup.

"At that time the troops were almost completely loyal to the government, and in a few instances they fired on the crowds. Only one company of the Pavlovski Regiment rebelled in the middle of the day. One of Globachev's last reports, on February 26, details conditions in the capital almost by the hour. He recounts the number of people and the number of police and troops who were injured and killed on various streets throughout the day. He further reports that members of revolutionary organizations were scheduling a meeting for later that evening, among whom would be Alexander Kerensky and a member of the State Duma by the name of Sokolov. Globachev proposed to arrest those present.[3]

"Recalling the February days, Spiridovich noted that Globachev realized that 'the revolution is coming at us.' Even though he was an outstanding officer, 'he was unable to influence the minister to act.' Later, Globachev claimed that he had warned Khabalov at about six o'clock that evening that the crowds refused to disperse even though they were fired on, and that he could not count on the troops billeted in Petrograd. Khabalov allegedly refused to believe this. Balk, however, stated that Globachev, supposedly, assured him that the troops were loyal and that the disturbances would calm down.

"On Monday morning, February 27, crowds were in the streets. The city was in chaos, people were looting, breaking into government buildings, etc. On that day Globachev sent his last dispatch to the Department of Police with a report of what was happening in the city. The dispatch was sent with haste to the office of Colonel Vasiliev, who was in charge of a unit in the Department of Police. This was Globachev's last day of service. The February Revolution had begun."[4]

Globachev's reputation as Chief of the capital's Okhrana Bureau was that of an honorable and capable officer; his record of effective investigations, arrests, and "liquidation" of revolutionary groups is documented in Alexander Blok's *Poslednie Dni Imperatorskoi Vlasti* (The Last Days of Imperial Power). There were a few who had doubts about him. An interesting observation was made by one of Globachev's colleagues, Major General Alexander Ivanovich Spiridovich, who had been in charge of Palace Security, but by 1916 had been appointed City Prefect of Odessa. Thus, he was no longer in the thick of what was going on in the capital. Spiridovich found Globachev to be "clever, industrious, efficient, dependable, and profoundly decent. He was a typically good gendarme officer, with a profound sense of duty and love for the Tsar and motherland. But he was soft and could not press his supervisors too much. He was good for peacetime, but soft for the coming troubled times. He did not have any of Gerasimov's mettle, who together with Durnovo and Stolypin, suppressed the first Russian Revolution."[5] Spiridovich's comparison of Globachev to Gerasimov fails to take into account that Gerasimov indeed had as his superiors, and supporters, Stolypin and Durnovo, both capable and formidable individuals, while Globachev's superiors were Vasiliev and Protopopov. In fact, Globachev "was not listened to by either the Director of the Police Department or the Minister of the Interior, Protopopov, whose only interest was in how security for Rasputin was organized."[6] In any event, Stepan Beletskii, who was appointed Assistant Minister of the Interior some time after Dzhunkovskii's dismissal, did not have much use for the latter—who, it will be remembered, appointed Globachev. Nevertheless, Beletskii had confidence in Globachev. After the February Revolution, Beletskii testified before the Provisional Government's investigative commission that he had approved Globachev's early promotion to Major General in January 1916 and supported him when others intrigued against him and, subsequently, found Globachev's surveillance and reports on conditions in Petrograd to be "entirely satisfactory."[7] It may be that his early promotion to Major General was associated with another promotion. The Tsar was thinking of making some personnel changes, and the Palace was unhappy with Major General Balk, the Petrograd City Prefect, and with Vasiliev, the Director of the Department of Police. Spiridovich had been lobbying to get the Prefect position in the capital[8] and, according to Globachev's daughter, Globachev was scheduled to be appointed Director of the Department of Police at Easter time, 1917, replacing A. T. Vasiliev.[9]

Globachev was known to others, and they had their particular point of view of him. Maurice Paleologue, who was the last French Ambassador to the Russian court, left an extensive, and dramatically written memoir of his tenure in St. Petersburg. As the crisis of political conditions in Russia grew, he wrote, "What is the Okhrana contemplating now? What plot is it weaving? I am told that its present Chief, General Globatchev [*sic*] is not altogether deaf to reason. But in times of crisis, the spirit of an institution will always prevail against the personality of its chief."[10]

Leon Trotsky in his *History of the Russian Revolution* refers to the "venerable General Globachev" (маститый Генерал Глобачев).[11]

17

Turmoil

SOFIA GLOBACHEVA

February 27 was a fateful day for Russia, and for everyone. Just the day before, the city came to a stop. The city was in semi-darkness, and there were all kinds of rumors going about. I won't go into details, but I will describe what happened immediately to my husband and me. My husband and all his subordinates were in the office the entire night. The morning report stated that crowds were on the way, demolishing government buildings and killing officials, and were moving toward our residence. Someone cut the telephone wires, and my husband, unable to establish communication with the authorities, decided to go to Morskoi Street, where there was an Okhrana office and where two of his senior subordinates lived. Upon hearing his decision, I quickly took our son (our daughter was in boarding school in Moscow) to some acquaintances who lived near us and asked them not to allow him to take a single step outside until I came back for him. I hurried back to my husband, who had already changed into civilian clothes and was sitting in the automobile with his senior assistant. I hopped in, and we drove off. As I left the house, I told our servant that if we were not back by eight that evening, she should dine without us. I did not think back then that I would never return to our apartment.

After driving off a little way, my husband decided to go back and got out of the automobile; his assistant drove on, holding me to keep me from following my husband. However, I jumped out and joined my husband. We headed toward home, but in front of the bridge that crossed the Neva River there was already a barrier, and armed soldiers holding their rifles at the ready. Some junior officer stated that nobody was allowed to go any farther. We had to walk to Morskoi Street against our will, where my husband telephoned the Winter Palace, where officials had gathered, and with whom he stayed in contact.

All evening and all night there was gunfire on Morskoi Street. From the apartment windows of my husband's subordinates one could see soldiers lying on the pavement shooting at soldiers attacking them with machine guns. A powerful cannonade lasted the whole night, because in the building adjoining the Security Bureau office was the main telegraph and telephone station. The revolutionaries wanted to seize it, but loyal soldiers were defending it. There were dead and wounded among my husband's subordinates, and he got a doctor to tend to the wounded. We were not able to shut our eyes for a minute. We were very tense and were waiting for the outcome of the fight for the station. Early in the morning, a servant suddenly ran in screaming that armed soldiers were coming our way. We went down a back staircase and exited into a courtyard, but soldiers were coming toward us. They had already stopped in front of us when suddenly there was intense rifle and machine gun fire—the revolutionaries were taking the station by storm. The soldiers were taken aback and for a moment seemed confused, and we took advantage of that moment and ran out into the street and quickly walked down the street while bullets were whistling past us. My husband and his assistant walked on, but I didn't have the strength and began to lag behind as machine gun fire continued without stop. The machine gun fire intensified so much that I couldn't stand it anymore, and I stopped and pressed myself against a wall. Some sergeant major had also pressed himself against the wall next to me, and we both waited to be killed any second. When the gunfire subsided a bit, I ran to try to catch up with my husband, but I saw that he had noticed that I wasn't behind him, so he became very worried and turned back to find me.

We decided to go to the train station and get to Tsarskoe Selo, where my husband wanted to report on everything that was going on in Petrograd. It took us four hours to get to the train station because we had to take all kinds of side streets to avoid the gunfire; there was not a single cab or wagon—not a trace of them. I cried; my nerves could not take all this, and I was terribly worried about our son. One of my husband's subordinates parted with us at the train station to stay in the city, and we bought three tickets and went to Tsarskoe Selo. When we got there we were surprised by the quiet and tranquility. Only the look of a cavalry Cossack guarding the road expressed alarm [and he said] that things were uneasy at Tsarskoe Selo and something was up. My husband made telephone contact with the palace, but in the absence of the commandant, General Groten, he spoke with the head of the palace police, Colonel Gerardi, and told him what was happening in Petrograd and asked him if Tsarskoe Selo could be defended, because my husband thought that by evening mobs would arrive there. Gerardi answered that Tsarskoe Selo was absolutely secure; there was a garrison of five thousand loyal troops who could repulse an attack, and machine guns protected the palace. He also said that the Grand Duke Mikhail Alexandrovich, who had just been there, had assured the Empress that she and her children were in no danger and that he himself was thinking of moving to the palace with his family. He persuaded the Empress to cancel her trip with the children to Mogilev, and so the train trip was cancelled. From his conversation with Gerardi, my husband came away with the impression that they did not fully understand the developing events and that everything pointed to a palace coup in favor of Grand Duke Mikhail Alexandrovich.

It was late, and I was so tired that I could hardly stand. We decided to get a room in some dacha for the night. Somewhere we could hear the shouts of incited crowds and single rounds of gunfire. It was not meant to be that we would get any sleep that night. I didn't even get a chance to undress when there was a knock on the door and a young man came in, the son of the landlady. He was pale and trembling. He was worried, and said to my husband that there was a police station across the road, and that crowds were getting closer and undoubtedly they would storm the station, and maybe even the dacha, so it would be best if we left. My husband thought that the own-ers were simply frightened and, not knowing who we were, thought that [my husband was] Protopopov, who was being sought everywhere.

Nevertheless, we had to go, so we went to the apartment of one of my husband's officers, whose duty was to live at Tsarskoe Selo. Nobody was able to sleep there, and everybody waited anxiously for the Tsar's train that was to arrive at midnight from staff headquarters. An officer was sent to the train station to await the Tsar's train, and he called my husband every hour. At midnight the train had not arrived, nor at two, and so on, and at five in the morning he telephoned that the train would not be coming because the Tsar had been arrested. This news hit us like lightning. We, the women, cried, and the men hardly kept back their tears. When the officer returned from the sta-tion, he changed into civilian clothes and we all parted. He left in one direction with his wife, and the three of us went to Pavlovsk, where the mother of one of my husband's officers had a dacha with a watchman who looked after it. It was a beautiful frosty morning; the snow glistened and crunched under our feet. The dachas were covered in snow, and all this gleamed in the sunlight. The beauty of this scene made it hard to believe that people could be of such a savage nature and could so irrationally and stupidly destroy their homeland. When we arrived at the dacha, we decided that I would go back to Petrograd to find out what was going on, because all we were hearing were rumors, and I was very worried about our son. My husband and his officer had to stay at the dacha and wait for my return. Before I left I made my husband promise that he would not go anywhere until I returned, and that he would not do anything to himself. I said this because I had overheard part of a conversation about a revolver and committing suicide as a last resort. Noticing that I had overheard, they had stopped talking.

When I got to Petrograd I went to my acquaintances where my son was staying. It turned out that their place had been searched twice at night. My son had not slept at all and was very nervous. I took him, and we went to some other acquaintances where there was less of a chance of their place being searched. After having coffee at their place and leaving my son with them, I needed to return immediately to inform my husband that the chairman of the Duma, Rodzianko, had issued an order that all military and civilian officials must come to the State Duma within three days. I was completely out of energy, and my feet were bleeding from walking. I had to walk the entire way from the train station, a very long way, but there was no other means of transportation. Everywhere was deserted except for the whistling of bullets coming from somewhere. So I had to turn around and make the wearisome trek back to the train station. I think that it was only extraordinarily strained nerves that gave me the energy to move. I seemed to trudge forward one step at a time, and soldiers I ran into warned me not to go in this or that direction where there was nonstop gunfire and dead bodies lying about, but I could not leave the road—this would have extended the distance I had to walk, and I did not have the strength to get to the station, yet I dragged myself there. To my great surprise, I met my husband and his officer at the station. They were very happy to see me and told me that as they sat in their room at the dacha they heard some acquaintances of the watchman say that in Pavlovsk there were people who were hunting down profiteers and killing them.

18

Allies and Adversaries

General Globachev

Participation of foreign governments in the Russian revolution. The German intelligence system before the war. Intelligence activities during the war. The Allied governments' relationship to the Russian revolutionary movement. Evaluation and responsibility for the revolution.

Now that quite a bit of time has transpired since the February 1917 revolution, many ask the question, "Is it true that Germany participated in its preparation?" I positively reject this idea. Germany participated in neither the revolution nor the preparation of it. The revolution was an unexpected pleasant surprise to Germany. In order to understand this, we need to consider how Germany conducted intelligence in Russia during peacetime and what this intelligence was based on.

All military, political, and economic data on Russia were received by Germany from German nationals in Russia—that is, from German commercial firms, financial and manufacturing enterprises, commercial travelers, and so on—and in those places where there were German colonists, from them. All this information was coordinated in Berlin, in the Central Bureau, where it was summarized. It was only from time to time that officers of the German General Staff were sent to Russia to verify the information. Thus, Germany based its intelligence about Russia on agents who were German nationals, who as patriots were working for their homeland. Only a minority were Russian citizens who worked for Germany for material gain, and this was mainly on our western borders.

Before the war, there was no point in Germany contributing to preparation for a revolution in Russia, as Germany was always prepared to support monarchical principles, not only for itself but also for its neighbors. Once war had started, the revolution in Russia was certainly to Germany's advantage, as any catastrophe in the enemy's territory would be. However, the Central Powers could not aid in preparation of revolt in Russia without first destroying the Russian army, because the entire apparatus at the foundation of German intelligence in Russia was destroyed when the war began. Indeed, with the declaration of war, Russia's borders with the warring nations were completely closed. Borders with neutral countries were guarded vigilantly with the establishment of the strictest controls: all German firms, commercial enterprises and banks, joint-stock organizations, and so on were closed; proprietors—German nationals who did not leave in time—were arrested; Russian subjects of German descent were sent to southern or Siberian provinces; German colonists were put under the strictest surveillance and isolation. Thus, the Central Powers, having lost the basis of their intelligence on Russia, had no chance for influencing public sentiment in Russia in hopes of aiding a revolution.

The only way that the Central Powers were involved in these matters was in assisting our revolutionary emigrants in spreading propaganda among Russian prisoners in concentration camps in Germany and Austria, and in supporting the Russian expatriate movement that had begun in 1915 by Socialist Party leaders. But these efforts bore their own fruit after the February Revolution, when it pleased the Provisional Government to allow this flock of crows, our emigrants, to pour into Russia across the long open borders of neutral countries. It is completely natural that, along with them, Russia was covered anew with a network of German espionage.

As far as any allied preparation for a revolution, I positively reject that. Some say that England supposedly helped our revolutionary center to overthrow the government through the aid of its ambassador Sir George Buchanan. I assert that throughout the war neither Buchanan nor any English national had any active involvement in our revolutionary movement, or in the revolution itself. It is possible that Buchanan and other Britons had personal sympathy for the revolutionary mood in Russia, thinking that a national army created by the revolution would be more patriotic and could smash the Central Powers—but not more than that. This view was created in Russian society as a result of the close relationship of the English ambassador with Sazonov, who was an avid Anglophile and affiliated with the Progressive Bloc, and other leaders of the revolutionary frame of mind, such as Miliukov, Guchkov, and others.

It is not even worthwhile to talk about France. Neither the ambassador nor any French allowed themselves to interfere in Russia's internal affairs.

Russian hands created the February Revolution in Russia. We already know whose hands these were, and who it was who needed a revolution. The revolution was needed by a small group of people of the Kadet Party and progressives, who affiliated themselves with the movement and who for the last two years had shouted about the need for a Russian government that could be trusted by the people—a government selected by themselves. The revolution was also needed by the socialists as the ultimate completion of their party program—that is, to overthrow the existing government. The people needed neither the revolution nor the people who supposedly had their trust. The Provisional Government consisted of individuals who sought ministerial positions, such as Prince Lvov, Miliukov, Guchkov, Shingarev, and others. There was only one member who was a socialist: Kerensky. The people did not elect them—they chose themselves. Did they enjoy the trust of the people? That is a big question. The people could only know them as an extremist opposition to the old regime; they contributed nothing to the people.

Why was there only one socialist, Kerensky, in the first government? It is because the Kadet Party established the first government and, in addition to that, there was not even a single individual who was worthy in the eyes of the socialists. The leaders of the socialist parties only got to Petrograd from across the borders and from Siberia after several days and even weeks, and they got there too late to get a piece of the public "pie." They did, however, get their share soon enough by being more energetic and talented demagogues. Within three months, the Provisional Government changed its character to a purely socialist one. The old actors were ousted, having played out their role, and they were replaced, as Kerensky said, "with true representatives of the people"—that is, with individuals who not only did not have the people's trust, but who also were not even known to the people. In fact, who knew all these, the Chernovs, Nekrasovs, Avksenteevs, Pereverzevs, and the like? Did the Russian people know anything of them? They were known only for their criminal politics and activities to the Department of Police and to the officials of the Special Corps of Gendarmes.

So, in essence, the order to take power into their hands and give Russia a government that supposedly would have the peoples' trust, the February Revolution brought Russia all the turmoil that followed. We do not see the end of our homeland's misfortune, and it may be that the present regime will bring her to her final ruin.

History will have to record that those who committed this dark criminal act were not the initiators of an ephemeral revolutionary victory, as they proudly proclaimed, but supreme criminals acting against their own homeland. History must also honestly and objectively judge the government at the time, which was perfectly well informed of the political situation and yet stubbornly refused to take decisive measures to prevent catastrophe.

19

My Husband under Arrest

Sofia Globacheva

Since my husband and his assistant were in civilian dress it was possible that they might be taken for profiteers, so they decided to go to the train station to wait for me. The news that I brought of Rodzianko's order came just in time for us to return to Petrograd, where they thought that some order was being restored. When we got there we parted with my husband's aide and went past St. Isaac's Cathedral to our acquaintances, where our son was staying. Bullets were whizzing past our ears, and I instinctively covered my head with my muff. Our son was very worried because it was already late and I had told him as I left that I would be back while it was still light. After having some tea, my husband was escorted by our acquaintance, who took along his orderly, so that it would look like they were escorting an arrested person to the Duma just in case they came across any soldiers running amok. When he returned, our acquaintance told us that he had successfully taken my husband to the Duma and handed him over to the commander of the guards.

The names of those who arrived at the Duma and were under arrest were published in the newspapers. A day went by, then two, then three, and there was no information about my husband. I was very worried, as I didn't know what happened to him. I decided to go to the Duma myself to find out. There was no transportation available, so I had to go on foot, and crowds of people were going about their business in the streets. I joined these crowds, but since I hardly ever had to walk about Petrograd, always having a vehicle available, and because my orientation was always bad, I did not know how to get to the Tauride Palace, where the State Duma was located. An officer was walking next to me, so I turned to him and asked if he could tell me the way. He told me he was going there and that I should follow along. I

FIGURE 19.1. Tavricheskii (Tauride) Palace—the meeting place of the Duma. The Petrograd center of the Revolution in March, 1917. meros.org.

asked him if there was any way I could get into the building, and I found out he worked there and had an entry pass. I got up my courage and asked if I could get in on his pass. He answered kindly that I should hold onto him and maybe the guard would let me in with him. That is how it turned out. There were two checkpoints where guards examined passes. The officer showed his pass, and I slipped in behind him. Thus, we were able to get to the corridor, where the officer introduced himself to me, giving me his last name, which I unfortunately forgot immediately in my anxiety. I thanked him from the bottom of my heart, and we parted. He went to the right into some room, after directing me to a door on the left that led into the State Duma hall, where almost all the Duma members were at that time. As I entered the hall, I could not take it anymore and began to cry. A number of people gathered around me and asked what the matter was, but learning that I was there to find out about my husband, who had been arrested, they quietly withdrew. Finally, a member of the Duma approached me. As I learned later, it was Zamyslovskii. In response to my tears and concern that something had been done to my husband, since I had no information about him, he calmed me and assured me that no excesses had been perpetrated, which they themselves had feared. However, when the War Minister, General Sukhomlinov, had been brought in, some soldiers tried to attack him, but Kerensky came running out. He shielded the general, saying they could get to him only over his dead body, and that the general would have to stand trial. After this act by Kerensky, most of the members of the Duma felt a great weight lifted from their shoulders; they understood there would be no excesses now. That same courageous member of the Duma went to find out where my husband was, and locating him, arranged for me to see him and gave me a pass to enter the Duma at any time. I made use of this pass even under the Bolsheviks, when the Soviet of Workers' and Soldiers' Deputies occupied the Tauride Palace. I showed this pass whenever it was necessary to get in, and I was allowed to enter without showing any other identification.

My husband was detained in the Ministerial Pavilion along with other high-ranking officials. I visited him often and took my children along. I had already taken my daughter from the boarding school in Moscow, since there were rumors that the Germans were approaching Moscow, and I was afraid she would be cut off from us. To visit my husband, it was necessary to go through a hall where there was complete chaos, noise, and uproar. Soldiers who had deserted the front were jumping on the platform, shouting loudly, thumping their chests, and making some kind of statements that could not be understood. It was obvious that they themselves did not understand anything, only that they could yell, make noise, and now indulge in excesses at will.

During one of my visits to my husband, I had to go to some room to get information, and I asked a Jewish woman who was in ragged clothes, dirty, and tattered shoes to show me the way. I was unable to control my indignation about all the noise, uproar, and chaos that was going on. Her answer to me was that all this would settle down, all would be well, and there would be a paradise for the people. Later I learned that the Bolshevik Kamenev had brought this Jewish woman into the organization, and many years later, when I was in America, I saw a photo of her in an American newspaper sitting at a dining table with representatives of various countries. She was splendidly dressed and bejeweled—she certainly got her paradise unexpectedly.

The arrested officials and generals had been detained in the pavilion for a whole month, and nobody had questioned them nor initiated any charges against them, since there was nothing to charge them with because they had served their Tsar and homeland faithfully and honestly. They were attended by politically active young people who treated them well and engaged them in conversation and debate. They told my husband that he never allowed them to get organized and was able to neutralize the activities of the underground, and that was why the revolution came as a surprise to them. All the detainees in the pavilion did not get to lie down at all during the month because there were no beds. They only dozed, fully dressed, in armchairs or chairs. They got laundry from home and changed clothes in an adjoining room. When we left our home during the first day of the revolution, we took absolutely nothing with us, so I was in a desperate situation of having to get changes of laundry for my husband, my children, and me from acquaintances.

During the first days of his detention, my husband asked me to go to see Rodzianko's secretary and tell him that it was vital for my husband to see the President of the State Duma to give him important information about the Bolsheviks—that they were planning to wait for an opportune moment to seize power. The secretary, I do not recall his name, informed Rodzianko. The next day, embarrassed at Rodzianko's lack of concern, the secretary informed me that Rodzianko's response was that he was very busy and did not see any possibility of meeting with my husband. The secretary added that Rodzianko, in general, did not know what to make of the Bolsheviks.

We, the wives of those arrested, showed unusual audacity and energy in trying to get our husbands released. It was not easy because we kept being told that they were being held for their own safety. The crowds, however, were not charged up, and were quite indifferent to the detainees after the first several days of the revolution. Leftist newspapers tried to inflame the crowds by printing all kinds of absurd hearsay. After some vile reporting, a crowd of several thousand people, instigated by agitators, showed up at the Tauride Palace one night demanding that the detainees be handed over to them for punishment. I always tried to be near where my husband was in case anything happened. I believed deeply, through some inner feeling, that at a moment of crisis I would find a way to save my husband. I did not know how, but even if this was an illusion, I believed it. I had to live through these frightening and agonizing moments when I was near the crowd that was screaming and howling to have them handed over. Suddenly everything went quiet.

Word spread that Kerensky had come out. Kerensky did indeed approach the crowd and was raised up on people's arms so he could be seen over the people's heads. He calmly exhorted the crowd to disperse and go home, assuring them that those arrested would stand trial and receive proper punishment (probably for serving their country faithfully). Kerensky spoke for a long time, and the crowd did disperse little by little. Fortunately, the detainees did not know what was going on outside the palace. The next day they were all to be relocated, some to the Peter and Paul Fortress, and some to the Vyborg Prison, known as Kresty [literally meaning "Crosses"]. I was very afraid that my husband would wind up in the Peter and Paul Fortress, where the regimen was very strict and the incarcerated were kept in solitary confinement. It was only later that they were allowed to have relatives visit them. I was sitting with my husband when Kerensky came into the room and announced that everyone would be moved out of the Tauride Palace. The next morning, the relocation began. My husband was driven to the Peter and Paul Fortress, but he was not taken out with the others; he was driven to the Vyborg Prison. I felt some relief, since the commandants of the prison from before the revolution were still in their positions. They were not cruel people, but quite responsive. It was possible to talk to them, and to visit one's relatives twice a week and bring clothes and packages. During my first visit to my husband in this prison, I found him very depressed. Upon leaving him I was worried, fearing he might do something to himself. Late that evening I telephoned the prison commandant and asked him to go to my husband's cell to see how he was. The commandant did so and informed me that my husband was perfectly calm. When I arrived at the prison the next day, my husband told me that when he was returning to his cell after our visit, he heard sobbing behind him. Turning around, he saw that the guard who was escorting him was crying. When my husband asked him why he was crying, he answered, "Your Excellency, it is so difficult, so difficult to see all this."

At first all the detainees were in one big chamber and had some freedom, but following one unfortunate incident, things got worse. One of the prison guards who had been fired telephoned the somewhat Bolshevik-oriented Moscow Regiment. Out of spite he told them that the detainees had rioted, were armed, and were trying to break out. The Moscow Regiment rushed to the prison, and having been joined by a crowd of people along the way, demanded in a threatening way to be let into the prison. The prison commandant, by the name of Popov, a Bolshevik who had replaced the previous commandant, was a decent and smart man who had three subordinate supervisors of the prison (the rest of the personnel had scattered). He went out to the raging crowd and ordered that the gates behind him be closed and bolted. For three hours he urged the crowd to calm down, and said that the detainees were in their cells and that they had no weapons. He proposed that the crowd should choose ten representatives from among themselves to go in and see for themselves that all was calm, and that they had been deceived by a spiteful provocateur. They agreed, and he let the ten into the prison. These ten chosen representatives burst into the chamber, cursing, and searched for weapons, which of course, they did not find. Seeing that on the beds of the detainees were straw mattresses, they tore them apart, saying they could sleep on planks. They forbade the detainees from having visits and packages, and then they left, demanding that all detainees be kept in separate cells, two to a cell or even in single cells. My husband was put into a cell with one of his subordinates. When the latter was released after three or four months, my husband remained alone. He told me that his psychological state at that time was the worst.

The next day there were rumors all over the city that the Moscow Regiment had burst into the prison and beat up all the detainees. Mothers, sisters, and wives rushed to the prison in tears. I had been on my way with my children to visit my husband. Hearing these rumors, something inside me told me that it was not so and that everything was all right. When we got to the prison, we were not allowed in. I asked to see Commandant Popov and asked him to tell me honestly, and he told me what happened. He added that it would be necessary to refrain from any visits temporarily, but that he would try to give my husband the parcel that I brought, if the guard on duty at my husband's cell was trustworthy. The guard was trustworthy.

From the start, when our husbands were under arrest at the Ministerial Pavilion, we wives ran around, among all the officials, demanding to know why they were being held and when they intended to release our husbands. Most often we went to the office of the prosecutor, Karinskii. This was a very dull man who kept us waiting in the reception area for a very long time because he never got up before eleven in the morning. He lived in the Justice Ministry building. His response to our questions was that the revolution had not yet ended and he did not know when our husbands would be released. One of the ladies announced that he would cause the wives to commit suicide in his office. This scared him, and he refused to see us after that. When the Bolsheviks took power, he had to flee, and he settled in New York.

I often had to go to the Minister of Justice, Pereverzev. I thought that since I had known him socially, he would be a kind person, but he was not cut out to be the Minister of Justice. He was neither logical, nor had any understanding of administrative matters. During the Tsarist regime I had the opportunity to meet senior government officials, so I could see the difference between the former competent and knowledgeable officials and those who now, by chance, wound up at the top. When I often spoke with them, it seemed to me that these were grown children playing at governing and not even thinking of the consequences. I also wondered how it could be that among all the Socialist Revolutionaries they could not find serious, competent people other than lawyers to fill all the responsible positions.

Pereverzev was a pleasant person who received us with civility. He sat in a cushioned sofa with a pipe in his mouth all the time. He was a bit affected when he rolled his blue eyes, which really were pretty, and, it seemed to me, he enjoyed talking to us—at least he never rushed us to leave on the pretext that he was very busy. Muravev, who was head of the extraordinary committee for developing any kind of charges against former government officials, was repulsive and completely unpleasant. We all hated him. Decent and self-respecting prosecutors, assistant prosecutors, and court investigators did not want to work with him and resigned.

I will now turn to Kerensky's personality, and I think that my opinion and impression of him—after the revolution, when he held all the power in his hands—will be at odds with other people. Not intending to defend him, I still have to say that, in my opinion, his fatal error was that he did not look before he leaped, taking as true every rumor and gossip that was spread about the Tsar's family and government. I heard that he was even startled at how many lies there were. Kerensky was always a Socialist Revolutionary and never denied that. Whenever the occasion presented itself, he lashed out and criticized the government. It seems to me then that one could not expect loyalty from him. However, he would still have to be held less responsible than those who would almost genuflect before the Tsar, but who then plotted to betray him behind his back and to betray their own country.

After the revolution, when Rodzianko tried to persuade the Grand Duke Mikhail Alexandrovich to refuse the throne and to wait for the people to choose him, Kerensky stayed on the sidelines, neither supporting nor rejecting the Grand Duke Mikhail Alexandrovich. He did this even though the Tsar was weak, and his last ministers were involved in intrigues among themselves with the goal of keeping their jobs—these were scoundrels, and major changes were happening. They were nothing in comparison to what the revolution did to Russia. If Kerensky, in achieving power, had recognized how much lying and rumor mongering was going on, and that not everything was as bad as it seemed to him, he could have taken Russia down a different road. Loving his homeland, he could have gotten a constitution, and Russia's condition, and indeed the whole world's, would have been different than it is now. In my opinion, Kerensky was an impulsive man. This I can judge from a session I attended of the Duma when Rodzianko read the Tsar's decree temporarily dissolving the Duma. Kerensky rushed out from an adjoining chamber and shouted in a frenzy, "Down with the police and the gendarmes!" and then disappeared. This was the first time that I saw him. The second time was just after the revolution. I decided to seek out Kerensky himself because I was trying vainly to find out from Pereverzev and Karinskii why my husband was arrested and when he would be released. I do not remember exactly what building he was occupying at the time, but as I entered the hall I saw many of the former officials decked out in their uniforms waiting nervously to present themselves to Kerensky. I approached a clerk, and he suggested that I see the Assistant Minister, since Kerensky was very busy. This did not suit me. I wanted to speak to Kerensky personally, so I sat down in an armchair, tired, my morale shattered, and not thinking of anything. Just then the office door opened and Kerensky came out surrounded by a whole group of followers and went into the Assistant Minister's office.

Those people who were waiting to present themselves bowed deeply and in a servile way. About ten minutes later, Kerensky returned back toward his office with his followers, and I never would have thought that I would do what I did, but I jumped out of my chair and ran toward him. Kerensky was taken aback, but he stopped.

"I need to speak to you," I said.

"What is your name?" he asked.

"Globacheva," was my answer.

"I will not approve your seeing your husband," answered Kerensky.

"I did not come about seeing my husband; I want to talk to you."

He thought for a moment and said, "All right."

This short confrontation is branded in my memory forever. An adjutant approached me and escorted me into a room adjoining Kerensky's office, where there were already some people waiting for their turn to see Kerensky. A bell rang from the office, and the adjutant went in. He came back out and called me out of turn to see Kerensky. I went in and sat down in an armchair, so agitated that a lot of our conversation was hazy and seemed to rush through my head. I do recall that we were both agitated. Kerensky walked nervously back and forth, and in response to why my husband was arrested, and as to when he would be released, he said that my husband was needed to give certain testimony, and as soon as the threat from the population to those arrested was past, which I do not think he even knew about, they would all be released. As I was leaving, I turned around and said that my son and I had nowhere to lay our heads, since all our papers were stolen, and without them there was no place for us. Kerensky hurried past me, impetuously, into the next room, where his secretary, by the name of Samov, was seated at a desk, and shouted, "Find this lady an apartment," and disappeared. The secretary looked at me with his sleepy eyes and did not know what to do. At that time it was impossible to find a room, much less an apartment, in Petrograd. So I told him that he should just give me and my son identity cards so that I would not have to be bothered being searched, questioned, or anything else like that. He took care of it.

The next day I visited my husband and told him everything about my meeting with Kerensky. The head of the guards, by the name of Znamenskii, who was always present and was a friend of Kerensky's, said, "Kerensky knows perfectly well that you are seeing your husband." From our conversations with Znamenskii, and his tactfulness, he gave the impression of a very decent and softhearted person. Meeting with Pereverzev, at that time already the Minister of Justice, I pointed out to him that he did not have the right to hold my husband so long without charging him, and that he must release him. He replied that he did not have the authority to do that since the Soviet of Workers' and Soldiers' Deputies would protest immediately. At that time the Soviets were getting stronger, and the Provisional Government was afraid of them. "All right," I said to Pereverzev. "Give me your word of honor that if I can get a document from the Soviet of Workers' and Soldiers' Deputies that they have no objection to releasing my husband, that you will release him."

Pereverzev agreed to this, and I did not see him again for almost two months, during which time I tried to obtain the necessary document.

I went first to the Tauride Palace with a pass that I still had from the State Duma. When I got there, I was surrounded by a group of young people who asked me what I wanted there. They were very nice to me once they knew what I was there for. They told me that they respected my husband very much and that his only misfortune was that he had been in the Tsar's service. One time when I was at the Tauride Palace, some artillery officer, a reserve ensign, came up to me and engaged me in conversation. In my subsequent visits, and I do not remember in what context, he told me that they had a terrible weapon that was not yet completed, but if some button was pushed, let us say from Petrograd, an entire city anywhere could be destroyed. I did not believe what he was telling me, and he took me to a room where there was some kind of machine that looked like a big movie projector. The ensign's last name was Mihailov, and I do not know whether he was a Socialist Revolutionary or a Bolshevik, but I think he was a Bolshevik, since after the Bolshevik revolution I met him in the street. He was all dressed up in a military uniform, seemed extremely arrogant, and did not acknowledge me.

There was one student by the name of Muravev who was always at the Tauride Palace, and who had extended me some sympathy. He introduced me to Chkheidze, who had been a deputy in the Duma and quite an important person. The student told him my situation, and Chkheidze directed me to the secretary of the Soviet of Workers' and Soldiers' Deputies. I did not give my name; I said only that my husband was a general and had been under arrest for very long without having been charged. The secretary of the Soviet stated to me that they had noted several times that the Provisional Government had held people under arrest without being charged. When I asked for a document stating that the Soviet did not object to my husband's release, he answered that there were already several wives of generals with similar requests, but they were refused. I demonstrated the necessity of getting such a document, and he finally promised that the next day there would be a meeting of the Soviet and he would bring up this petition. I came back three days later and was told that I should make a request to the Soviet of Workers' and Soldiers' Deputies. Returning home, I thought for a long time what kind of heading to put on this document; to write "request" to the Soviet of Workers' and Soldiers' Deputies made me feel belittled, so I decided simply to write "Application of the wife of the Chief of the Security Bureau of Petrograd, S. N. Globacheva." I showed up with the document to show to the Secretary of the Soviet. He received me quite pleasantly, but when he opened the document and saw the heading, he turned red and shouted, "How is it possible that there are no charges against the head of the Security Police? It is not possible." I kept my calm at his outburst and said, "It may seem strange to you from your perspective, but there are no charges that can be produced, other than that he honestly carried out his duties and responsibilities." Little by little, he calmed down, took my application, promised he would hand it over to the Soviet of Workers' and Soldiers' Deputies for their decision, and said to come back in a week for an answer.

A week passed, and I set off to find out the result. The secretary handed me a note that said they had no objection to the release of my husband and left the matter of his release to the Provisional Government (I still have that note, though it is in very deteriorated condition). I have often wondered why, at the beginning of my meetings at the Tauride Palace to get the required papers for Justice Minister Pereverzev, the Bolsheviks were not hostile to me. I supposed that among them remained principled individuals who had become disillusioned with what was happening and gradually left or were removed and replaced by Bolsheviks of a different sort with different methods of fighting, including deceit, terror, and lies. As an example, not knowing where former officers lived, the Bolsheviks started employing deceit, and shortly after coming to power they issued a decree that all officers should register so they could get assignments. Many did so, even though my husband warned them that this was a trap. Indeed, the Bolsheviks, having access to their addresses, arrested and shot them all.

I returned home happily with the note from the Soviet of Workers' and Soldiers' Deputies, and the next day I set off to see Justice Minister Pereverzev.

"Here is the paper. Now you must release my husband," I said.

"I cannot release him," replied Pereverzev.

"Why?" I was indignant.

"Because he was the Chief of the Petrograd Security Bureau," was his answer.

"But you gave me your word that you would release him as soon as I brought you the paper from the Soviet of Workers' and Soldiers' Deputies."

"Well, that was then, and things are different now," answered "justice minister" Pereverzev.

"Have you any other charges, other than that he held that position?" I asked.

"No," was his reply.

What kind of response could there have been to all of this? Since there was nothing more for me to talk to him about, I left and I had no more to do with him. I continued to work with the former deputy prosecutor, Popov, who stayed on to work in the Provisional Government and remained as honest and decent as he had been under the Tsar, not having changed, as so many other officials of the previous regime had done. It was through him that I requested Justice Minister Pereverzev to transfer my husband from the prison to Furshtatskaia Street, where the headquarters of the Corps of Gendarmes had been. Also at this location were the naval officers from Kronstadt (the base near Petrograd) who had been arrested by sailors who accused the officers of demanding that the decks be clean. Other officers were accused of tightening discipline for untidy sailors, for being too strict, and so on, but none of them was accused by the sailors of being abusive or rude. Deputy Prosecutor Popov forwarded my request to Pereverzev, who said that he would first have to go to the prison to speak to my husband.

I had to ask Popov several times to press Pereverzev to go to the prison. Every time I got the same answer—tomorrow. Finally, Popov came and said that Pereverzev was on his way, but by this time I really did not believe him. He calmed me by telling me that Pereverzev had gotten on the phone in his presence and ordered a car, so he really was going. I asked Popov to let me know by telephone of the results of Pereverzev's trip. Pereverzev gave orders that my husband was to be transferred to Furshtatskaia Street, and he was indeed transferred the next day.

The routine there was not strict; the individuals who were under arrest were more like in a guardhouse. There were several individuals per room, they could walk in the yard without guards, and they were allowed visitors who could bring parcels every day. The head of the guards was a young Georgian officer by the name of Nadjarov, who was not bad, but quite stupid, so the inmates referred to him as a "lamb." There were two guards, both day and night, who sat on chairs all the time and slept with their rifles in their hands. One could easily have walked out of there, but these were all individuals of the Tsar's regime, and such a thought would never enter their minds. By the way, some of the arrested individuals there were General Khabalov, commander of the Petrograd Military District; War Minister General Beliaev; Lady-in-Waiting Vyrubova; Justice Minister Dobrovol'skii; General Balk, the Petrograd City Prefect; and also the naval officers from Kronstadt, some army officers, and many others. Those who came to visit their husbands, sons, and brothers became acquainted with all the other individuals who were under arrest.

One time when I was visiting my husband after his transfer from the prison to Furshtatskaia, I asked him what he spoke about with Justice Minister Pereverzev in the prison. It turned out that Justice Minister Pereverzev came to ask my husband to help them understand how the Security Bureau operated. My husband agreed to clarify and explain how everything worked, but it seems that the new regime consulted among themselves and decided they should not resort to asking the Chief of the Security Bureau for explanations and assistance, as the matter never came up again.

Some of the officers that we became acquainted with said that as soon as they were released they would head to the south of Russia. Others decided that they would stay, since the army was falling apart and they would be needed to maintain discipline in the army—otherwise the Germans could take Russia with their bare hands. The incarcerated were allowed to read and to play chess and other games, but not cards, and I would bring various games for their diversion to the room where my husband and others were. The meals were not bad, but not much; the same food was cooked for the incarcerated as for the guards. Even though food was distributed by ration card, I was sometimes successful in bringing my husband and the others a whole box of eggs that I was able to get, without a ration card, from a shopkeeper who gave them to me, once he knew that it was for the individuals who were under arrest. My husband would sometimes tell me amusing stories about some of his roommates. For example, General Balk and his assistant, old General Vendorff, who had planned to retire even before the revolution, would sit down every evening across from one another on their bunks and would imagine that they were dining at the restaurant Cuba, the best in Petrograd, and in their imagination they would order the tastiest of dishes and dine, and only then they would go to sleep. It was also just as strange to see an official as important as the former Justice Minister Dobrovol'skii going to the kitchen with a tea kettle to get some boiling water for tea. Later, in exile, we gradually got used to this, but at the time, it was difficult and painful to witness. After his release, Dobrovol'skii headed south to Crimea and was brutally murdered by Bolsheviks in front of his wife.

The days dragged on, one after the other, and the situation grew more alarming as the Bolsheviks grew stronger and the Provisional Government grew weaker, taking no action against the Bolsheviks. In one of my visits to my husband, he told me that he heard that his case was in the hands of a special investigator, Stavrovskii, and that I should go to him and ask him to hurry up and question my husband and end this dragged-out situation one way or another. I went to Stavrovskii and explained the situation to him. I was surprised that investigator Stavrovskii was very agitated; he rushed about the room and shouted, "I will show you right now the material I received to hold your husband accountable for his responsibilities," and he showed me some papers from the prosecutor Karinskii, charging my husband accountable and responsible for having had secret agents, and attached to these documents were clippings from some worthless newspaper that named some of the secret agents. Knowing that my husband was the head of the Security Bureau, and obliged to have agents, just as every government has, Stavrovskii was very embarrassed by this senseless paper from prosecutor Karinskii's office. He told me that he would go to see my husband tomorrow, not to question him, but to talk to him, since there was nothing to question him about, and he would give orders for his release. He did as he said he would, and my husband was released immediately.

20

Imprisonment in the Tauride Palace

General Globachev

My arrest. General Sukhomlinov's arrival at the State Duma. The Ministerial Pavilion. The composition of the guards. The commandant of the Tauride Palace place of incarceration. People who visited those who were under arrest. The mood of those under arrest and the guards. Kerensky's visit. Pereverzev. Burtsev. The incident with Admiral Kartsev. Transfer to the Vyborg Prison.

The State Duma, now under the banner of the February insurrection, became during these nightmarish days the headquarters of the revolutionaries and the central repository of the incarceration of the arrested Tsarist government officials, and in general of all persons whom the revolutionary committee believed to be dangerous to the revolution. The revolutionary committee met in the Duma Building, as did the Soviet of Workers' and Soldiers' Deputies, which had been established on the spur of the moment on February 27.

The Ministerial Pavilion was assigned to those arrested for more serious offenses, while the Tauride Palace was assigned for the less serious offenses.

I was delivered to the State Duma on March 1 at about 7 p.m., and before I was assigned to a final location, I had to wait for about two hours in a room where the State Duma representative, Papadzhanov, assigned those who were in custody. There were about thirty people here, waiting their turn as decisions were made on the disposition of those under arrest. Some who had been detained were released by Papadzhanov, who thought they posed no danger, while others were assigned to one or another detention area inside the Duma.

It seems that, at first, Kerensky showed a lot of energy and influence as to who should be detained. As I waited my turn, I noticed with some interest a disturbing scene. When General Sukhomlinov was brought in under arrest, it is impossible to describe the noise and shouting that began from the drunken soldiers, from the members of the Duma who were in charge of our fate, and from some suspicious individuals who were there. All were shouting, cursing, and swearing at the unfortunate general. More than anyone else, it was Kerensky who raged and shouted, ordering that Sukhomlinov's epaulets be torn off, after which Kerensky played out a scene of extraordinary noblesse, declaring that Sukhomlinov must not be harmed, so that he could be tried by the lawful revolutionary court and punished as a traitor to Russia, and that the crowd could harm Sukhomlinov only over Kerensky's dead body. The latter had apparently forgotten that just a short while before it was he who instigated this violence when he ordered the general's epaulets to be ripped off. The soldiers obeyed Kerensky, and Sukhomlinov, with his torn epaulets, was led past the line of soldiers preceded by Kerensky to the yelling and whooping of hateful epithets.

Finally, after some short questioning and brief paperwork, I was handed over with a note to some young man who led me to the Ministerial Pavilion and handed me over to the head of the guards.

The Ministerial Pavilion consisted of a meeting hall, two spacious offices, a public area, and a toilet. One door connected the pavilion to a lobby, and the other door opened onto a garden that surrounded the pavilion. The prisoners were put into the hall and offices, while the guards were in the public area. Running the entire length of the hall, which was not all that big, was a cloth-covered table around which the prisoners sat, about twenty to twenty-five individuals, and around them stood ten guards with rifles. In each of the offices were fewer prisoners, also with guards. The garden outside the Ministerial Pavilion was surrounded by guards, ordered to fire on anyone attempting to escape or even to be at a window. This guard was made up solely of the 4th Company of the Preobrazhenskii Life Guards Regiment. They had earned this honor because they were the first company to join with the rebellious training command of the Volinskii Life Guards Regiment. The head of the guards was Ensign Znamenskii, and his assistant was noncommissioned officer Kruglov.

After a preliminary search by Kruglov, I was led to the hall and seated at the table with the other prisoners, all of whom I knew: the Chairman of the Council of Ministers, Prince Golitsyn; Trepov; Secretary of State for Finance, General Markov; General Renenkampf; City Prefect, General Balk, and his deputy, General Vendorff; Police Chief, General Grigoriev; Procurator of the Holy Synod, Prince Zhevakov; Senator Chaplinskii; Finance Minister, Bark; Gendarme General Furs; Kazakov; Colonel Pletnev; the director of the Naval Academy, Admiral Kartsev; Adjutant General Bezobrazov; General Makarenko, and others. In addition, the other rooms held individuals who had arrived later or had been transferred in: A. A. Khvostov; S. P. Beletskii; General Klimovich; Adjutant General N. I. Ivanov; Adjutant General Baranov; the Governor General of Finland, General Zein, along with his chancellery head, General Nikol'skii; the Director of Police, A. T. Vasiliev; former ministers Makarov, Maklakov, and Shcheglovitov; General Count Meklenburgskii; General Spiridovich; General Gerasimov; General Riman; S. E. Vissarionov, and others. The general population of this citadel of the Russian revolution, as the commandant of the Tauride Palace called it, was about sixty individuals. There were only two women: the former lady-in-waiting, A. A. Vyrubova, and the former publisher of the newspaper *The Populace*, Poluboiarinova. Later, the wife of General Riman and the wife of the Governor Kreton of Vladimir were taken into custody, but they were quickly released. The women were held in a small room near the guards' area.

Conditions were quite severe for those who had been arrested earlier. For example, during the first three days we were not allowed to speak to one another, only to answer questions put to us by guards or authorized individuals. Everyone had to sit in silence for hours and, when ordered, would stand up simultaneously and walk around. We slept in the armchairs that we sat in; that is, we slept seated. Those who were luckier got to sleep on the small sofas against the walls of the hall, of which there were no more than six. A guard escorted those who had to use the toilet. Any meetings with relatives or acquaintances were under the guard of a noncommissioned officer or corporal of the guard and were conducted in the corridor that connected the pavilion to the lobby. Our twice-a-day meals were quite tolerable, and we also got hot water for tea. The worst was that we were not allowed to speak to each other, and we could not get undressed to go to sleep.

The head of the guards, ensign Znamenskii, who was quite decent, conducted himself correctly. He did not taunt the detainees, even though he was a member of the Party and had suffered for his revolutionary activities in the past. The same cannot be said of noncommissioned officer Kruglov, who was an absolute beast. He was an Old Believer from the Nizhni Novgorod province who was drafted from the reserves—an uncultured, bitter man. He was forty years old, taller than average, had a light-brown beard, and small, angry, deep-set eyes that gave such a repulsive appearance that detainees called him "Maliuta Skuratov." Kruglov generated fear and commanded respect, not only from the entire guard but also from the leaders of the new power structure. Even Kerensky, who was appointed Minister of Justice, the Prosecutor of the Petrograd Judicial Chamber, and Commandant Perets would shake his hand and obviously ingratiate themselves to him. Kruglov extended no deference to them; he considered himself to be the most important of all personnel in the Ministerial Pavilion. He treated all detainees with great contempt, considering them his personal enemies, and allowed himself to indulge in all kinds of mockery and rudeness.

The commandant of the detention area of the Tauride Palace, and later of the entire palace, was Colonel Perets, a rather base individual who constantly ingratiated himself with the soldiers, and especially with Kruglov. To please the soldiers, he was as rude and malevolent as possible to the detainees. When he first showed up at the detention area I recognized him immediately. He had served in the Warsaw Military District in 1912 as a military investigator for the Warsaw Military District Court. When a senatorial inspection was formed by imperial command to revise the office of the Warsaw Governor General, the inspecting senator, D. V. Neigart, appointed Lieutenant Colonel Perets to look into some military matters. Incidentally, he was also assigned to investigate some matters pertaining to the head of the Plotz Military District, Colonel Efremov. Perets wanted to make a mark and further his own career, so he patently shuffled the testimony of witnesses, falsified records, and fabricated evidence to incriminate Efremov. Perets's forgeries were established in court, and to put a stop to this matter, he was transferred to the Kazan Military Court District, where he was caught in some swindling activity and fired from government service. He wound up in Petrograd at the moment of the revolution and attached himself immediately to the new leadership. I think he was the commandant for only a month, after which he published a brochure costing fifty kopeks entitled "In the Citadel of the Russian Revolution," in which he described his impressions of individual detainees. This booklet was written in a brazenly biased manner, with the goal of ridiculing those who were now in such unfortunate straits and arousing as much hatred among the masses as possible.

There were also the spontaneous leaders over the detainees, so to speak, consisting of quite a few rabble individuals who had easy access to the detention facilities supposedly to provide hygienic services and to raise the morale of the detainees. In actual fact, these were journalists, curious people, released political and criminal convicts, some kind of nurses who were totally unnecessary, male and female students, and others. All these people frequented the Ministerial Pavilion every day and would get into conversations with the detainees and try to find out something interesting that they could later recount in a distorted manner in some newly established newspaper. These people would boast impertinently to the detainees how they had won the revolution and had the effrontery to agitate on behalf of the new regime. Some of these visitors would enter into real political debates and discussion with the detainees. Among this rabble were many of my former clients, who complained that the Security Bureau did not give them the possibility to participate in revolutionary activities. From conversations with them, it became clear that, regardless of the revolution, the squabbling within the party would go on for a long time. It was doubtful that the socialists would be able to establish a united democratic front. These young people—for the most part students, male and female—behaved correctly to the detainees. But there were some who had nothing to do with politics; these were simply criminals and adventurers who had been released from prisons and now presented themselves as having suffered in the past for their political views. In all this confusion, these people indulged in robbery, settling old scores with detainees, and getting their share of dirty deals. As an example, in the first several days of our detention, a young man, about thirty years old, identified himself as a physician by the name of Count d'Overk. He claimed that he had been of great help to the revolution by instigating street riots against the defenders of the old regime and in pursuing and arresting Tsarist ministers. He recounted his participation in Rasputin's assassination and talked a lot of other nonsense. Incidentally, I knew clearly from past experience that this man had been listed on a police department circular as having been involved in robberies in Petrograd. He had fled to Kazan, where he was involved in further robberies and other criminal activities. Not long before the revolution, he was arrested in Vladivostok under an alias and was delivered to Petrograd. By background, he was the son of a janitor by the name of Overko, and during the Japanese War he was a medical orderly. However, soon into his new position of power, he was exposed and arrested for both his old and newer crimes. During the time that he participated in the revolutionary upheaval, he executed search warrants on various individuals and robbed them of up to 35,000 rubles in cash.

Another individual was the Jew, Baron, who would tell impossible cock-and-bull stories about himself. He visited the detainees every day, ate almost all the canned food that was given to the detainees, and smoked their cigarettes. He soon disappeared, but not before announcing to everyone that he was leaving for Kuban, where he was chosen to be military leader. There were also some thieves who were unmasked and sent back to prisons.

As I have mentioned, the soldiers, incited by their leaders, first treated us rudely and impertinently, as if we were personal enemies, but as time went on, their attitude improved. They began to engage us in conversation, and some even shared their views on current events.

In all their talk, they justified what had happened. There were some, however, who quietly asked us, "Well, what will we gain from this revolution?" Among the guards I recognized noncommissioned officer Shevelev, who had been one of my students when I taught at the training command when I was in the Keksholm Regiment. He recognized me, too, and treated me with considerable respect. He told me in secret that he had barely escaped getting into big trouble. He had recently applied to the Special Corps of Gendarmes and was to have been assigned to it, but the revolution intervened.

During the first several days after the revolution, everyone from the commandant down to the soldiers were depressed, even worried. They were afraid that the new order would not be stabilized and would be suppressed by veteran troops from the front. They did not even try to hide their concern, and talked openly about this peril. After the suppression of the move on the capital by the Georgievskii cavalry unit and the arrest of Adjutant General Ivanov, everyone cheered up and calmed down.

As for the detainees, they were all in a depressed state, which was perfectly natural; each fully understood the significance of Russia's collapse and the abyss into which these adventurers who were now in power carried the country. The detainees experienced their misfortune in different ways: some were terribly nervous and completely dispirited, while others were calmer. Some of these individuals had held high offices and been decisive, bold, and energetic; now it was sad to look at them—they looked so lost. For example, one individual had been a public prosecutor, and he assured me that he would either be shot or made to stand trial as accountable under Criminal Code 102—that is, that he belonged to a secret organization that had as its goal . . . and so on. When I assured him that this could not happen, since he served in the government and not in a secret society and that the laws of the Russian Empire had not been repealed, he continued to stick to his perception. It is true that in the end he was shot, but this was under the Bolsheviks in 1918. The Provisional Government had released him without charging him.

Three days after my incarceration, Kerensky came to see us for the first time. He gathered all the detainees and announced that the Tsar had abdicated, that the Grand Duke Mikhail Alexandrovich had done the same, that the composition of the Provisional Government had been established, and that he, Kerensky, had been appointed Minister of Justice. He also announced that from now on Russia would enter a time of truth, justice, and fairness; moreover, from his words we understood that in these matters Russia would be responsible to him, Kerensky, who as the prosecutor general would have unabated supervision over all these matters. Further, Kerensky magnanimously announced that those individuals who conducted themselves courageously in the war would not be kept under arrest; thus, he ordered the release of two holders of the St. Vladimir Cross: Adjutant General Bezobrazov and Major General Tiazhelnikov, who had been General Khabalov's Chief of Staff. It did not bother Kerensky to re-arrest Tiazhelnikov the next day and imprison him in the Peter and Paul Fortress. General Renenkampf's release was not included, even though he was a holder of the St. Vladimir Cross. It became clear that having been awarded the St. Vladimir Cross did not mean freedom.

The best result of Kerensky's visit to us was that from that day on we were allowed to talk to one another.

Two days later, Kerensky returned. His arrival occurred in the following manner: we were in the hall, arguing heatedly about something, and did not notice his entrance. To inform us of the arrival of his important personage, he began to bang a cane on the floor, announcing, "The Minister of Justice is here." We all stopped talking and awaited what he would tell us. He sat down at the table and asked us to sit also. He spoke for a fairly long time about the collapse of the monarchy, of the new enlightened future, and again about truth, justice, and fairness once he was the Prosecutor General of the Republic. After this introduction, Kerensky said the following: "There is a traitor among you—an executioner who executed innocent victims of the Tsarist regime. I hope that you do not want to have him in your midst." We did not know what he was getting at and kept quiet, but even so, several voices were heard saying, "Of course not." Then Kerensky yelled out, his voice cracking, "Colonel Sobesschanskii, stand up!" Sobesschanskii stood up and wanted an explanation, but Kerensky screamed out in a cracking, hysterical voice, "Soldiers, tear off his epaulets, take off his St. Vladimir Cross, and isolate him in a certain place until you get further instructions." After this, Kerensky left. The next morning Sobesschanskii was taken to the Peter and Paul Fortress, where he was incarcerated in a damp cell. He spent four months there and was released without being questioned at all.

After everything that Kerensky had said about truth and justice, this crude scene astonished us and showed us who we were dealing with. It became clear that truth and justice were pretty words, but at present the Minister's role was vengeance against his political enemies.

Where did Sobesschanskii's guilt lie? Only in that he had been the head of the Shliselburg Gendarme Command, and that it was his duty to be present, along with the deputy prosecutor, at the sentencing of individuals and in the carrying out of the sentence. As it was, he was an ordinary gendarme officer about to be discharged.

During the first several days, many detainees were transferred from the Ministerial Pavilion to the Peter and Paul Fortress, and Kerensky himself put this list of names together. New detainees took the places of those who were transferred; some were even brought in from the provinces. The following were brought in: Count Frederiks, Prince Meklenburg, Governor Kreton, General Riman, Governor Shidlovskii, Adjutant General Ivanov, and others. Some were kept a day or two and then released.

Kerensky came by a few more times and always tried to impress us with his rhetoric, but the general substance of his speeches was no different from what he had said earlier, and it was not interesting. On one of his visits he called me out and began the following conversation: "It is definitely clear to me that you were involved in placing machine guns and are guilty of the bloodshed of the people." I told him that I absolutely rejected such an accusation, but that I witnessed machine gun fire when I walked along the streets between February 24 and March 1. Then Kerensky announced to me, "We have witnesses who can testify against you."

"Who are these witnesses?"

"I will not tell you who they are, but the matter will be investigated."

"And I am asking you to do just that, and when you have investigated, you will see that it was workers who placed the machineguns."

"Don't tell me that, these are fabrications," said Kerensky, and then he asked me, "Is it true that there was a tunnel under the Neva that led from the Okhrana to the Winter Palace? I ordered a sapper company to verify this."

I answered that I did not know of such a tunnel until now, but with the assistance of a sapper company one could be built.

Kerensky got angry and said, "If you are going to answer like that, then we have nothing more to talk about," to which I answered, "As you wish," and I added, "Pay attention to the notice in the newspaper that the Okhrana had a rooftop radio telegraph and an armored car in the garage; that is about as true as the tunnel story."

For some reason, Kerensky said, "Well, that is nonsense." Then he asked me one more question: Why did I, who had graduated from the General Staff Academy, join the Special Corps of Gendarmes? When I answered him, "By conviction," he became completely angry and rushed out of the room. After that I never had occasion to speak to him again.

Immediately after he left, I was informed that I should get ready to be transferred to the Peter and Paul Fortress, but after two days I still had not been transferred. It turned out that the fortress and other cells were being repaired; so in the meantime I remained at the Pavilion.

We were visited by other personages, such as the S.R. Pereverzev, not a very good lawyer, who was appointed Prosecutor of the Petrograd Judicial Court, and by the new chief of prisons (I have forgotten his name), who was an old S.R. party worker whose party alias was "Comrade Golden Eyeglasses." Both of them went out of their way to impress us with the wonderful new regime and what a paradise awaited Russia now that she had cast off the shameful fetters of the monarchy. They both tried to show off the beauty of their rhetoric and to impress us no end. Commandant Perets came by every day, talked all kinds of nonsense, lied a lot, and found fault in the smallest things just to annoy the detainees.

Moreover, the detainees were visited by various soldiers' and workers' deputies to confirm that all the detainees were present and to see those who were considered enemies of the new regime. These visits were very unpleasant because the leaders set them up as presentations, as if the public was at a performance. I will never forget the visit of the deputies from the naval guard crew that was headed by an incredibly tall sailor who had a fierce look. Kruglov gave this sailor a briefing, and then, stopping in front of each detainee, he introduced the detainee and added an epithet. For example, in introducing Dobrovol'skii, he added, "The Justice Minister issued unjust laws." When Dobrovol'skii noted that the Justice Minister did not issue laws, Kruglov immediately put a pistol to Dobrovol'skii's head. Introducing General Klimovich, he added, "The City Prefect, who tortured people." When Klimovich objected, Kruglov played the same scene with his pistol, and so on.

Photographers were brought in to take our group pictures, with the goal of publishing them in Russian and foreign journals with corresponding commentaries, but we declined this honor.

The old revolutionary V. L. Burtsev visited us, mostly interested in talking to me and other gendarme officers to try to find out who our secret agents were. Their names had not yet been found in the materials that survived the destruction of the Security Bureau's offices. In his conversations with me, he asked about secret agents using their code names; he asked me to clarify who these agents really were who were hiding under one alias or another. I did not satisfy his curiosity by telling him that I did not remember, and in many cases I did not know the real names. Burtsev also asked me to write my

FIGURE 20.1. Vladimir Lvovich Burtsev. Wikimedia Commons.

personal perception of the Russian Revolution and to mail it to his apartment. I declined, knowing full well that he needed this to get published in the Russian and foreign presses, with his personal conclusions and his unwarranted commentary added.

My impression of Burtsev: a narrow-minded individual obsessed with exposing those who he called political provocateurs. It must be said that Burtsev did not belong to any political party. As an old revolutionary, who in the eyes of the socialists had suffered under the Tsarist regime and who hated the monarchical system with all his might, he was very popular with the new regime during the early days of the revolution. One of the first tasks that he took on was to go through the materials of the Okhrana that had survived. In addition to that, he began to publish the journal *The Past*, which was subsidized by the Provisional Government. Burtsev spent a major part of his life outside the country as a political emigrant and returned to Russia only two years before the revolution, having received permission to return from the Minister of the Interior. At first he lived in Tver, and later he applied to move to Petrograd, citing his need to access libraries for his literary efforts. He was given permission, and he moved to Petrograd and established residence in the Balabinskii Hotel on Znamenskii Square. At first the police maintained external surveillance over Burtsev, but once all of his contacts were identified, the surveillance was discontinued, and Burtsev was not considered any kind of threat. It was known for quite some time that this was an old maniacal exposer of agents who, by the way, was not always successful. Indeed, it was established that in Burtsev's early days in Petrograd, surveillance over him caused him to become paranoid. Sensing that he was being watched, he would attack strangers, demand that they accompany him to the police station, write down the license numbers of cabs, and in general give the impression of being abnormal.

In exposing agents, he often made mistakes; he accused innocent people and defended actual provocateurs. In his heart he was a benevolent person, but gullible and not bright. He tried to calm all the detainees when he came to visit, and never accepted any accountability for Russia's collapse. He tried to convince everyone that everything would be well and that a paradise was in the offing. Burtsev was able to get some of the detainees released on his guarantee. Some of those released were re-arrested very soon afterward and incarcerated. Burtsev was dismissed from his assignment of going through Okhrana materials and replaced by a certain person named Kolontaev.

Our life was monotonous; we read newspapers and exchanged views. New detainees and visits from officials, which I have mentioned, brought us some diversion. There were some excesses, though, including this one particular incident. Among our detainees was Admiral Kartsev, who had been the Director of the Cadet Naval Academy. From the first day of his arrest, he showed signs of experiencing a nervous breakdown. One day, around 4 a.m., he jumped up from his armchair where he slept and attacked a guard, with the intention of grabbing the guard's rifle. Another guard shot at him, and the bullet hit him in the shoulder. A third guard fired, and wounded Colonel Pirang in the neck. A fourth guard began firing in the adjoining room but did not hit anyone. Kruglov came running in with his pistol in one hand and a whistle in his mouth. It was only because all of us who were awakened by the noise and gunfire remained calm that we were able to avoid mortal danger. Kruglov told us later that if any of us had gotten involved in any way, he would have blown the whistle, which was the signal for the guards to shoot us all. Kartsev was dragged away from the guard he had attacked and handed over to two medical aides. It turns out that he had become severely deranged, and his intention was to seize a rifle from the guard and do away with himself. While his wound was being tended, he somehow deceived the medics and tried to attack a guard again, but was only able to grab the end of the rifle and stab himself in the chest slightly with the bayonet. He screamed all morning long and was finally dressed and taken away somewhere.

There was also gunfire directed at the windows from the outside guards, but we got used to it and paid little attention. Almost three weeks went by, and not a single detainee was charged or questioned. We were all at a loss as to why we were being held and what our fate might be.

Finally, on March 23, five others and I were ordered to get ready to be transferred to the Vyborg Prison, known as "the Crosses." Our transfer became a pompous occasion. Six detainees were put in a small bus with two armed guards; two other guards were on the rear door's running board, one on each front fender, and two on the roof. In order to make the transfer longer and to show how important criminals were transferred, we did not go straight down the Shapalerov Boulevard to the Liteiny Bridge but made a big swing along the Kirchnoi.

21

Incarcerated Life

General Globachev

The layout of the Vyborg Prison. The prison hospital's surgical unit. The makeup of the prisoners and their living conditions. The prisoner's typical day. Medical service. Visitors. The head of the prison. Investigators. Muraviev's special commission. Selective releases. Attack on the prison. Transfer to individual cells. The internal routine and election of leaders. Conversations with Pereverzev. Transfer to detention cell.

"The Crosses" prison was across the Liteiny Bridge on the Vyborg side of the Neva. Each of the three three-storied stone buildings was in the shape of a cross, which is how the prison derived its name. Each building had more than a hundred individual cells, structured in the American concept. Each cell had a window to the outside and a door that opened to an interior corridor that ran the length of the building, and its height was from the first floor to the roof. The cell doors on the upper floors opened onto balconies in the gallery that extended along the length of the corridor. An interior staircase connected all these galleries on the different floors. At the corners of each floor were toilets. If one stood at the intersection of the corridors, he could see all the galleries at once, so fewer guards were required. In addition to the main buildings were an infirmary outbuilding and a housekeeping building. A high stone wall surrounded the entire prison.

The prison was damaged during the February Revolution when prisoners were freed. The cells were repaired quickly because they were without heat, light, or water. It seems that only one building was left intact, but it was already filled with prisoners arrested by the Provisional Government. That is why our group, after all the formalities in the prison office, was sent to the other wing—the surgical wing of the prison infirmary.

This separate wing had two stories and one entrance. Along the length of the outer wall, each story had a fairly wide and light corridor along which were doors that led to guardrooms, a toilet, and halls that were used as cells. Our group was put into the largest room on the first level, with windows looking out onto the prison yard. This room had been planned for patients, but now there were fifty-six individuals here and, by the way, only ten beds, three of which had straw mattresses. Ten lucky prisoners got beds, and the rest had to find a place to sleep on the floor. The population was the most diverse: there were generals, security police officials, gendarmes, city policemen, line officers, journalists, private citizens, and others. Convicts populated the cell next to ours. God knows why these people were re-arrested after their release in February. Other cells housed young petty thieves and pickpockets, and still other cells mixed criminals with political prisoners. The situation on the upper levels was about the same. The entire wing was filled beyond capacity. Our room was very stuffy and so crowded that there was not enough room on the floor for everyone to sleep lying down, so some had to sleep in a sitting position.

Although the regimen was easier here than at the State Duma building, the hygienic conditions were more difficult; the overpopulation created a lack of air and awful dirt.

The daily guard was the Moscow Life Guards Regiment, and while their mood was revolutionary, they did not inhibit the prisoners. There were no guards in the cells, but guards were posted in the corridor. There was a certain amount of freedom; the cell doors opening to the corridor were open, so it was possible to leave the cell, enter the corridor, drop into the adjoining cells, and go up to the next level. On the other hand, there was the unpleasantness of having to interact with criminals.

Our daily routine was to get up at six in the morning, wash either in the bathroom or kitchen, and get hot water to make our breakfast. In addition, each cell had to be cleaned, which was the responsibility of the person assigned to be the duty officer of the cell. Each cell had a duty in its turn to keep the corridor, kitchen, and toilet clean (the criminals handled these chores for us for an agreed-on price). We also had yard exercise during which we walked about for half an hour under the surveillance of the guards, but we were not allowed to talk. Our lunch was brought to us at noon. The first course was a bucket of hot water in which an uncleaned herring that had gone bad floated, or else some cabbage. The second course consisted of undercooked lentils. It is understandable that almost nobody was able to eat this stuff. So our meals consisted simply of black bread and tea, or canned food that our relatives or friends brought. At six o'clock our dinner was brought in. It consisted of watery gruel, which nobody touched as it was about the same quality as the lunch. At nine o'clock we were locked in for the night.

Twice a week a medical assistant came to take care of the sick and pre-scribed the same powdered medication for all maladies. A doctor visited us only one time. His specialty was psychiatry, and he was a Socialist Revolutionary. His talk was strictly about the victorious revolution, not about offering medical assistance to the indisposed.

The prisoners spent their time in conversation, reading newspapers, which we were allowed to buy from the prison supervisors, and strolling along the corridor. Some entered into conversation with the guards, and there were some, such as Vladimir Gregorievich Orlov, an old member of the Union of Russian People, who got into propagandizing for the monarchy, and even had some success.

Prisoners were allowed to meet with relatives and acquaintances, and were conducted under escort to the prison office, where visits occurred. The people who came to visit us were escorted into a central hall, while we were in small cells along the wall, separated from the visitors by a double metal net. One could talk through this double metal net, but nothing could be passed through it. Food and other items were handed over to the office, where they were examined and even cut up, before being given to the prisoners. In spite of this difficult situation, the visits were comforting moments for each prisoner and brought some diversion to a monotonous existence.

Other people and deputies also visited prisoners. Ensign Popov, who was the head of the prison, came to see us often. He treated us very correctly and even showed us some care. He referred to himself as a member of the Union of Republican Officers. Subsequently, Popov played a considerably prominent role with the Bolsheviks by being appointed Commissar of the Moscow office of the Government Bank. Burtsev also visited us and sang the same old song about the delightful revolution and the paradise that awaited us all. General Gerasimov and S. E. Vissarionov were released on his recommendation, but, as we learned later, they were re-arrested and incarcerated in the Peter and Paul Fortress. Burtsev was removed after the investigation of the Security Bureau, and his task was handed over to a certain young man named Kolontaev who, in his own words, had distinguished himself during the revolution. This gentle-man visited us often and interrogated me, and sometimes some of my former subordinates. Initially he was concerned with the issue of the placement of the machine guns and, just as Kerensky had done, he accused me, but this matter was soon dropped because the investigation concluded that neither I nor the others were involved. As I had affirmed before, the machine guns were placed by the workers themselves. After this, Kolontaev tried to expose who the secret agents were, but here too he was unsuccessful—he got nowhere. He expended a lot of energy and resources to uncover whatever illegalities the Security Bureau committed, but having spent almost half a year on this, he uncovered nothing. By September his mission had borne no fruit, and the Security Bureau building was converted into a court for juvenile criminals.

The persistent wish of all of us who were locked up was to find out what we were being charged with; therefore we insisted that we should be questioned and specifically charged. Finally, all the political prisoners were taken to the prison office, where two former deputy prosecutors arrived and handed out papers and pens and suggested that we write down what we did during the revolutionary days of 27 and 28 February—that is, before our arrest. This did not seem like we were being questioned; rather it was more an accommodation to our demands and, indeed, we saw no results to these written statements.

Just before Easter, which was in early April, some of the prisoners were released little by little, even some police officials. We began to breathe a little easier; in our cell there were no more than twenty-five individuals left. At about this time, Kerensky ordered that the sentence of convicted criminals be cut in half, and those willing to go to the front were freed. Almost all the convicts volunteered for the front. Afterward, in private conversations, they told us, "So we fools are going to do battle; we will be given uniforms, we will be fed, and at the very first station we will desert." Political prisoners were not given this opportunity.

The famous "Extraordinary Committee" was established around this time to investigate abuses committed by officials of the Tsarist regime; its president was the barrister Muraviev. This committee operated for the entire time that the Provisional Government was in power. It had a large and varied staff, occupied a lot of space in the Winter Palace, but it did not complete its task.

After Easter I was often taken before the Committee to give testimony on various matters. I was taken there escorted by two guards, which meant we had to walk from the prison to the Winter Palace. I was asked questions about my efforts to abolish one group or another. I was also asked about ministers, about Rasputin, and so forth. In addition to the investigators who questioned me, some other men were also taking notes. I think these were journalists or socialists who belonged to different parties and who were mostly interested in my secret agents. Most of the Committee's investigators were former precinct investigators or left-wing prosecutors who became true servants of the new order. One thing was clear from all this interrogation—the Committee wanted to go after any possible abuses, but not finding any, they simply wandered in the dark and went after anything. For example, and strange as it was, the former prosecutor of the Orlovsk Regional Court, a man named Zavadskii, questioned me about the former Minister of the Interior, A. N. Khvostov, and what I knew about half a million rubles given to Khvostov through a credit office that was personally approved by the Tsar Emperor. I expressed my complete bewilderment about this, since I did not know that Khvostov received such money, nor what the purpose was for such funds. Not only that, but Zavadskii put the following question to me: Didn't Khvostov give the money to me for safekeeping, and did I not have a safe in one of the banks? To this I answered that I was not a relative of Khvostov's, that there was a professional distance in our relationship, and that I had no safe—and, by the way, he could easily verify this. So, this was the nonsense to which the former prosecutor resorted.

Going to these questioning sessions was pleasant in only one way: it allowed me to breathe fresh air and provided some diversion from the tedious prison regime.

After Easter, with the approval of the prison administration, we were supposed to be transferred to individual cells, or, as they were called, "singles," that had been remodeled, but an incident occurred that merits mention. It was April 11. At about 7 p.m. there was some loud noise in the courtyard, along with yelling and the clanking of rifles in the corridor. Soon after, the door of our cell was opened, and a gang of drunken wild people broke in. The head of the group, as we later learned, was a commissar of the local militia, a young man who looked to be from the Caucasus region. He had a dagger in his teeth, a Browning and a Mauser in his hands, and ammunition belts across his chest. He was followed by twenty individuals, a various group of soldiers, workers, and vagabonds. They all made a racket, and it was so menacing that we did not know what they wanted. Finally, the commissar said that they were here to have firearms surrendered to them. Of course we could not surrender any firearms because we, as prisoners, had none. Then one of the prisoners in our group got the idea that maybe a penknife was considered contraband, so he handed his penknife over to the commissar, and this inadvertently turned the whole situation into a joke. Nevertheless, the commissar put the matter to a vote as to whether the penknife was contraband. The gang graciously decided to leave the knife for cutting bread. Then the search began like a storm. Everything was turned over, damaged, and the three mattresses that were shared by twenty-five prisoners were declared an extravagance. The drunken gang finally left, having cursed us in the most vile language, and proceeded to the next cell. The noise died down, but within ten minutes another gang of drunks burst in. This time they were mostly soldiers, and no commissar was with them. They did not demand the surrender of firearms; they just began their search. They found somebody's tea biscuits and announced that we were authorized only black bread and hot water. After their search, everything was in a pile in the corner of the cell. The soldiers aimed the bayonets on their rifles at us and ordered Colonel Riman to step forward. He did so. Then the soldiers began to vote on what to do with him: "Hang him or shoot him?" They were ready to carry out their vote when a soldier spoke out, "Comrades, he is a member of the Semenovskii Regiment; I remember that he was good."

This changed the group's mood right away, and someone said, "Well, the hell with him. Comrades, let's go." The entire group left to carry on disgracefully in another cell. Finally, around 9 p.m., when we were able to calm down from what happened and lay down to sleep, a third gang came in that included sailors and workers. To our relief, the head of the prison, Popov, was with them and was able to keep them calm so that they only searched the cell and left.

We were completely unable to understand the reason for these raids, all within a two-hour period, but finally it became clear. Someone had made a phone call to the Moscow Life Guards Regiment and reported a riot in progress at the Crosses: political prisoners had disarmed the guards and were escaping. That phone call was enough to get six thousand workers and soldiers gathered in front of the prison, and many of them picked up machine guns along the way. Initially this mob decided to take the prison by storm, but when the head of the prison came out and explained to them that what they heard was not true but only a provocation, it was decided to have a limit of three delegations search the prison and report back to the crowd gathered outside. That is the background to what occurred in the wild raids I described above.

We read the newspapers in prison (we were allowed to buy them) to keep track of the Provisional Government's politics and the public mood. By comparing the various newspaper reports of excesses, the information that we received from our former agents who wound up in the Crosses, and the provocateurs who had ties with the inner circles, it became evident that the Provisional Government would not last long and would lose out to the Bolsheviks. This became especially clear when Kerensky proclaimed the slogan to "deepen the revolution," and the Provisional Government began to tear down the old administrative institutions without replacing them with anything.

In the middle of April, we were ordered to move into single cells in the first prison block. We political prisoners were lodged in the top tier of one of the wings of the building. There were still not enough single cells for everyone, so some were occupied by two prisoners. I was assigned to share a cell with one of my former subordinates, Captain M. T. Budnitskii, and this made me happy. We were able to exchange ideas and thoughts, which gave us some respite from the tedium of sitting around alone. This lasted only two weeks, and then my companion was released and I was alone again.

A single cell was a room of four steps long by three steps wide. The ceiling was vaulted, and one could touch it with an outstretched arm. At the top of the facing wall, almost at ceiling level, was a deep opening with a small barred window. The furniture consisted of a bunk with a mattress, a small table, and a stool. A sink and a toilet were in the corner. If there were two bunks, there would be a very narrow space between them. There was a small-hinged pane in the door that was used to pass food and also used as a peephole through which the entire cell could be seen. A prisoner spent all his time either sitting or lying down because there was no room to walk about. This was the routine for the "singles." The prisoner got up at six in the morning, the cell was opened, the prisoner stepped out into the gallery and went to the bathroom, and then the cell was cleaned and aired. This took about 10 minutes. Then the prisoners went back and were locked in, and bread and hot water were passed through the slot in the door. At nine o'clock the prisoners were taken out to walk in the courtyard. This exercise lasted for fifteen minutes, twenty minutes at most, and was under heavy guard. Lunch was at noon and was the same meal as breakfast, and at six we had dinner. After dinner we were let out for 10 minutes to wash and go to the bathroom, and at nine o'clock it was lights out.

The prisoners of each gallery selected a head and his assistant from among their number. Political prisoners did not have the right of such selection, so these responsibilities were assigned to convicted criminals by the prison administration. For example, our leader was an old convict, and his assistant was a young thief under investigation. Both of them operated as go-betweens in dealing with the prison administration in distributing books from the prison library and buying newspapers, food supplies, and other items. Of course, in all these exchanges they took in a considerable profit and were able to make out well at the expense of the political prisoners.

In spite of our repeated demands that we be presented with charges and be examined, none of this occurred, and we were forced to conclude that we were being held illegally and simply for the order of the revolution. However, each one of us was presented with the Provisional Government's law stating that arrested persons must be charged within twenty-four hours, or otherwise be released. It was only rarely that investigators visited us and questioned everyone, political and criminal prisoners, but their questions were more surveys than anything else.

And so I spent a month in a single cell. Finally in June, I was called to meet with Justice Minister P. N. Pereverzev in one of the lower vacant rooms. Pereverzev had it in mind, if not to plead for my help, to seek my advice as to "how the new government should fight the growing anarchism in the capital." It was true enough, based on newspaper articles, that the anarchist movement was growing, and the government was unable to cope with it. The anarchists had taken over Durnovo's country house outside the Moscow Gates and established their headquarters there. They conducted raids and robberies that kept the population of Petrograd terrified. In response to Pereverzev's question of how I would deal with the situation, I answered, "The same way as before the revolution, when anarchist groups were neutralized in a timely manner and its participants were sent to prison. There is no doubt that when they were freed after the revolution they began to set up their anarchist cells. Thus, it is imperative, if any of the Security Bureau's materials have survived, that their names and addresses be determined, and all of them should be liquidated. Later incorporate a system of agents and assign the entire matter to a good court investigator to conduct surveillance and plan complete liquidation. Experience has taught us that anarchists are close to common criminals in their thinking and they gladly bear witness to that."

Pereverzev responded that the new government could not resort to the unworthy methods of Tsarist times—that is, to the use of secret agents. Hearing this, I concluded that we were not even speaking the same language, and that Pereverzev was showing himself to be completely obtuse and lacking an understanding of the situation. Even so, I asked him, "By what means are you able to know what your enemies are planning and exactly what their actions are?" Pereverzev responded, "Thanks to rumors, gossip, and anonymous reports." I answered him, "You will fill your prisons with innocent people, but the ringleaders will deal with you quickly. You are lucky if 1 percent of anonymous reports are accurate." Nevertheless, as Pereverzev was leaving, he announced that I would be taken to the Security Bureau, where I would identify anarchists, and for this help my routine in prison would be made easier and I would be transferred to another prison.

22

Imprisonment Continues
and the Bolsheviks Rise Up

General Globachev

The detention cells. The routine. The commandant and guards. The makeup of the prisoners. The Kronstadt sailors. The rise of the Bolsheviks in July. The consequences of the rise of the Bolsheviks. Changes in the laws that applied to political prisoners. Charges of exceeding authority. My release.

After about two or three days I was transferred to a detention area set up in the former headquarters of the Special Corps of Gendarmes at No. 40 Furshtatskii Street. Those under arrest were held on the third floor, which had been the Chief of Staff's apartments. There were only ten rooms, and the largest was converted into a reception area and dining space. Two separate rooms were allocated to A. A. Vyrubova and to the former Minister of War, General Beliaev, each getting their own room because they were ill. The remaining seven rooms were organized as cells for the detainees, with each cell holding five to six individuals. The routine in this place was very easy and the conditions quite humane. Meals were prepared for guards and detainees alike, and were quite good. The second floor was occupied by the Soviet of Metal Workers, and the commandant and guards were on the first floor.

The commandant was a young ensign by the name of Nadzharov, a very stupid Georgian, who bragged about the importance of his position because, according to him, he had been a personal aide to the Justice Minister. The detainees named him "little lamb" because of his supposed wit and Georgian background. His activities consisted primarily of betting on horses and profiteering on rations, and it seems that in these areas he was nobody's fool. Evidence of his dishonesty eventually surfaced. Due to his abuse of office and the theft of 35,000 rubles from the safe of the Special Corps of Gendarmes that were in his keeping, he was arrested and jailed, and a new commandant replaced him.

The security of the place was slipshod, really awful. One external guard was placed at the entrance to the building, and a second in the dining area. When we had our exercise in the courtyard, there were no guards. One side of the courtyard opened onto Voskresenskii Prospekt and was separated from it by a very high wooden fence, against which winter firewood was stacked. The inside guard often would leave his rifle in the corner of the room and leave. At night, the rifle was often left in the corner while the guard slept on an oilcloth-covered couch. Under these conditions—and if you add to this that counts of the detainees rarely occurred—escape would have been very easy, and it is surprising that this never happened.

The composition of the detainees was privileged people, mostly officers and officials. Many had been transferred from other detention sites and, like me, were given an easier routine. The individuals that I came into contact with were General Khabalov, General Beliaev, A. A. Vyrubova, General Kommisarov, former Minister of Justice Dobrovol'skii, Madame Dubrovina, City Prefect General Balk, General Vendorff, and others. Almost every day, new detainees arrived, some from other detention sites and some newly arrested.

In early June, nearly all the police and Gendarme officials had been released, and now many rooms were vacant. But soon the trial of the Kronstadt sailors began, and the detention cells filled up once again, mainly with naval officers from Kronstadt. About one hundred individuals from Kronstadt were assigned, twelve to fifteen per room. They were charged with absurdities such as being too strict with the sailors or spending too much time training the sailors. As an example, one midshipman spent four months incarcerated because when he learned that Guchkov had been appointed Naval Minister, he had said, "What kind of sailor is he? He probably only saw the sea in his dreams." By the end of June, all the naval officers had been freed.

In early July, the detainees experienced some awful days, particularly July 3–5, during the ascendancy of the Bolsheviks. Early in the morning on July 3, a mass movement of Bolshevik troops and a crowd of armed workers began along Furshtatskii Street toward the Tauride Palace. This crowd was passing the windows of the building we were in, and we were able to observe the mob's movement. The crowd was moving in complete silence, and we could see their anxiety, uncertainty, and even fear as they energized themselves by carrying posters and being heavily armed. It seemed to us that just one or two shots would disperse them, but this did not happen. The movement continued slowly, with those in the crowd, rifles shouldered, looking cautiously at the windows and doors of buildings they passed. By evening, things got even livelier—an armored car showed up, and there was rifle fire and the rat-a-tat-tat of machine guns being fired.

Our commandant was completely confused. When we asked him what was going on, he said that a coup was in progress and that he could not count on his guards, who had been incited by the Bolsheviks. We concluded that he would either flee and leave us to our fate, or he would join the Bolsheviks along with his guards. All day long, on July 4, the situation was frightening, and the commandant did not show up at all. By July 5 it looked like everything had ended. The commandant appeared and told us the Bolshevik uprising had been put down. Indeed, on that same day, some newly arrested detainees arrived, Bolsheviks, who were put in a separate room. They were kept isolated, but when questioned they answered readily and tried to incite other detainees. After several days, they were all released.

After the Bolshevik uprising, the Provisional Government established a special commission to investigate the incident. In early August, the commission's court investigator came to see me to ask for my thoughts on this matter as a witness to these events. I told him I had no idea about this matter—how could I when I had been detained under guard for the past five months? It turned out that Kerensky and his entire clique decided to connect the Bolshevik uprising as a counter-revolution to the Tsarist government and to monarchist groups that, it must be added, did not exist at this time.

By the way, I was asked if Lenin had been a secret agent of the Security Bureau, to which I answered that, unfortunately, he had not been.

A second question was: "But did not Lenin come to St. Petersburg during the war and meet with you?"

I answered that if Lenin had come during the war, he certainly would have been arrested and, by the way, during the war the Bolsheviks were the only ones who had shown any activity, and the same could not be said of the other revolutionary parties.

Then followed another question: "If Lenin was not an agent of the Security Bureau, then was he an agent of the Department of Police?"

I answered, "That could be. I do not know who the Department of Police's agents were, but I personally do not think that Lenin was one of them."

Subsequently, this investigator kept returning to the same questions, and summoned me even after my release. He was especially interested in the failed uprising of the workers and of our political emigrant groups during the war. The commission did not come to any conclusions about the Bolshevik uprising of July 3–5, and the commission's activities ended at the same time as the October Revolution.

Because of the detainees' persistent demands to be presented with charges and reasons for our being detained under guard, Justice Minister Pereverzev came up with a new law, "extrajudicial arrests," which was mainly copied from the 1881 law on state security, but with some questionable addenda and corrections. It was hard to determine to whom these laws applied and under what circumstances. It turned out that the law was developed exclusively to justify the actions of the Provisional Government to arrest and detain people who were considered enemies of the state. This was proven when the law was published. Many arrested individuals were given a maximum sentence of three months, not including the time they had already served as detainees prior to the law being issued.

My situation did not fall under this law; my "crime" was considered more serious. The prosecutor of the Petrograd Judicial Court, Karinskii, assigned Stavrovskii to the most serious cases and to bring me to trial under Chapter 2, page 342, of the Penal Code—that is, exceeding or in criminal negligence of my authority. The basis for these charges was that I had used secret agents—or as they were now called, provocateurs—illegally. The evidence against me included two volumes of the Bulletin of the Provisional Government in which 152 named individuals were exposed as secret agents. Prosecutor Stavrovskii, having gone through these materials, did not find any criminal case, about which he informed me. He asked me to give testimony on this matter, which I agreed to do. I demonstrated that it was my duty to carry out the struggle with the revolutionary movement and to use secret agents as a resource, that this did not violate any laws, and, in addition, this system had been in use for decades. Thus, if I had *not* used secret agents, I could more rightly be accused of criminal behavior as found in Chapter 2, page 342, of the Penal Code, that is, dereliction of duty. Stavrovskii concluded his investigation and issued a decree that the matter was closed and that I would be released. A day later, I was released on Stavrovskii's order to the detention area's commandant. As I found out later, my release really upset Karinskii and Pereverzev, and because Stavrovskii refused to prosecute me, he was forced to resign.

And so, having spent almost half a year in detention, I was again free.

23

My Husband's Release, but Now Fear

SOFIA GLOBACHEVA

Special Investigator Stavrovskii resigned shortly after this, not wanting to serve any longer under such circumstances. Fortunately, my husband was released just in time, because soon after his release the Bolshevik revolution occurred, and the Bolsheviks shot everybody who was still under arrest. Those executed included the former Minister of the Interior Khvostov, Assistant Minister Beletskii, Vice Director of the Department of Police Vissarionov, and many more. After his release by Stavrovskii, my husband was assigned to the reserve staff of the Petrograd Military District, and even received a salary. After the Bolshevik Revolution, everyone who was in the reserves still received a salary for another two months, and then they were allocated only soldiers' rations. Within another week or two they were discharged. Without money and without things that we could sell to buy whatever food we needed, my husband, our two children, and I had to stay in Petrograd living on extremely minimal rations. We awaited a new arrest that would end in execution this time, and there was no way for us to get away. My brother helped us with money, and we lived on this. All my family jewels that I had kept at home I thought were safe, since our apartment was in the Okhrana building. However, things turned out differently, because in the very first days of the revolution they were stolen, as were all our possessions: money and important documents that were in the government bank were confiscated by the Bolsheviks.

My husband lost weight and strength, not day by day, but hour by hour, because his system was sapped by his long incarceration.

A short time after the Bolsheviks had triumphed, they began to order everybody to show up for communal work, cleaning streets and doing snow removal; both men and women were required to work. An apartment house committee was formed, elected by the apartment dwellers to ensure that people went to work. The committee took orders from the Bolsheviks. My husband went to do this work, but I never did, despite the fact that the head of the house committee warned me that I could be shot for failing to obey their order. I responded, "Let them shoot me, but I will not unquestioningly submit to the wild orders of the Bolsheviks." The head of the house committee gave me a dismissive wave of his hand and left me alone.

For the people who arrived for work there was a roll call by last name, and they were given shovels and pickaxes, and after work there was another roll call to find out if everyone had worked. Even here people were able to get around working; some would answer the first roll call and then would put their shovels and pickaxes in some secluded place, leave to go about their business, and return for the second roll call. The workers made quite a strange sight. Women wearing expensive fur coats and fashionable hats lazily tapped their pickaxes on the ice for the assigned work hours, chatting with each other all the time, and after the second roll call they went home.

After the Bolshevik Revolution many of the socialite ladies opened various cafes. The majority of their customers were Bolshevik sailors, but soon enough all these cafes went out of business due to a lack of provisions. At the beginning of the revolution it was still possible to get cereal and potatoes at the markets, but soon after, the Bolsheviks began to banish the merchants from the markets, arrest them, and confiscate their goods. Thus, the last opportunity to buy produce was lost, and we had to live on what was provided, assuming we had money and a ration card. Soon even getting provisions with a ration card diminished, because products completely disappeared, and having a ration card got you nothing. Meals for the four of us were a quarter of a loaf of bread mixed with something like sawdust, and that was a two-day ration; mornings and evenings we drank tea without sugar, and sometimes we could buy cod at three rubles a piece, but we stopped buying it because it was impossible to eat.

Our children helped with work in the apartment cooperative, for which they occasionally received some dried vegetables for soup, in addition to potatoes. This, then, became our dinner; the soup was made only with water, and of course without meat or fat. Sometimes when I went to the railway station at five in the morning, I would manage to meet some farmer coming from the country with bread and I would buy a whole basket of bread for ten rubles, fighting off others who wanted the bread. What joy when I brought the bread home—it was incredible good luck.

One of our female acquaintances who was in charge of a large cooperative house risked being arrested by giving us an extra bread ration card of the first class that allowed bigger rations to those who worked. This saved us from complete emaciation. As soon as the Bolsheviks began to increase the number of occupants per apartment, the wife of General Kaznakov invited us to live with them. On one beautiful morning, the Bolsheviks came to the house to search for weapons. I was not home, and my husband was sick in bed. They ransacked through everything, and no weapons were found, but they took all the documents there were. Without them, it was not possible to survive. Also among all these papers were some important ones that my husband had received from certain sources after his release concerning various former officials and officers who were now in the employ of the Bolsheviks. The next morning I set out for the regional commissariat to get them back. It was terribly noisy and chaotic there, and I barely got the necessary information from one of the Bolsheviks who seemed more reasonable. It turned out that the papers were there, and they were getting ready to send them to the Cheka on Gorohovaia Street, but it was not certain when.* I suggested to them that they give all the papers to a messenger boy in their employ, and I would go with him to Gorohovaia Street. They agreed, and just in case, I wrote down the number that they had assigned to the packet of papers. I have to say that before their rise to power the Bolsheviks on the whole were completely disorganized; they did not know much or understand much, and you could see this clearly in

FIGURE 23.1. Moisei Solomonovich Uritskii. Wikimedia Commons.

their confusion and actions. Because of this it was possible to communicate and interact with them at first, but day by day they learned quickly, got stronger, and began their terrorist programs.

Arriving with the messenger boy and packet at Gorohovaia Street, which had been the City Prefect's office and apartments, where we often visited, I carefully tried to size up everything. At the entrance to the building right by the front door and vestibule was a turret with a machine gun, and two soldiers who never took their eyes off the entrance. Entering the room of a clerk, a young man about eighteen years old, I told him that I wanted to see the Bolshevik commissar of Petrograd, Mr. Uritskii—and I gave him my pass with my real last name—and said that I was there because of the search that had been done at our apartment. The clerk left and came back soon and said that Comrade Uritskii was in a meeting that would last a long time, and that everyone should go home. Besides me, eight other people were there, and they all left, but I stayed and said that I would wait, since the meeting would have to end sometime. I had arrived at Gorohovaia at nine in the morning and had not eaten anything all day. I was still there at eight in the evening when I saw that the clerk was getting ready to go home, and I talked him into letting Uritskii know of me. He went in, and on his return he said that Uritskii would send for me when he was free, and then he left. I thought the clerk had lied, but sure enough within half an hour the former valet of the City Prefect, who knew me personally, came down the staircase and escorted me upstairs.

There were a lot of rumors in town of mass executions every night in the basement of the house on Gorohovaia Street. I wanted to find out if these rumors were true, so as I waited for Uritskii I approached a seated guard and asked him how long he had been there, what his pay was, and if it was true that executions were carried out every night. He seemed like an honest enough chap who had recently come from the country, and he willingly replied that he had been a guard for two months, received 250 rubles a month "for grub," as he put it, but he had heard nothing about executions, and if that did happen, the guards that he replaced would probably have talked about that. Whether it was as he said, I don't know.

I saw about twenty Bolsheviks in a dining room on the second floor, mostly young people dressed in khaki uniforms, dining and talking about how much of an abundance of everything they had. I was interested in seeing what they were eating; every place setting had a plate of cereal (not very big), a glass of tea, two pieces of sugar next to the little tea saucer, and a small piece of bread. I entered another room adjacent to the dining room and, seeing a number of people there, I asked which of them was Uritskii, and a well-dressed, European Jewish-type gentleman in civilian clothes came up to me. He led me into his office and asked me to sit down. After hearing what the situation was, he said that so far he had not seen the papers, that maybe they had not yet arrived, and so he was not able to say anything about it, and that I should come back in two or three days. My answer was that I had been sitting there since early morning, and it was so hard for me to get to see him that I doubted I could go through this a second time. I added that I knew the papers were there because I accompanied the messenger boy who had brought the packet, and the packet had a certain number assigned to it. Uritskii wrote down the number, rang a bell, and told the person who came in to bring the numbered packet unopened. As I sat waiting and listening to the reports that were being given to him, I thought that his instructions were reasonable.

The packet arrived, and we went through the papers together. He seemed to be going through them superficially and handing them to me; I was very nervous that Uritskii might read one of the papers that listed those who were working for the Bolsheviks, and I almost yanked these from his hands. There was also a plan that had been developed by my husband at the request of the apartment house dwellers that dealt with maintaining security of the house in light of the growing number of robberies and attacks on apartments. Uritskii kept it, saying it could be useful. Back home, they were very worried about me because I had been gone so long, and they thought all kinds of terrible things could befall me. When I was leaving Uritskii, having thanked him, he said that he had to warn me that if there would be a second search, things might end very badly.

I was worried that he might know that I was the wife of the head of the Security Bureau, since I did not hide my last name from him, and in his official capacity he had to know who I was. I was also surprised that during the entire time that I was in his office he did not once ask me who my husband was or what he did, and then that strange warning—all of which was a mystery to me and to my husband, and it has remained a mystery. Rumors were going around that Uritskii was against mass executions, and that there were many more in Moscow than in Petrograd under Uritskii. Even so, about two to three weeks later, he was murdered by a young Jew supposedly upset by the execution of officers. The Bolsheviks arranged a magnificent funeral for Uritskii. His body was under a splendid canopy, and the procession moved for several hours down the major streets of Petrograd. The Bolsheviks were all dressed in various uniforms carrying innumerable posters with various menacing inscriptions and slogans. I don't think any earthly king ever had such a luxurious funeral.

After Uritskii's death, things got awful. Life became unbearable. Every night trucks arrived at houses, and people were taken away and shot. After the search that was done at our apartment, and fearing a second one, we moved from General Kaznakov's to the apartment of a naval officer who had left for the south with his wife and young son. His father rented the apartment to us furnished with full household accommodations. Later, Bolsheviks in Yalta killed the naval officer and his wife and child. His last name was Schumacher, and given that at the time the Germans had a lot of influence on the Bolsheviks, the little wooden plaque over the door with his German name saved us for the time being. I think it is for this same reason that the Bolsheviks did not bother General Kaznakov, who even before the war had a good relationship with the German ambassador assigned to Petrograd after the peace treaty with the Bolsheviks.

But it soon became dangerous for us to stay even in that apartment; now several trucks would come to houses every night and search each apartment. I didn't close my eyes at all at night, listening as trucks drove by, as the elevator went to some floor and stopped—this was not living, it was complete torment. The porter of the building, who had been there even during Tsarist times, hated the Bolsheviks and addressed my husband in the old way: "Your Excellency." He forewarned me that if the Bolsheviks came at night he would give us three warning rings and my husband should then leave by the back stairs and he would let my husband out into the street. This was little comfort, because the Bolsheviks usually came through the front door and up the back stairs at the same time. It finally happened that trucks got to one of the adjoining buildings, so we could not delay any longer. We had to do something. We decided that my husband would go to my brother, an artillery officer who had been chosen by a soldiers' committee to be their commander. Not wanting to be in this position, my brother had left to join his family in Gatchina.

On the day that my husband was supposed to go to Gatchina, he suddenly had some kind of misgiving and decided to go the next evening. I sent my son along to accompany my husband and told my son that he should go into my brother's place first to make sure that everything was all right, and then to go back and get my husband, who would be waiting at the train station. My son found my brother's wife and children in despair. The day before—that is, when my husband had the misgiving and postponed his trip—my brother had been arrested, taken away somewhere, and perished under the Bolsheviks. My husband and son returned from Gatchina to Petrograd immediately. The next day, having received a letter from an acquaintance of the cashier of the international sleeping-car train, we set out to get tickets. However, although the cashier wanted to help us, there was nothing she could do because all tickets were sold out for the next two months, even all the standing room in the train's corridors.

We started to leave in despair, with no hope of getting out of Petrograd, where each passing day could mean death. As we passed the ticket booth for local trains, something clicked for me, and I told my husband to get in line.

We were clutching at straws, because everyone in line was turning away, having found out that all the tickets were sold. Just then, as the cashier put up a sign that all tickets were gone, and my husband and I headed for the exit, a real miracle happened. Some woman came into the station and shouted, "Who needs a ticket?" In an instant I was next to her, saying that I needed it. By the time others surrounded her, the ticket was in my hands. I paid her, not knowing where the train was going or when, but it didn't matter—my husband had to get out of Petrograd. When I finally asked the woman where the ticket was for, she answered, to my great joy, "To Orsha," namely, where my husband had to go: south.

Orsha was an industrial city on the Dnieper River some sixty miles south-west of Smolensk. It was also on the railway track from Petrograd, and it was on the boundary border of Ukraine, which in 1918 was occupied by the Germans. Below, a Russian historian provides an excellent description of the limited choices that Tsarist officials had in terms of fleeing the Bolsheviks.

"Fleeing as the red terror was beginning they only had two directions: north to Finland or south to Ukraine, which had recently declared its autonomy from Russia. The Finnish border, very near to Petrograd, was heavily guarded. It is enough to say that even such a capable political operator of the old regime who had an opportunistic character, such as the famous I. F. Manasevich-Manuilov, using forged documents to get across the Finnish border, was recognized by vigilant revolutionary soldiers and shot on the spot.

"Fleeing south from Soviet Russia seemed more promising, and most people preferred to put their fate at the boundary of Ukraine, where Bolsheviks generally allowed people with Ukrainian documents to pass. Thus, Gerasimov and Vasiliev were able to take advantage of this situation. Less fortunate was General V. F. Dzhunkovskii: in October 1918 he was removed by watchful police agents from a hospital train in Orsha . . . on which he was hiding trying to get to Ukraine, and he was arrested and sent to a Moscow prison under guard."[1]

As the reader will see, even the flight south was fraught with danger.

24

The Revolution Deepens

GENERAL GLOBACHEV

My personal situation. My assignment to the reserve ranks of the Petrograd Military District Staff. The revolution deepens. Anarchy. Petrograd's appearance. The Bolsheviks. The mood of the citizenry. Sabotage. The initial system of labor. The officer corps. Counter-revolutionary uprisings. Uritskii's murder. Mass searches and arrests. Flight to the south of Russia and Ukraine. My escape to Kiev.

The first order of business was to organize my personal situation, which took two weeks. Nothing was left of my former apartment. Everything right down to the smallest item was plundered and stolen, and what was too big to be taken was broken, ruined, soiled, and turned over to the guards who now occupied my former apartment for their use. Somehow I had to start all over again.

Since I had not received any orders from the Provisional Government that I had been discharged, I enlisted in the Petrograd Military District Reserves and continued there until December 1917, when the Bolsheviks abolished the reserves and dismissed everyone over a certain age limit (by express order) from military duty.

It was sad to see the formerly brilliant and disciplined Staff of the Petrograd Military District. The personnel, especially the clerks and minor officials became totally insolent. There was no order or discipline. Anyone who wanted, especially soldiers, but civilians too, could enter into whatever rooms without authorization, rummage through drawers, and even look through confidential documents with almost no objection from staff workers. Clerks slighted generals and staff officers shamelessly. Most offensive was the behavior toward former gendarme and police officers. The leadership of the staff and the commander of the staff himself, General Bagratunii, was completely in the hands of the various deputies from different Soviet organizations and were not only unable to exercise any initiative but could not even give orders that they were authorized to give under law. Hundreds of people jammed the staff headquarters every day, and most had nothing to do with military matters. These people were mostly individuals involved in shady enterprises, public speakers, and agitators. The staff headquarters was more like a meeting club. Every former commander had an assistant in his office—a soldier deputy from the Soviet of Deputies.

The number of the reserves was five thousand strong. They did absolutely nothing, but they did draw salaries. This remarkable number of the reserve unit is explainable by the collapse of the front and the retreat of commands to the rear. The Provisional Government wanted to do something to rid itself of this cancer, not only in Petrograd, but in other military districts as well, but it was unable to come up with any ideas.

At this time I had nothing to do. I was just a witness to the mood of the population and the activities of the Bolsheviks as they tried to bring down the incompetent and strange Kerensky government.

Kerensky's slogan of the "intensification of the revolution" became ineffective and showed its true face. The government broke up the entire structure of the administration and army and did not replace it with anything. In the meantime, the Bolsheviks were working with extraordinary energy, giving the dregs of society a new perspective on freedom—that is, complete lack of accountability in manifesting their predatory instincts and in their lying promises that they could participate in governing the country.

The work of the Bolsheviks was made easier because they were sprinkled throughout all government institutions, and they were represented mainly in the Soviet of Workers' and Soldiers' Deputies, an institution that hung like a weight around the Provisional Government's neck. The major Bolshevik ideological leaders were freed from prison after the July uprising because Kerensky's socialist conscience could not keep his brothers in spirit under arrest. The latter went underground and orchestrated the preparation for the October Revolution.

Anarchy ruled in Petrograd during all of September and October. Crime increased to an unimaginable level. Robberies and murders occurred every day, not just at night, but in broad daylight as well. Citizens feared for their lives. The population saw that it could not count on the nominal government for help, so people began to organize themselves. Buildings had security and defense organized in the event of any attacks by robbers. Armed individuals stood guard at night at each house, but even this did not help, as robberies did not decline. The appearance of the city was awful; the Nevskii Prospekt looked like a huge filthy marketplace; people traded in almost anything. In general, the streets were crowded with soldiers who were trading and chewing seeds. All the beautiful buildings—monuments, palaces—were covered with posters and placards. Streets had not been cleaned in months. If you add to this the constant gunfire that could be heard sometimes here, sometimes there, and the fright of the people who were in mass meetings, this gives an accurate picture of Petrograd at that time.

There was one moment of hope for the citizens to be delivered from the coming Bolshevik offensive—this was the Kornilov uprising. Everybody thought that Kerensky would understand the imminent threat to the nation and join Kornilov hand in hand against the Bolsheviks, but this hope went unrealized. Kerensky betrayed Kornilov and thus hastened both the destruction of Russia and his own downfall.

The revolution occurred on October 24 (on the Old Style calendar). The Kerensky government fell, and power passed into the hands of the Bolshevik Party, calling itself the Workers' and Peasants' Government.

I will not describe the details of the successful revolution, since I could observe it only from the side, but I will say that it succeeded easily and more painlessly than the February revolt. The entire matter was done in one day. At that time it really did not matter to me whether Kerensky or Lenin ruled Russia, but if one looked at the entire issue from the point of view of a citizen, then I must say that at first the new regime lightened the burden of the citizenry. This was because the new regime acted decisively against robberies, which made life more tolerable for the citizens. I have to add a reservation, however. This was only in the early days, before the new regime got into the fierce struggle against the sabotage by the bourgeoisie that was instigated by the Socialist Revolutionary Party and the Kadets.

Before the revolution, the Russian people and even the educated among them, did not understand or discriminate among the goals and missions of the various socialist parties. One may say that the Russian people in general were politically ignorant. Just as they did not know Kerensky, Chernov, Avksenteev, and others, they also did not know Lenin, Trotsky, Nakhamkes, and so on. It seems that it was a matter of complete indifference who would rule Russia after a monarch, Kerensky or Lenin. So, the people should have seen the October Revolution the same as the February one, and to accept the fact that in the first days of the Bolshevik takeover they did much less damage in governing and in the social structure than was done by the Provisional Government. Then why is it that even though the citizenry breathed easier after the October Revolution and after the nightmarish period of the Kerensky government, that the very same citizens, especially the intelligentsia and officialdom, turned in opposition to the new regime of Lenin? It was because the Socialist Revolutionaries and Kadets and the Bolsheviks pulled the people, and even more the intelligentsia, into the struggle. Since the very first day of its existence, the Provisional Government was constantly under the threat of Bolshevik attacks and had neither the will nor the desire to take decisive measures to neutralize this danger. The politicians of the Provisional Government only fanned the flames of frightening the public in speeches and in the press, the same way that a nanny frightens little children with all kinds of terrors and demons. After the unfortunate uprising of the Bolsheviks in July, and Kerensky's betrayal of Kornilov, the unknowing citizen considered the Bolsheviks to be the same kind of irresistible evil. This is why, after the October Revolution, minor officials, members of the intelligentsia, and even some groups of workers readily began to sabotage the new power structure by inciting agitation and making promises on behalf of the Socialist Revolutionary Party and Kadets.

Thanks to this, the new regime was put in a difficult position. By placing their own commissars in all the major posts of government, they did away with the experienced bureaucrats and workers. Thus, the government institutions, especially the central ones, stopped functioning effectively. The Bolsheviks had to employ whomever they could, people with no special skills or experience, at least to keep the administration operating. The central organ of the new power structure issued decree after decree. However, enforcing the decrees was extremely difficult because of the government's disorder and the sabotage by personnel.

The strikes and sabotage by the Socialist Revolutionary Party, especially by those in government, struck a major blow to Soviet power. Special committees that provided leadership to the strikers and supported them financially organized these actions. The Socialist Revolutionaries planned to do away with the new power structure within two to three months. It turned out that it was not that easy to accomplish. The Bolsheviks reacted to this danger with a series of repressive measures that started a bitter interparty struggle into which non-party individuals got pulled, especially the officer corps. The populace mostly did not get involved, but those who did become involved on one side or the other when the Civil War started were coerced to do so.

The sabotage and strike committees had only enough money to support the striking government workers for a month and a half, after which these people were left to their fates, and many of them, now in need, sought employment with the regime they had been boycotting.

Few changes occurred at the Staff Headquarters of the Petrograd Military District during the early stages. The commander and higher-ranking officers disappeared and were replaced by Bolsheviks, but the lower echelons remained at their posts. The relationship between these echelons and the reservists and the general public changed dramatically; they became unusually polite, even-handed with all and, I would say, fair. It can be seen that the changes above stunned and frightened the Bolsheviks. It became noticeable that the higher-ups had no trust in the officer cadres, and they did not differentiate between police, gendarmes, guards, and army at all. I will say also that line officers were the least trusted by the Bolsheviks. By November, the Civil War had begun in the south, and officers who had lost their commands at the front due to its collapse, and who had lost all their authority thanks to the Bolshevik decrees, naturally went south to join Kornilov, where an officer's profession and dignity were respected.

The Bolsheviks did away with the reserves quickly. At first they took away salaries and left the reservists strictly on soldiers' rations. In December the reserves were demobilized, and all ranks were dismissed from service and relegated to the status of citizens of the Soviet Republic. From this time on until September 1918, when I had to flee from Petrograd to Ukraine, I had no connection with any government organization. I was just a bystander witness to what was going on. I will not describe what everyone already knows about how the Bolsheviks destroyed all the branches of government and social life, but I will share my perceptions with the reader of some of the events that led to this destruction.

As I have said, the Soviet power structure took the reins of government from the Socialists under very difficult conditions. Banditry, raids, robberies in broad daylight—common occurrences at that time—were intolerable to the Bolsheviks unless it was done for the good of the party. Meanwhile a lot was going on under the guise of various political organizations that were even more extreme than the governing Bolshevik Party. The Anarchist-Communists were particularly active in their struggle at this time. Lenin came to a rational decision from the perspective of the party's evolution; he announced that the Bolshevik Social Democratic Party was communist and the Soviet government was communist. While this action might seem to have little meaning to the average citizen it yielded very positive results. By this action, Lenin absorbed all the Anarchist-Communist groups and paralyzed the propaganda of the more extreme political groups, and the extreme left had nowhere to go now. From this time on, anarchistic groups, as political organizations, began to disappear. By the way, a year before, if any Bolshevik had even mentioned communism, Lenin might have branded them a traitor or a renegade. Protecting himself thus from the left, it was now necessary to guard against the right—that is, to defeat his most dangerous enemy, the S.R.s and Kadets who were still quite powerful and who organized uprisings here and there and tried to regain the power they had lost.

The Bolsheviks did not even bother with the monarchist organizations because they were small in number and passive. To paralyze the danger from the right, the All-Russia Extraordinary Commission (Cheka) was formed. It was organized as a government agency to fight counter-revolution and profiteering; that is, it was a political/criminal investigative agency that subsequently turned into a punitive/judicial organization and simply into a torture chamber. All the provincial bureaus of this central agency had the same mission and received their directives and orders from the center; this was the Cheka. At first the Cheka's operation as an investigative agency was extremely ineffective because, on the one hand, its staff was selected casually from among the poorly qualified, not having special knowledge or experience. On the other hand, the technical aspects of the work was weak. The whole system was based on bribing opposition groups, betrayals, and the crudest of provocations. Even so, notwithstanding its results, the Cheka's actions justified its existence. Conspiracies and attempts at uprisings were uncovered and liquidated one after the other. The Soviet government spent a countless amount of money on this struggle. It understood perfectly well what the issue was: for its very existence as a power and the need to fight internal enemies, money was a powerful resource.

At this time I worked on gathering information for a secret organization, and I had agents in several Soviet establishments and in the Petrograd Cheka. I knew that many secret organizations, especially the officers' organizations, were being liquidated by Soviet agents infiltrating them. Now the once-respected officer corps was corrupted with big money bribes. At the same time as this treachery was going on, many agents of the White Movement infiltrated Soviet agencies as government workers. This gave considerable advantage to the counter-revolutionary movement, but its power weakened later when the Soviet system of mass terror all but paralyzed the counter-revolutionary activities. Even so, during the worst moments of the terror and the height of the Civil War, the connection continued between the White front and the underground activities of the counter-revolutionaries in the rear amidst the Bolsheviks.

Among the officers who were kicked out at this time, a totally unworthy type of criminal/investigative agent appeared, who for the most part had no ideological foundation and just treated what he did as a job. Soon this individual became recast as a counter-intelligence agent working for the White Movement or a Chekist working for the Reds. Many of these agents were totally unprincipled and served both sides equally; they would sell their services to the side that was least dangerous and most advantageous to them. These were called double agents; and so, an entire contingent of officers—counter-intelligence agents—was created who disgraced the counter-intelligence agencies of the White Movement during the Civil War.

The persecution of officers began in the summer of 1918, when officers became involved in the S.R. insurrection and conspiracies under the leadership of Savinkov. He was able to attract not only irresponsible officers, but even some monarchist groups who claimed they were for the restoration of the monarchy, even if it was only to overthrow the Bolsheviks. After the failed Yaroslavl uprising led by Savinkov, the Soviets understood that the officer corps was the basis for the S.R.'s power and that the officer corps constituted the same kind of threat as did the White Movement in the south of Russia under Kornilov. Thus, the Soviets decided to finish off this threat once and for all. Officers had to register, and then there were mass arrests, first in the major cities and then in the provincial towns. Some of those arrested were shot, while others were distributed to various prisons, but the capital punishments had not yet reached mass proportions. It was only after the attempted murder of Lenin and the murder of Uritskii, who was the head of the Petrograd Cheka, that the mass terror and a system of executions without trial began. In like manner, the terror was also aimed at the bourgeoisie, who the Soviets considered a no less serious threat to their existence. In short, the pursuit and extermination of the intelligentsia began.

Here is how the procedures of the mass arrests worked: its implementation was delegated to the district Soviets, who proceeded to execute searches in their districts. The information for this came from the registration data on the officers, building records, and information derived from questioning doormen and janitors. Red Army soldiers would surround an entire block, and each building would be searched by Cheka agents. Every former officer and suspected bourgeoisie was arrested. These measures produced several thousand arrested persons, who filled the prisons in Petrograd and Kronstadt, and none of them had any substantive criminal charges lodged against them. Still, these measures completely paralyzed the activities of the counter-revolutionary organizations by snatching away many serious counter-revolutionary workers and cutting existing ties. These same measures were also carried out in the Petrograd suburbs so that it was extremely difficult for a former officer to hide out. Masses began to flee to the Don and Ukraine. It became impossible for anyone who did not recognize Soviet authority to remain. There was also another reason for a sensible person to flee Soviet Russia—imminent starvation.

The decrees on nationalizing, socializing, and restricting trade almost to a complete stop put inhabitants in a bleak situation; even if they had money, they would either have to starve or enter Soviet service to get food rations. The principle was established that only those who worked for the good of the workers' and peasants' republic had the right to survive. Everyone else was outlawed and should perish one way or another. Thus began the mass flight of the intelligentsia to the south of Russia, but even here the Bolsheviks wanted to prevent the growth of the White Movement's ranks, and they tried to make it harder for anyone to leave the major cities. Anyone who wanted to leave for Ukraine had to prove their Ukrainian descent, but this was difficult because few people had kept the needed documents, and it all took a lot of time. Leaving the major cities also required the official approval of various Soviet agencies, and especially of the Cheka. It is understandable that under these conditions, only an insignificant percent of the population was able to leave, after lengthy ordeal, while the majority escaped either with forged documents or with no documents. The system of mass terror combined with the economic conditions created a situation in which some people energetically refused to recognize Soviet authority and fled to fight it later, while others were shot or imprisoned to await their fate. The Soviet government was able to purge its territory, as it stated, of counter-revolutionary gangs.

Personally, I could not count on getting out of Petrograd legally, even though I had the right, since I was born in Ekaterinoslav, which made me a Ukrainian citizen. This could have taken a long time, and I could possibly have been detained somewhere along the line, as happened to many others, even those with valid documents. In addition to the certification in my name that I was dismissed from the reserve staff of the Petrograd Military District, I also had a forged certificate under a different name that I was on a secret mission authorized by the Central Investigative Commission to the city of Orsha. I had no other documents. I was able to get the latter document thanks to my connection with a representative of this commission working secretly for the Whites. I decided not to use this document except in an extreme case, because I was not sure that I could pull off the role I would have to play. It would be better to avoid using any documents along the way. Luckily, I was able to get out of Petrograd, thanks to the chance to buy a railroad ticket to Orsha from a young man who had gotten approval from the Soviet government to leave the city. Even though I settled in the corridor of the international sleeping car, where there were about twenty passengers, this was still to my advantage because I had no luggage with me and I could easily avoid inspections. Truly, by the time the train arrived at Orsha, documents had been inspected ten times and luggage searched by young soldiers who were armed to the teeth and very thorough. Because I had no belongings, and no assigned seat, I was able to employ various ruses to avoid this unpleasantness, and I calmly stepped off the train at Orsha.

The border between Soviet Russia and Ukraine was between the passenger station at Orsha (Soviet side) and the cargo station (Ukrainian side). I had to find a way to get across the border as painlessly as possible. It took me two days to do this. According to Bolshevik rules, the local Soviet Deputy had to authorize a person's crossing the frontier. It was possible to get such a document under the pretext of needing medical treatment in the south of Russia and bribing with a handsome amount of money. I could not risk that since I would have to show up personally at the local Cheka, and I surely would be asked to produce my papers. I might even be recognized. As a result, I began to reconnoiter the local border crossing. It took me all day to learn how I could get across the border. Having seen enough of how the border crossing operated, I showed up early in the morning, at least an hour before the customs office opened. The office was right at the border crossing and heavily guarded. I asked one of the customs clerks to let me go to the Ukrainian border guard, but not to cross into Ukraine. The Ukrainian border booth was about three hundred feet from the Soviet side, with barbed wire strung along the border. I was asked to produce authorization from the Soviet Deputy, but I explained that I was not planning to cross the border since my luggage was still loaded at the admissions area waiting to be examined, and that I would be returning for it, but that I had to make some necessary inquiries at the Ukrainian border-crossing booth. After some hesitation, I was given permission, but of course I did not return, for I had no luggage. At the Ukrainian booth I told the Ukrainian commissar who I was and asked that I be allowed to enter Ukraine. A German officer who was present noted that I had no luggage and gave me authorization to cross. He personally escorted me past the barbed wire fence. Once again, having no luggage saved me.

25

Our Flight South

Sofia Globacheva

The ticket was for a train leaving that same day at 2 p.m., and we did not have much time. It was eleven in the morning. We ran home, buying food provisions from street vendors on the way. At home we packed some laundry and the food we bought into a small suitcase, and I accompanied my husband to the train station, but I walked a bit to the side of him so as not to draw any attention to him by my nervousness. The doorman of our building had warned us that many people trying to leave were being arrested at the station. When the train left, I breathed a sigh of relief. My husband and I had an agreement that when he got to Orsha he would send a prearranged telegram addressed to an old lady acquaintance of ours, and then a second telegram, also in her name, once he was across the border and beyond the reach of the Bolsheviks. That evening, after many, many sleepless nights, I fell asleep soundly, not fearing the sound of trucks or the sound of an elevator stopping at some floor.

The next night I received the first telegram from Orsha, and then a second, but I really did not trust the latter. My husband could have sent it without having crossed the Bolshevik border, just to calm my anxiety. That is exactly what happened. My husband would later tell me of how he was able to escape the Bolshevik passport check on the train by going from one car to another and hiding in the restrooms. He rode in a compartment with two ladies he became acquainted with who were also heading south. After arriving in Orsha everyone spent the night at the railway station. In the morning my husband asked these two ladies to take his suitcase along with their baggage to go through the Bolshevik passport control checkpoint. He could not risk getting across the border where the Bolsheviks were checking passports, so he took a roundabout way to where a sentry stood guard at the border. He told the guard that he needed to check some cargo depot that was on the other side and that he would be right back. Seeing that my husband did not have any luggage, the sentry let him through.

Arriving at a railway station that had been occupied by the Germans ever since their peace treaty with the Bolsheviks, my husband approached a German officer, identified himself, was saluted by the officer, and was escorted to a train bound for Kiev.

I stayed in Petrograd for another two months with my children, and during our stay there the savage murder of the Tsar and his family occurred in Ekaterinburg. At first there were vague rumors about this incident, but nobody wanted to believe it, and the Bolsheviks were keeping quiet. Apparently they wanted to see how people would react to these rumors, and when things were seen to be calm, they announced, about a week later, "On the night of 16–17 July 1918, by the sentence of the regional Soviet of Workers' and Soldiers' Deputies, the former Tsar Nicholas was executed, as well as his wife Alexandra Fedorovna and daughters Olga, Tatiana, and Maria." The heir and Anastasia were not mentioned. This struck me, and I asked others about it, but they concluded that it was just the newspapers' error not to mention those names. I have often wondered about this, and when I was already in America and news of a pretender Anastasia appeared, I remembered the Bolshevik announcement of the death of the royal family.

While we remained in Petrograd I went constantly to the Ukrainian Committee to speed up the arrival of our Ukrainian passports, because when my husband was still in Petrograd he registered with the newly formed Ukrainian Committee to get Ukrainian passports on the basis that he was born in Ekaterinoslav. However, he could not wait for the passport and left while I continued to go to the committee to try to get one. It was also necessary to have the approval to leave from the Commissariat of Internal Affairs. I was afraid that if I went there for the needed papers, they might hold me hostage, and so I did not risk going there. I left Petrograd with my children and without the authorization.

Within half an hour of our train's departure, the Bolsheviks came through the train, checking passports. A little Jew came into our compartment with two soldiers and demanded our papers. I gave him our Ukrainian passports. He asked me if I had any other documents, and upon my saying, "No," he declared that he would not give me back my passports and we would be removed from the train at Dno, where the train was scheduled to arrive in a while. I became very worried and asked him who he was that gave him authority to hold on to my passports. "I am a commissar," he answered. "Show me your papers to prove it," I said. He dutifully got out some paper and handed it to me, and I put it behind my back and told him that I would not return the paper to him. He lost his composure and turned to the soldiers and said, "Comrades, what the heck is this?" The soldiers looked vacantly and apathetically at all this and did not answer. I thought better of it and handed him back his papers and lay down to go to sleep. My children were worried, and I calmed them down, assuring them that if I could sleep everything would be all right.

The train arrived at the Dno station. The passengers, who were worried for me after my argument with the commissar, knocked on my compartment door to wake me up. They suggested that I myself should go to the Bolshevik commandant, to whom the commissar had already rushed with my passports. It was a still night but pouring rain. I ran out dressed in only my dress, and ran in the direction of the commandant's office, when suddenly this commissar was hurrying toward me and stuck my passports into my hands with the words, "You may move on." This was the second mystery, just like Uritskii's, and has also remained unresolved. That same night at the Dno station, thirty families, some even with little children and no baggage, were removed from the train. We continued on our way, and when we arrived at the station in Vitebsk, peasant women came up to the train with baskets of bread for sale. We were faint with hunger and could not believe that we were seeing all this bread in abundance being sold freely.

We finally reached the city of Orsha, and had to have our belongings inspected by the Bolshevik Cheka. I put forward two baskets. One held my husband's military things that had been ordered even before the revolution, which I had retrieved from the store before our departure. There was a new general's overcoat with silk lining and epaulets, and two pair of black lacquered high boots. I thought that all of these things would be useful once this nightmarish Bolshevik turmoil ended. I had put these things in the bottom of one of the baskets and covered them with children's things and books. My acquaintances had been horrified that I would take these things and insisted that I should at least rip out the coat's silk lining and remove the epaulets, but back then I really believed in my luck, and so I took them with me. My children knew which basket had my husband's things, and when the Bolsheviks ordered me to open one of them, my daughter nervously pointed to the one that did not have those items, but then the Bolsheviks ordered me to give them my key, and they opened the basket that had my husband's things in it. One of the guards reached into the bottom of the basket and pulled out a boot.

"What is this?" he asked.

"As you can see, it is a boot," I answered calmly.

He then pulled the other boot out and reached his hand to the bottom, where the overcoat lay. To tell the truth I was really frightened, and some instinct overcame me, and I began to yell at them that they were ransacking the whole basket and it would be me, not they, who would have to repack it again and all there was were books and children's things. This obviously evoked a reaction, as a more senior Bolshevik who had been watching over this inspection told his comrade not to disturb things so much, and to repack everything accurately. They closed the basket and gave me back my key. So I was not wrong—my luck held out.

We left the station and headed into town to spend the night. We stopped at a Jewish hotel called "The Silver Anchor." We had hardly fallen asleep when a loud knocking came on our door and a voice demanding that we open it immediately. These were Bolsheviks who were searching for someone, as we learned the next day. We could hear some kind of talk on the other side of the door. Apparently the owner of the hotel was accompanying the Bolsheviks on their rounds, and he told them that there was a woman and two children in this room. We had just managed to jump out of bed when we heard the same voice say, "You can go back to sleep."

The very next morning began my ordeal in trying to get across the border. First, I rushed to find out if we could get across the Bolshevik border without authorization. Cab drivers used to charge three to four thousand rubles to get people across, and I did not have that kind of money. Now the cabbies were afraid to do this, since cavalry patrols were arresting and shooting cabbies and passengers in the fields and on the roads. There was only one thing left for me to do, and that was to go to the regional Bolshevik committee and explain to them my urgent need to leave and that I did not have time to get the authorization to leave from the Commissariat of Internal Affairs.

When I arrived there, I addressed myself to the secretary of the committee, a young Jewish man named Semkin, and he told me that without authorization nothing could be done. He recommended that I go to the head of the Ukrainian detachment, which was about to cross the Bolshevik border into Ukraine with a group of Ukrainians, and that I should ask him to register me into the group. I ran there, but the head of the Ukrainian detachment decided not to register me without the written approval of the regional Bolshevik committee. What to do? I was losing my composure, and I rushed back to the committee. Many people were in the adjoining room, and I was told that there was a meeting of the committee next door discussing the German closing of the borders and not allowing anyone through. I thought to myself that if the borders were closed and the Ukrainian detachment left, my children and I would never get away from the Bolsheviks. So I decided on a desperate move. I burst into the meeting room, where there were twelve Bolsheviks, and I ran up to the secretary, Semkin, and stuck a paper in his hand and asked him to sign it immediately since the head of the Ukrainian detachment was getting ready to move. Semkin turned the paper over in his hand indecisively and turned to the committee explaining the situation to them. All at once a Polish Bolshevik woman stood up, the only woman on the committee (I do not remember her name), and demanded that I be returned to Petrograd immediately. I was standing in front of the table where the Bolsheviks were meeting. I was pale and terribly angry, and I said to her, "I am astonished that you, a woman, can be so heartless to demand that my children and I should be returned to Petrograd. Will you give me money for the trip back since I have no money?" After my impetuous outburst, a middle-aged man, a Jewish doctor as I later learned, spoke up. He was apparently chairing the meeting, and he said that in his opinion, this time I should be allowed to pass, but that they should write to Petrograd that such situations should not happen again. I was delighted, and I turned to the Polish woman again and said, "As you can see, men are much better than women." Following what I said, the men all agreed with the chairman, and I got the authorization. I rushed out, ran to the Ukrainian detachment's chief, and arrived there just in time, as he and the Ukrainian group were already moving out, and wagons loaded with the belongings of the impoverished had already moved out in single file. There was just one more Bolshevik inspection point where belongings were searched, as well as people who had to undress because the Bolsheviks thought they would find something hidden on these people. Fortunately, just as these searches had started, some Bolshevik men arrived and took their Bolshevik women to some kind of festival, and they ordered the inspection point to be closed down. We were finally free of any more searches. We walked at a snail's pace and finally reached the village of Pustynki on the shore of the Dnieper River, where we were supposed to wait for a ship that would get us to Kiev.

We spent two days and two nights in this village. Most of the people spent the night by the river's shore around campfires, but some, including me, found peasant houses where we could sleep on benches. German soldiers, who were quartered in this village after the peace treaty with the Bolsheviks, joined people at the campfires, offered them coffee and cigarettes, and asked them about the Bolsheviks. Some of the wealthier peasants listened in horror to what we told them.

On the third day we were informed that the ship was not coming because the Bolsheviks had fired on it from both shores of the Dnieper. So the decision was made that we would walk some miles to a cargo depot occupied by the Germans, and there we would get in wagons.

It was a beautiful autumn day when we got on the road—the day clear and the air fresh. Our caravan of carts moved slowly, creaking along the path. As we walked through the woods, the sun's rays came through the treetops to light our path, and the yellowing leaves rustled under our feet. It was a picture of tranquility, and for the first time I felt a calm in my soul.

Along the way we became acquainted with some nice people who were also from Petrograd, and with whom we continued to be friends in our later wanderings. We arrived at the station and were billeted into third-class compartments on the train (there were no other classes available) and so we got to the town of Gomel, whose population was almost entirely Jewish. The dirt on the streets was impassable, and when my children and I and another lady got into an open carriage, I was so tired that I was like a lifeless body being bounced around from one side to another as the carriage traveled over potholes. My children held onto me so I would not fall out while going over a bump. If I had fallen, I would have just lain in a puddle, not having the strength or inclination to get up. When we reached the hotel—this one was called "The Gold Anchor"—I was so exhausted physically and psychologically that I could not think, and I just fell onto the bed dressed and slept right through to morning, seeing and hearing nothing. My children and my lady acquaintance took care of things.

The next day we left Gomel and set off for Kiev. The train moved very slowly, sometimes stopping for hours in an open field. The provisions that we had been able to grab were all gone, and so at one of the long stops I left the train and walked along the cars, hoping I might get some bread from soldiers traveling in heated cars. One softhearted soldier cut his loaf in half and gave it to me for three rubles. I shared the bread with my children, and also gave a piece to a passenger sitting across from us and looking at the bread with hungry eyes. On our way to Kiev a passenger who was a supervisor at a factory in Ekaterinburg boarded the train at one of the stations. He told us that he had quit his job because he could not stand everything that the workers were doing; they broke expensive machines, did not do their jobs, did not follow rules, were unruly, and they drank. He dropped everything and ran away, and now he was going to his family. I asked him about the Tsar's family, and he confirmed they were all shot. When I said that it was strange that the Bolsheviks did not mention the heir or Anastasia in their announcement of the execution, he answered that he did not know anything about Anastasia, but when it came to the heir, there were persistent rumors going around Ekaterinburg that the heir had died before the execution of the family from the shock of a bomb that exploded near the window where he was standing.

After many hardships, we finally made it to Kiev, and I found my husband alive and unharmed. He was already working at the Department of Police in the government of Hetman Skoropadskii and living with his stepbrother (Leonid Axenov), a physician, and we moved in with him temporarily, too. When we arrived in Kiev we were emaciated from our long starvation and could not be satiated. When we would leave the house, we would spend the day going from one bakery or confectionary to another, eating an incredible number of buns and cookies, and drinking coffee several times a day, and yet we still felt starved. The Kievans looked at us with amazement, seeing how many buns and cookies were put on our table, which we quickly downed. We paid no attention to their amazement; it did not matter to us because we knew that a well-fed person does not understand a starving person. While going to these bakeries, some amusing incidents occurred. We would sometimes head for home separately, and somewhere along the way we would bump into each other in yet another bakery or confectionary, and we would again eat nonstop. This continued until our physical systems no longer required such excessive feeding.

Kiev made a splendid impression on us. The marketplace was remarkably beautiful, set on a hill overlooking the Dnieper River with a big, beautiful amphitheater in the middle where, in more peaceful times, music was played in the evenings. Kiev was famous for the Kiev-Pecherskaia Monastery, revered by Orthodox believers and to which massive numbers of pilgrims traveled from all over Russia. Kiev also had many beautiful, distinctive buildings.

But during our stay in Kiev we saw something terrible. I was walking down one of Kiev's streets with my children, and we saw fourteen coffins being carried out of a church to be taken to a cemetery. These coffins held the remains of fourteen young officers who had been savagely tortured by the Bolsheviks. The officers were bivouacked in a small hamlet when they were surrounded at night by Ukrainian Bolsheviks, who seized them and violated

FIGURE 25.1. A major avenue in Kiev, approximately 1900 to 1915. Marinich collection.

them, cutting off their lips, burning their noses with candles, putting out their eyes, and cutting their ears off. To this day, it is terrifying to remember and to think what extremes people can go to. Beasts.

After staying with my husband's stepbrother for some time, we moved to the Hotel Gladyniuk, and even though the Whites held Kiev, we lived as on a volcano, waiting for the White front to collapse any day and the Ukrainian Bolsheviks to arrive. Indeed, soon after our move to the hotel, after a persistent battle, the Petliurovites entered Kiev. They were those same Ukrainian Bolsheviks under the leadership of Petliura, a former country teacher. They entered the city in triumph, with music accompanying the troops, but they were met by machine gun fire from those Whites who remained in the city.

We were standing in the street when they entered, and ran through a gate when the shooting began. It did not last long because the Whites had to retreat and leave the city. At some point during the first few days of Petliura's arrival, the owner of the hotel approached my husband and suggested that he go into hiding since that very day the Bolsheviks had come to the hotel, arrested two colonels, and took them away to be shot. My husband left that evening for his stepbrother's, and I had to stay at the hotel with my children.

I had accompanied my husband when he went to his stepbrother's, and returning to the hotel at night I suddenly stopped, surprised by the exceptional scene before me. On the street that I was walking down there were huge bonfires everywhere, with Bolshevik soldiers standing around illuminated by the fire with their rifles in piles. The huge glow from the fires extended a great distance across the sky, while shells were exploding all the time over the train station, destroying it. At some distance from the glow, the clean dark sky shone with countless stars and a full moon peacefully illuminating the land that had so much bloodshed on it. The contrast was indescribable, and I was so stunned by this scene that I was not conscious of the danger of the bursting shells. I then proceeded with my search for any kind of food for the children. The hotel had no food since Petliura arrived, and all the stores were closed, so I had to wander the streets for quite a long time until I came upon a little store that was still open so late. I bought sausage and bread and returned home. After supper we went to bed.

Late that night there was a loud knock on the door and a voice demanding us to open up. My son, who was sleeping in the front room, tossed on a coat and opened the door. The hotel manager stood at the door looking very pale, and there were two officers and several soldiers carrying rifles. The officers entered the front room while the soldiers stayed at the door. My daughter and I were in another room that also had an alcove. "Where is the general?" asked one of the officers. I was in bed and did not get up. I answered that he had left on business, but I did not know where he went. When I was asked when my husband would return, I said in about two or three weeks. Then the officer who was dressed in a Ukrainian uniform and had a scalp lock said in broken Ukrainian (obviously he was a Russian who turned Ukrainian) that they would come back when my husband returned. He then ordered me to clear out immediately because they would need the room for Petliura's staff. It was night, and the arrogance of this officer raised my indignation. I jumped out of bed, tossed on a peignoir and slippers, and rushed out to him. As I passed a mirror and saw myself in it looking as I did, I could not help but smile bitterly. I argued with him heatedly that I couldn't be tossed out into the street with my children and belongings. The officer in the Russian uniform tried to convince the Ukrainian one not to insist on immediate eviction. The Ukrainian put on airs and was obstinate, but finally he backed down and "graciously" allowed us to stay until morning. We were certainly not able to sleep the rest of the night, and as soon as the Bolsheviks left, I ran downstairs to the office to see how we were registered in the hotel—that is, where we had arrived from. I was afraid that if the register showed we had come from my husband's stepbrother's place, where we had stayed until we moved to the hotel, the Bolsheviks could go there and arrest my husband. But we were registered in the book as coming from Petrograd.

In the morning I went to see my husband and told him everything that happened. We decided we would move to Slobodka; this was a settlement in the Chernigov province, on the other side of the Dnieper. In Slobodka, there were separate huts among the gardens, and we would settle into one of them where my husband's stepbrother's friend, an engineer, lived with his elderly mother, both of whom had fled from the Germans in Warsaw during the war.

After we decided on this, I returned to the hotel and my children and began to pack our things. Around noon, a military truck drove up, and a young, short Ukrainian officer showed up who was quite cheerful and polite. He apologized profusely, expressing his sympathy that we had to give up the room, but Petliura's staff had nowhere else to go. He then ordered the staff's things to be carried in. Many huge crates were brought in, all filled with bottles of champagne, wine, and vodka. That same officer was already tipsy when he arrived. So, we had to move again.

Having packed our things, we loaded them onto a cart, and my son went with them to the new residence, the settlement at Slobodka, where he waited for us. Our nightmare of an existence began again. Every day my children and I had to go from Slobodka to Kiev because I did not want the children to miss school. Regardless of where we wound up, my children were always enrolled in school. We had to walk across the Dnieper on a long bridge from Slobodka and then take a narrow gauge train to Kiev. Along the entire way we would see corpses lying on the ground. When we went out, we would return home trembling in fear that maybe my husband would have been arrested and taken away while we were gone. My husband did not go out at all, as Bolshevik patrols were everywhere, stopping passersby, checking papers, and arresting many. Our life in Slobodka was quite difficult. Everyone had to sleep on the floor on mats filled with straw because there were no beds, and only I was afforded the privilege of sleeping on a camp cot. The little old lady housekeeper made coffee for us every morning. Feeling sorry for us, she kept the stove in our room stoked so that when we returned after being out we could warm ourselves. It was cold out, and snow was already on the ground, and we had no warm clothes. We would have supper at the home of a woman who lived in a little house across from us, and for relatively little money she fed us very well. She gave us a three-course meal: first soup, then the second course might be goose, duck, chicken, or roast, and then dessert.

When my children came home from school they would go to get dinner and bring it back and put it on two chairs, which was the only furniture we had in the room. We had no table, and our landlord could not give us theirs, since these refugees from Poland had almost no furniture. So we ate standing up, or sitting, if one could fit on the camp cot. Given that there was enough of everything in Kiev, especially food provisions, we often thought with sadness that even here the Bolsheviks would indulge in their ruinous behavior, completely destroying the good, well-organized life of the people, and there would be hunger, poverty, and executions, just as in Petrograd. Indeed that did happen shortly after the Bolsheviks occupied Kiev.

One time when my children and I were returning to Slobodka, we were walking down one of the major avenues of Kiev and saw a crowd of men standing, and coming toward us was a poor peasant woman peddler with a basket of apples who was crying loudly. I asked her why she was crying, and she told us that a young man wearing a civilian overcoat was walking down the street, but a military uniform could be seen under his coat. An armed soldier walking toward him noticed the uniform, stopped the officer, and dragged him off to a wagon to take him to some commandant, or maybe just to shoot him along the way. She was in this crowd and seeing what was going on, she grabbed hold of the soldier and cried and yelled that this officer was a human being, like us all, and demanded that the soldier release the young officer. The soldier broke away and rudely pushed the woman so that she fell down, and then he took the officer away somewhere. I was indignant that nobody in this crowd of men even tried to come to the aid of this officer who was being hauled away by only one soldier. I turned to the men and reproached them and told them that I was at a loss as to why they remained passive when this was happening before their very eyes. "We do not know, it was as if we were mesmerized," was their answer.

Searches began in Slobodka, and we had to move again, even farther. We still had the same baskets that we brought with us from Petrograd, but we could not leave with both of them, so one night the servant of our landlord dug a big pit in the cellar and buried the basket that contained, among other things, the already-mentioned general's coat and my husband's lacquered boots that I took such risks in getting out of Petrograd. My husband was waiting for just the right time to leave. At the first possible opportunity, he left alone again, for Odessa, and my children and I followed later.

At the railway station, as we were leaving, what was going on was unimaginable. All the trains were overloaded with soldiers and civilians trying to save themselves from the Bolsheviks, and people were even sitting on all the tops of the cars. We barely found places in the third-class section, thanks to giving the porter a good tip for his efficiency. Above us sat soldiers with their legs dangling in front of our faces. We could not even move around, the air smelled awful, and I got such a headache that I could not even move. Unruly, noisy, belching, cursing Bolshevik soldiers went from car to car looking for someone. After this awful traveling situation, we finally arrived at the Odessa cargo station. There we had to transfer to wagons and go through a Ukrainian Bolshevik checkpoint, where belongings were searched. A soldier approached our wagon and, learning that we had nothing other than a basket of clothes and children's books, he let us through without a search. He was probably sick and tired of all these procedures and too lazy to inspect them. While we were en route from the station to the checkpoint, we could hear gunfire, and a few times bullets whistled past us. This was obviously the fighting between the Ukrainian Bolsheviks and the retreating Whites. We got through the Bolshevik zone and into Odessa, which was still free because of the White presence there. We were reunited with my husband, and we moved into the Hotel France.

26

The Situation in Ukraine

General Globachev

Ukraine. Personal impressions. Kiev and the general situation in Ukraine. Department of Supreme Security. The Hetman, Germans, and the army. The separatist movement. The fall of Kiev. Petliura.

I will not describe my impressions or my mood as I traveled through Ukraine to Kiev. These would be fully understandable to anyone who had been under the Bolshevik regime in 1918, and finally able to tear himself away from this insane asylum. There was order, law, and private property here in Ukraine, and the Germans supported it. However, it could be seen that although the revolution and the governmental system had devastated this once prosperous part of the world, a more normal life was beginning to be restored. Although Ukraine called itself a sovereign government, one could see the German hand everywhere, and the overall impression was that Ukraine was a conquered region occupied by German troops.

Kiev, the capital of Ukraine, in contrast to Soviet cities, presented a favorable impression immediately to anyone coming to the city. There was a normal lifestyle, trade, plenty of goods, lawfulness; all this was a healing balm to the physically and emotionally tortured refugees from the north. But after being there a short time, I became more or less aware that life there was far from normal. All of this apparent prosperity could be temporary, depending on how the political situation turned out. The government of the Hetman was extremely new, not yet fully established, and not yet strong enough. Anyone could see that this regime was surviving only because German bayonets were present.

Because of the influx of refugees, mostly from Soviet Russia, Kiev was extremely overpopulated. This did not affect food supplies, of which there was enough, but it made living accommodations critical. Moreover, this concentration of people looking for work saw the development of speculation and transitory occupations. Restaurants began to pop up, as did pastry shops, clubs, and all kinds of entertainment establishments. People were looking to make fast and big profits. Gambling developed to an extreme. The political situation was very unsettling. The separatist-republican party was unhappy with the lack of order and dreamt of complete autonomy without Germans, and so they stood in opposition to the Hetman, the Germans' protégé. The Bolshevik-communist party worked underground to annex Ukraine to the Russian Soviet Federated Republic and was subsidized by Moscow financially and materially. The official representatives from Moscow and Rakovskii led these efforts jointly. The Volunteer Army had its agents who were trying to increase their strength by drawing on officers and soldiers who were in Ukraine in large numbers at that time. There were people of various political leanings around the Hetman, everyone from monarchists to Socialist Revolutionaries; thus, the Hetman's government was in no shape to take a firm direction in its policies. The government and the Hetman himself were constantly in a state of vacillation.

FIGURE 26.1. Hetman Pavel Petrovich Skoropadskii. Wikimedia Commons.

Thus, both the political and the social atmosphere in Ukraine were unhealthy. It could be seen that much effort had been made to introduce a monarchy, the one that was in the recent past, but this got nowhere because there was nothing to build it on, and it was also clear to anyone that the Hetman's government would fall apart like a house of cards once the Germans left. Even so, the intention to establish order and governance was noticeable in the government's business-like mood.

In my search for work, I was able to get a job as an official in the commission of the 5th Class of the Department of Government Security (that is, the Department of Police), where I met many of my former colleagues. This department was still in its formative stage, and even though it was functioning, other offices under its jurisdiction had not yet been established under law. The Department of Government Security was an exact copy of the former Department of Police, but on a smaller scale. The department had a number of missions to carry out, and a special bureau had the same name as it had had in the previous Department of Police. An Information Bureau, as it was called, was set up in every province, whose function was to perform the same political tasks as the former provincial Gendarme administrations, as well as the criminal investigations of the former investigative agencies. All the police departments and the railway police reported to the Department of Government Security. The major task of all these agencies was to fight forcefully against Bolshevism, but to only maintain surveillance over the activities of the socialist and separatist parties. The head of this organization (in September 1918) was a former prosecutor of the old regime, Akerman, of very right-wing ideology, who was able to employ experienced and competent people. Thus, the Department of Government Security could have dealt perfectly with the political and criminal investigation tasks it was assigned in the rather small territory of Ukraine if it were not for the constant changes of the Hetman's policies toward the separatists. Petliura's subordinates were under arrest until November 1918, when the Hetman's position toward them changed dramatically. He ordered them to be released and, strictly speaking, created the opposition to himself that hastened his downfall.

During the German occupation of Ukraine, the Germans allowed the Hetman to organize an insignificant number of combat troops, but even this was made up exclusively of Ukrainians who were called "the camp of multicolored jerkins." This group consisted exclusively of Ukrainian separatists. Thus, the Hetman did not have troops loyal to him except, it seemed, for one cadre of a division that the German command allowed that was not composed of a strong Ukrainian nationalist group. Among the top military and civilian heads of the government, a considerable number sided with the separatists and maintained contact with their leaders. Thus, when the Hetman freed Petliura and his colleagues, the latter moved with lightning speed and gathered all the nearest Ukrainian troops under their banner at the White Church and moved openly against the Hetman, who was now left with no military support.

The Hetman had to turn to the officer corps, of which there was a large unemployed number in the city, for his defense of Kiev and in his struggle with Petliura. A volunteer officer corps of not more than three thousand was hastily organized under the command of General Kirpichev, and it was surprising how this small handful was able to defend the city for a month against a much greater enemy force. The Hetman initially gave the major overall command to Count Keller, but later they had a falling out over political issues, and the Hetman transferred command to Prince Dolgorukov.

I transferred from the Department of Government Security to work in Kirpichev's staff in intelligence and investigation. This organization initiated an active struggle in the city against the Bolsheviks and Petliura, but all this effort was too late and produced no changes. The lower classes in Kiev were all on Petliura's side. The intelligentsia, most of which had newly arrived, generally did not want to be involved, and simply continued to engage in economic speculation. The city was full of Petliura's agents, who had no difficulty in instigating uprisings, and there were repeated untimely attempts to suppress them by force. In general, the entire responsibility of the struggle was on the shoulders of the officer corps, as it was at the front, so also in the city. These three thousand men had to defend a huge perimeter of the city. Of course this fluid front was finally broken by Petliura's troops, who entered Kiev on December 14.

The Hetman's power ended, giving way to the Ukrainian Directorate, with Petliura at its head. Repressive measures began at once, targeting anyone associated with the previous government. Initially, the terror came down on the officer corps as the defenders of the previous regime. The horrors of this terror exceeded even those of the recent measures carried out by Soviets. Uniformed officers were killed like dogs in the streets of Kiev. Anyone who had any chance either hid out with the underground or fled from the city. As for me, I had to hide out for ten days across the Dnieper in Slobodka, after which I fled under a fake identity through Nikolaev to Odessa. The train ride from Kiev to Nikolaev was an absolute nightmare; in addition to the train being overloaded with people, there were uninterrupted inspections and searches of the passengers and all kinds of taunts that drove the passengers to near nervous breakdowns. From the Dolinsk station to Nikolaev, heated trains were crammed full of baggage and people, and the train ride dragged on for more than twenty-four hours.

The forces of Ataman Grigoriev already occupied Nikolaev. Having spent two days at the train station, it was with some difficulty that I was able to get on the ship *Rumiantsev*, which was leaving for Odessa. This was the last ship that Petliura allowed to leave from the port in Nikolaev.

27

Odessa's Defense and Evacuation

General Globachev

Odessa. The city defense by officer detachments. Grishin-Almazov. The French occupation. The Russian influence in Odessa. Cooperation between French and Russian authorities. French policy in Ukraine. The mood of the population. Bolshevik propaganda. Crime and speculation, and the investigative agency's struggle against them. The new Russian government. General Shvartz. Bolshevik propaganda among the French troops. The evacuation of Odessa.

With the beginning of Petliura's uprising in Odessa, as had happened in Kiev, officer detachments that had been left behind by the Hetman began forming, but since the city was a port, and a rather small allied fleet had shown up after Turkey's defeat, the allies decided to support the defense of the city. Petliura's bands almost reached the harbor but were forced to stop because of the steadfast resistance of the officer detachments and the shelling from the sea. Deribasovskii Street had been set up as a neutral zone, but by the time of my arrival, it had been pushed back to the train station. Odessa's rescue was partly due to the French fleet's threat, but the main reason was the courage and direction of General Grishin-Almazov, who was able to organize the defenders almost at the embankments of the harbor and still defend the city. He was the only commander able to save the city from Petliura's bands. In joining with the volunteer White Army, he assumed the position of Commander in Chief of the city.

At that time, the French decided to occupy the Odessa region, and had already landed the first echelon of troops with weapons and brigade staffs. Grishin-Almazov in turn organized a brigade from the officer detachments under a young brave General Timanovskii. This brigade saw to the immediate defense of the city against the encroaching Bolshevik and Petliura bands.

FIGURE 27.1. Major General Alexeii Nikolaevich Grishin-Almazov. Wikimedia Commons.

The city was divided into two sectors: (1) the French—the port, under French command, and (2) the rest of the city, under Russian command. This was the situation by January 1919.

Russian authority was organized in the following manner. At the top was Grishin-Almazov, and his civilian deputy was A. I. Pilts. The City Prefect was V. A. Markov. All the administrative offices remained as they had been under the Hetman. I was assigned to be in charge of the political investigation branch reporting to the City Prefect, and I was also assigned the information branch that was the local investigative office of the former Department of Government Security.

Grishin-Almazov was quite a young man, about thirty-two years old, and he did not even look that old. During the German war he was promoted to captain of artillery, and nobody was really sure how he got the rank of general. He said of himself that he had recently come from Kolchak's army. In any case, he was bold, decisive, and even talented, but too hot tempered. He did not quite have that composure or administrative experience. He reminded me a little of Kerensky in his personality and manner of speaking. He was susceptible to being influenced, and in good hands he could have been a fine administrator.

Initially, the French did not intrude into Russian governmental affairs, but as newer echelons and staffs arrived, the French command, apparently wanting to expand its occupation, painlessly appointed General D'Anselm and Colonel Freidenberg as his Chief of Staff. The latter got into politics exclusively, which consisted of attempting to establish relations with Petliura's representatives and handing Odessa over to him under conditions that would be advantageous to the French. The negotiations between Freidenburg and Petliura's Ataman Zmiev went on all the while that the French were in Odessa, notwithstanding that the Volunteer Army under Grishin-Almazov was at war with Petliura. Ataman Zmiev mercilessly shot Russian officers who were under the protection of the French, even as he arrogantly came to the negotiating meetings in plain sight of the defenders of Odessa. As it turned out, Freidenburg was not able to conclude his negotiations because Petliura and Vinnichenko lost power in Ukraine, and negotiating with the Bolsheviks was not possible at that time.

Under such conditions, with France supposedly trying to ally itself with Grishin-Almazov on the one hand, and negotiate with his enemies on the other,

Figure 27.2. One of the main streets of Odessa. Wikimedia Commons.

Grishin-Almazov's situation became more untenable. His relationship with the French command intensified. With the Bolshevik Revolution in Ukraine, the zone expanded to about seventy to one hundred kilometers to the north and east to include Nikolaevsk. Allied forces continued to flow in (especially the Greeks), and it seemed that the French command wanted not only to take over Ukraine but also to fight the Bolsheviks. If this was indeed their intention, they backed off quickly. The Bolsheviks brought out their most powerful weapons—propaganda and agitation.

At this time, Odessa was exactly like Kiev had been in the fall of 1918. The intelligentsia that had fled there from both the capitals added to those who fled to Odessa from Kiev and other Ukrainian cities after the fall of the Kievan Hetman. There were a considerable number of unemployed officers and various shady individuals. There were all kinds of speculators who tried to profit personally from the situation. All this overpopulated Odessa, which created a major crisis in the number of allocated apartment ration books. With all this going on, the working and lower classes, which had already had a taste of Bolshevism at the beginning of 1918, but had not yet experienced its nastier side, looked forward to a Bolshevik regime and provided fertile soil for propaganda and agitation. The bourgeoisie of the city, along with the socialist-oriented city Duma, sulked and discussed matters, but offered no support to the local authorities, so they were a good conduit for the spread of Bolshevism. The Jewish population in Odessa was also inclined to Bolshevism, with the exception of the wealthier bourgeoisie. Thus, while the Russians and the allied (mainly Greek) forces defended the front against the advancing Reds, the latter's agitation within Odessa was operating at full force, not only among the Russian population but among the French forces, who did little and were undisciplined. The French troops in Odessa conducted themselves in a completely unbridled manner. They indulged in drinking and socializing with Jews, among whom were no small number of Bolshevik agitators who spoke French. Propaganda was successful not only among the soldiers, but also among the officers. The result was that by February there was ferment among the land forces, and even among the sailors, who were tired of the war and wanted to go home. There were also those who went over to the Bolsheviks for ideological reasons. One such person was Captain Sadul. In addition, the French intelligence agencies were not able to counter Bolshevik propaganda since they did not know the local conditions and lacked competence because of their hasty employment of line officers.

A major problem at this time was that Odessa was crime-ridden to an unimaginable degree. In January 1919, a citizen felt worse in the city than in a forest camp of brigands. Apartments were robbed at night, and street crimes were committed in the light of day. Odessa had always been a crime center, but now it was beyond all limits. Lawful measures had no effect and came to nothing, so the City Prefect, General Markov, had to initiate extreme measures. Robbers who were caught in the commission of their crimes were to be shot like dogs. These measures worked; within a month the crime rate decreased considerably, and citizens could breathe easier. One of the big problems that the police had at that time was the gang of a certain "Mishka Iaponchik," who was very influential in criminal circles and terrorized everyone with his criminal activities. Subsequently, after the surrender of Odessa, he held some important post with the Bolsheviks, but then they shot him for some reason or other.

The Russian political investigative agencies fought with all their might against the Bolsheviks, who focused their efforts mainly on workers' organizations. These agencies had the full support of the civilian and military authorities, but had to struggle constantly with the city government and its head, Braikevich. The socialist makeup of the city Duma was patently on the side of the workers and was unwittingly helpful in strengthening the Bolshevik position. None of this hindered Braikevich and other members of the city Duma, who were the first to flee Odessa during the French evacuation. Meanwhile, the organizing and agitating work of the Bolsheviks in Odessa was very intense, and, notwithstanding the liquidation of many of their ranks, they continued to enlist new supporters from the masses, who were favorably inclined toward them.

The speculators who sold the most necessary products that were needed by the population profited from the inflated prices. The guiltiest of these were the old-time speculators, especially those who were the sugar manufacturers and owners of sugar refineries during the war. They were Kharii, Gepner, Zlatopol'skii, and others, and they were virtually the economic dictators in Odessa at this time. This group was finally arrested by the military counter-intelligence in spite of the protests of the city Duma. The materials that were gathered during the search fully proved the pernicious activities of these speculators.

By March, the French command seemed to have decided to disassociate itself completely from the Volunteer Army and its Commander in Chief, General Denikin, regarding anything having to do with Odessa. A new Russian authority was set up in Odessa that was required to operate solely under the French command. Lieutenant General Shvartz was invited to become the Commander in Chief of the Odessa Region, and he organized the Defense Council as the government agency. General Grishin-Almazov and his Chief of Staff, General Sannikov, who had been assigned by General Denikin, were both asked to leave the Odessa Region within twenty-four hours. Both left on the first ship for Novorossiisk. Grishin-Almazov's deputy for civilian affairs, A. I. Pilts, had left earlier.

The Defense Council consisted of Andre, Rutenberg, Iliashenko, Braikevich, and some others. Although Andre was in charge of internal affairs, the dominant role in the Council was that of Rutenberg, an old Socialist Revolutionary—the same man who shot the not unknown Gapon in 1905 by order of the party. Rutenberg humiliated his colleagues on the Council with his insolence, his peremptory and categorical decisions, and by the authority he claimed that he represented the party. Andre, who had been the head of the Volynsk Region (governor) during the Hetman's regime, was clever, energetic, and ambitious. He was not a government man, and even had a touch of an adventurer. When he was in Kiev he assured everyone that he was Ukrainian, and in Odessa that he was pure-bred French, a descendant of one de Lanjeron, which is why he called himself Andre de Lanjeron. The other members of the Defense Council did not play much of a role. The president of the Council, General Shvartz, was a decent and honest man, a brilliant engineer, not a statesman, but he was weak willed and could be influenced. Such was the government established by the French, or more accurately, by the Chief of Staff of the French occupation forces, Colonel Freidenberg. The administrative apparatus of the area remained the same as before.

The new government did not improve things; rather it impeded matters, as all decisions had to be dealt with in a collective manner, which meant procrastination. The French, as before, influenced all decisions.

The Bolsheviks continued with their activities to prepare Odessa for a future government should a coup succeed there. They concentrated their efforts on the professional union of workers, and in March the Union of Unions declared itself as the future ruling Revolutionary Committee. My work in neutralizing some of the workers' organizations yielded documents that proved this.

In order to paralyze the internal work of the Bolsheviks, circumstances required that there should be a major liquidation of the organizations and the removal from circulation of the major leaders. I insisted on this in my report to the Defense Council, but Rutenberg turned this down and tried with all his might to delay any liquidation. Thus, the Defense Council decided not to hurry with any liquidation, but to wait until some as yet unknown circumstances became clearer. It was strange that Rutenberg, upon being given forty-eight hours by the French Command to leave Odessa, insisted on my liquidating those organizations that he had previously refused to deal with. It was not possible to carry out his orders, because all the agencies that would be involved were already preparing to evacuate. Rutenberg's persistence became less strange as Odessa's abandonment became evident, and it was my deep conclusion that his behavior was simply provocation.

Propaganda among the French forces progressed, with results that showed at the front as well as in the rear. The French concealed the unreliability of their troops, but even so it was clear that the infantry refused to engage the Bolsheviks, and on one French cruiser there was a revolt and the red flag was hoisted.

Одеса 1919. Суда інтервентів за рейдом
під час евакуації.

FIGURE 27.3. French ships ready to evacuate Odessa. Wikimedia Commons.

I think that this was the main reason that the French decided to evacuate Odessa. All kinds of commentaries mentioned changes in France's policies and even alleged that there were forged telegrams initiated by the French General, Franche D'Espere, but the truth for the evacuation probably lies in the breakdown of the French occupation forces.

Be that as it may, on April 2, 1919, the French staff issued an announcement that they would evacuate Odessa within forty-eight hours. One can imagine how hastily and in what disorganization the Russians had to turn about to get loaded onto the ships, of which, it must be mentioned, there were not enough, and those there were were not prepared for such a sudden departure. The embarkation was disorganized, and there was already gunfire heard in the city. The only people who were able to get on the ships were those who were at the pier on April 4. Many were not able to get out and so remained in Odessa. In a short while they paid for that with their lives.

The French did, however, evacuate several thousand people from Odessa. Some of the ships sailed for Novorossiisk, and the rest for Constantinople. I got on the French cargo ship *Kavkaz*, along with the entire Russian staff of General Shvartz, and all the civilian administration of Odessa. There were over two thousand men, women, and children on this not very large ship. We were on the ship for thirteen days under the most awful sanitary conditions and the rudest treatment by the ship's French administration. There was no difference among us to the French. The Russians were all just one refugee mass, all of whom were treated sternly. This is where we first felt the depth of our misfortune; we had lost our homeland, and this despair translated into physical suffering during this nightmare of a trip.

28

Evacuation from Russia

Sofia Globacheva

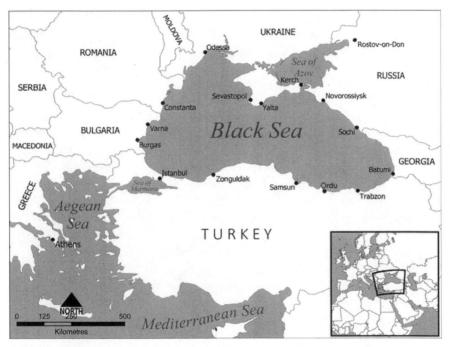

Map 2. The Black Sea, showing some of the major locations mentioned in the Globachev memoirs: Sevastopol during the outbreak of World War I, Odessa, Rostov-on-Don, and Novorossiysk during the Civil War, and Istanbul (Constantinople) after the evacuation of the White Army. (Source: Wikimedia Commons.)

My husband was already employed as head of intelligence in Odessa. Rumors began to circulate very soon that the Bolsheviks had pushed the Whites back, and were approaching Odessa. Even though the Whites had shown marvelous courage, strength won out. There were more Bolsheviks at the front and relatively few Whites. The staff of the White Army began to send their families to Varna (Bulgaria). My husband bought tickets for me and the children to leave for Varna by ship, but I refused to leave and announced that either we all left together, or we would stay with him. After a few more of such anxious moments, the allies slowly and inconspicuously began to leave Odessa, and one fine day everyone was unexpectedly ordered to board the French ship *Kavkaz*. The ship was loaded in a hurry, and there was no order in people boarding the ship. General Shvartz, the commander of Odessa's defense, was on board, as was Archbishop Anastasi and his clergy. We sailed away from Odessa in beautiful weather. We were given space in the hold of the ship, and were to sleep side by side on planks covered with some nondescript, dirty-looking grass. One of my acquaintances and I chose not to lie down on the planks; they were disgusting and awful, and looked as if all kinds of worms and insects could crawl out. So we sat in the dining room of the ship for two days, resting our heads in our arms at the table. By the third night we could not take it anymore, and we threw ourselves exhausted on the planks and slept like the dead. While we were at sea we were fed some kind of broth and beans.

When we had sailed some distance from Odessa, Archbishop Anastasi and his clergy came on deck and conducted a service, praying for those left behind in Odessa, and praying for all of us who left their homeland and were sailing into an unknown future. The picture that this presented was solemn and sad; as prayers were chanted, the sun gleamed and carefree dolphins leaped around the ship. Not only did the women cry, but many of the men too.

We were on the ship for twelve days. We arrived in Constantinople late at night and dropped anchor in the Bosporus. What a beautiful impression the lights of the houses on the hill made. So, too, did the white palace of the Sultan, with its marble terrace and stairway leading down to the sea, and the silhouette of the Hagia Sofia Mosque set out in the night sky, and other mosques with their minarets. We disembarked from the ship and were sent to Halki Island,[1] which was under French jurisdiction. On the island most of the refugees were lodged in a Greek monastery, on a fairly high hill. We were settled into rooms in families, and the families were separated from each other by sheets. Somehow we adapted to all this, and lived as if we were in a Gypsy camp—except we were not in the open air but within the walls of a Greek monastery. Some of the people who had arrived were able to rent rooms from Greeks and Turks.

We rented a room from a Greek widow who spoke French, as did her daughter. In appearance, the room looked tidy, and the furniture had white covers, but at night what happened was awful. Some kind of peculiar, very long bugs came out of all the cracks and from under the furniture covers and gave us no peace. When we complained to the landlady, she suggested indifferently that we should just gather them up. In every room that was rented from the Greeks it was the same thing. We could see this as we walked along the streets at night and saw the flickering of candles and the moving shadows of Russians occupied with fighting these bugs. The day after our arrival on Halki, I got up in the morning and looked out the window. A black African woman stood at the well, covered from head to foot in a loose white garment. She had a jug filled with water on one of her shoulders. Before my eyes, the sea sparkled, and a mullah on a minaret loudly called the faithful to prayer. This was all so beautiful after the horrors we experienced in Russia that an indescribable calm came over me, and I did not want to walk away from the window, afraid this would all vanish.

Halki was one of the four Prince's Islands situated not far from Constantinople, and communication with the islands was by small boats, called sherkets. Any time these little boats came from Constantinople it gave the residents of Halki great pleasure. Halki is a fairly hilly island covered with woods, and these Prince's Islands at one time were the meeting place of the League of Nations. In general, our life on Halki was not bad, and the French, in the person of the commandant and his staff, treated us well; they were cordial and polite. For the most part, our meals consisted of rabbit, which we did not eat but gave to our Greek landlady.

We arrived on Halki in the summer, and the weather was marvelous. We often went for donkey rides around the island, especially on moonlit nights. At that time mainland Greece was governed by Venizelos, who was evidently very well liked by the Greeks in Constantinople. Often at night when they rode their donkeys, these Greeks would loudly sing the same song praising Venizelos all night long without a break, not allowing anyone to sleep. We were told that the Constantinople Greeks were sharply different in their ways from mainland Greeks. The Greeks on Halki were very miserly and tried to squeeze as much money as they could from us poor refugees, while the poor Turks neither wanted, nor took money from some refugees who rented from them, saying that when the refugees had money again they would then repay them. The Turks turned out to be very likable people; they treated the newly arrived refugees with considerable respect and sympathy. At the beginning of our stay, they would point to us and whisper to each other, "Rus, Rus." They were, after all, the first to run into the mass of peacefully inclined Russians— their former mighty enemy.

One of the noticeably remarkable sites on Halki was the naval cadet academy, which was on the shore and surrounded by a high, latticed iron fence. On a big plaza in front of the academy building, the cadets trained. We would stop by the fence and watch them march and train in their clean white naval uniforms. Shortly after our arrival on Halki, we made the acquaintance of the director of the naval academy, a cultured and educated man. We also met all the naval officers, who spoke German. They had learned German when fighting the Russians under German leadership, so we were able to talk to them, since most Russians who came to Halki were of the intelligentsia and also spoke German. All the naval officers were cultured individuals from the best Turkish families. They led us on tours of the naval academy, strolled with us, and were attentive and interested in what was going on in Russia. One time an entire group of us Russians were strolling with them, and one of them, who was married to the Sultan's sister, said that he was on the battleship "Goeben" when it shelled Sevastopol. Learning that we were there at the time, he said in jest that if he had only known we were there, he definitely would have given the order to stop the shelling. Another young naval officer, who was in the company of some Russian young ladies, swore on Allah that knowing the Russians he would never again raise a weapon against them.

This was all so kind and pleasing to hear, and to see the consideration given to us, who were now unfortunate refugees. The Turkish civilian population also treated us with respect and was attentive to us Russians. They invited us to their clubs and were delighted when we learned how to pronounce numbers in Turkish and shout them out when we played Lotto with the Turks. This gave them great pleasure, and they smacked their lips in approval. I think they were surprised at our abilities. There was a lot of hostility between the Greeks who lived on Halki and the Turks, and when we praised the Turks, the Greeks became indignant and remonstrated that we did not know them very well and criticized them.

During our time on Halki, I became acquainted with a very kind young couple. The husband was a young naval officer, and his wife was a very likeable, educated Englishwoman. We often got together. Once a big fire started on the island, and people rushed to put it out. It turned out some hooligans took advantage of the turmoil and began looting things. The Englishwoman and her husband were at the fire, and they recounted the event to me in detail. A Turkish policeman, who was guarding the saved items and chasing the hooligans away, could not cope with them because the hooligans called for more of their comrades to help, and there was total robbery. It was only when more police arrived that the hooligans were arrested. As it turned out, these hooligans were Greeks, and the resident Greeks of Halki sent a telegram to the Greek Patriarch crying out that the Turks were knifing Greeks. The Patriarch took the matter to the English command, and an English officer was sent to investigate the incident, and also to question my Englishwoman acquaintance as a witness to determine how everything happened.

Because of a strange Turkish custom, I wound up in an embarrassing situation at that time. I went into a confectionary that was open to Russians and ordered a coffee. Turkish naval officers frequented this place often, and when I sat down at the table and drank my coffee, a waiter came up to me and put a plate of ice cream in front of me. I was surprised and told him that I had not ordered it. He turned and pointed to a Turkish naval officer, with whom I was not acquainted, sitting at the far end of the room, and said that he ordered the waiter to bring me the ice cream. I was extremely indignant at such behavior, which in Russia would be an extraordinary affront. I ordered the waiter to take the ice cream away immediately, and without even finishing my coffee, I left. The Turkish officer had been watching all this intently. The next day I met some of the naval officers, and I had hardly finished telling them of this incident when they informed me that their comrade felt very hurt by me because it was their custom that if you wanted to express your deep respect for someone, even for someone you did not know, you would order some kind of refreshment. Laughing, I told them that under the circumstances I would like them to relay my regrets, because I had not understood his intentions, but from then on, this officer avoided me.

Among the Russian refugees on Halki was our acquaintance, Veletskaia, whose daughter had been a lady in waiting to the Empress, and who was with her right up until the Tsar and family left Tsarskoe Selo. Various officers from the south of Russia, with whom Veletskaia was acquainted, would visit her. My children and I were at her place when an officer by the last name of Markov was also about to visit her, supposedly on his way to join Admiral Kolchak in Siberia. We were ready to leave when Veletskaia detained us, saying that this officer could be arriving soon and he would tell us some marvelous things about the rescue of the Tsar and his family. Of course, we stayed.

This officer told us that many Guards officers and army officers, wanting to save the Tsar and his family, pretended to be Bolsheviks and were assigned to Ekaterinburg, where the Tsar's family was. They were deliberately rude to the Tsar's family so that the Bolsheviks would not suspect them. When they learned that the local Soviet of Workers' and Soldiers' Deputies had set a trial date for the Tsar, they decided to act. They disguised Prince Dolgorukii, who was there for the substitution, as the Tsar. They dressed the Tsar and the heir in peasant clothes, and the Empress and Grand Duchesses also in peasant clothes, with kerchiefs on their heads. At night two wagons drove up. The Tsar and heir got into one, and the Empress and Grand Duchesses got into the other, and the wagons went in a prearranged direction. He, Markov, supposedly was one of several individuals who were escorting the Tsar and his family, and when they were riding through the forest, early in the morning, a peasant woman was riding in a cart in their direction. Markov rode up to her and ordered her to turn around, which she did in fear, and the convoy moved on. Markov and some other officers brought the Tsar and his family to a certain point, where a different escort replaced them, and they rode off in different directions. In this way the Tsar and his family were transferred from one point to another, and the escorts were changed each time, so that nobody would know the final destination. All the gold and diamonds were thrown into a bonfire as proof that the family had perished.

We reacted to this story with considerable skepticism, although the investigation of the murder of the Tsar and his family by the special investigator, Sokolov, who had been appointed by Admiral Kolchak, had not yet been undertaken. When Sokolov's book about his investigation of the family's murder finally came out, I paid particular attention to one part in it that concurred with this officer's story of meeting the peasant woman in the cart in the woods, and that Markov supposedly ordered her to turn around.

Who was this officer really? An individual dedicated to the Tsar and his family, or someone sent by the Bolsheviks to spread rumors of the rescue to further obscure this savage murder?

After a two-month stay on Halki Island, we began to hear news from Russia that the Whites were hurling back the Reds (that is, the Bolsheviks). People began talking about returning to the south of Russia. Many people were getting ready to join Admiral Kolchak in Siberia via Vladivostok, and the allies assigned the ship *Jerusalem*, which was to come for us, and which we awaited on a daily basis. But its arrival kept being postponed, so a lot of people felt they could not keep waiting and left, not to join Kolchak, but to join General Denikin in the south of Russia.

29

A Short Return to Russia

Sofia Globacheva

My husband, who had been ready to take passage on the *Jerusalem*, decided not to wait any longer for the ship, and left for Rostov-on-Don. I remained on Halki with my children for another month, and then we left to join my husband in Rostov. The Turks were sorry to see the Russians leave; they tried to talk us into staying, saying that we would relive the horrors we had already experienced and would return to Constantinople. And they were right!

When we returned to Russia, Rostov-on-Don was overflowing with both a civilian and military population. We were not able to find a single apartment, not even a single room. My husband had a room so small he could hardly fit into it, but we all were able to squeeze into it those first few days. Later we were able to get an apartment of a government employee who lived in Rostov-on-Don year-round, but he was away visiting a relative in Yalta. We moved into the apartment, and it was quite tolerable compared to our other experiences. My husband kept his room, and my children and I settled into this apartment, since the apartment's owner was not expected back for a month.

One night, about two in the morning, while we were sleeping soundly, there was a loud knocking on the door, and then another knocking at the window. We jumped out of bed, thinking it was the Bolsheviks. My son went to the door and asked who it was and what they wanted. An angry voice responded that it was the owner returning, and who were we to be occupying his flat? It would have been strange not to let the owner of the apartment in, so we asked him to wait a moment while we got dressed. Upon letting him in, we saw that he had brought a friend of his, a colonel and his wife, thinking that the apartment was unoccupied. The owner turned out to be a kind and courteous man, and he told us not to worry and to go back to sleep, and that he and his friends would take care of themselves. He arranged for the colonel's wife to sleep on the table in the dining room, and he and the colonel somehow settled in the kitchen by the stove. We felt ashamed that we had inconvenienced him so much, but he said we should give it no thought and that we could stay there until we found new lodgings. He even promised to help us find a place. There was, however, an inconvenience. We did not want to disturb the owner by going through his room to the bathroom, so we would go out into and through the courtyard, but at that time there were storms and strong winds, and I was afraid my children and I could get sick.

This is how we lived for a while, until my children and I were assigned a room in a nice big apartment that had belonged to the director of a bank in Rostov. His widow lived there, as well as her young adult daughter and a son. The widow's husband had recently committed suicide in this apartment, and an older daughter, after that tragedy, had hanged herself in that same apartment. The widow was an unpleasant and tactless person. She would come into our room around six in the morning and wake us up by making phone calls to someone about some matter or other. I finally lost my temper and protested; after that, we hardly spoke to one another, but at least her early morning visits to our room stopped.

When my husband arrived in Rostov-on-Don from the island of Halki, he was appointed to Headquarters of Supply. The job was uninteresting and deadly boring, and my husband did not like it. So, when he was offered the job of organizing a naval counter-intelligence service for the city of Sevastopol, he readily accepted. He left on the ship *Nicholas*, sailing out of Novorossiisk. He promised he would write to me just as soon as he arrived in Sevastopol.

At that time my children and I had our meals in a dining hall that was set up for military and civilian personnel and their families, since prices in restaurants were very high and rising even more. I was waiting impatiently for my husband's letter, but it was not coming. Some acquaintances of mine, dining in the same hall and seeing my anxiety, did not tell me that the ship *Nicholas* was caught in a terrible storm and two passengers had been swept into the sea. Their identities were not known. I finally found out about this incident, and having no information about my husband and knowing he liked to stroll on a ship's deck during stormy weather, I became so anxious that I developed a sleeping disorder. I slept all the time, and whether I was at dinner or visiting friends, or just speaking to someone, I could not control myself and would get very sleepy.

A month later, I received a telegram that my husband had sailed on a minesweeper with some admiral (I don't remember his name) and was scheduled to arrive at Rostov-on-Don by a certain date. Though I calmed down, my sleeping problem continued for quite a while, even after my husband's arrival. It seems he had sent several letters that never reached me. This happened often due to the inconsistent passages of ships carrying mail. My husband did not stay in Rostov-on-Don because the rumors were that Bolsheviks were advancing. Since almost all the White troops were at the front, with very few remaining to defend the city, volunteers were being sought.

I recall going up the Don River to meet some friends who were supposed to arrive by ship from Yalta. On my way to meeting them, I was surprised to see the former Petrograd City Prefect, General Balk, on one of the streets, and about thirty elderly men, all in their sixties, marching with rifles. I approached General Balk and asked him what was going on, to which he answered, with a smile, that he was training the city's defenders.

A strange thing happened to me as I was returning home, after not having met with my friends because they had not arrived. Walking home along the bank of the River Don, lost in thought, I didn't notice a gypsy woman who was walking toward me. She stopped and fixed her eyes on me and said, "There is a cross behind you of which you are not yet aware." Three days later I ran into Colonel Skvortsov, formerly a member of the General Staff, who was married to the sister of my brother's wife. I had not heard anything of my brother since his arrest by the Bolsheviks in Petrograd. I asked Skvortsov about him, and he said that the Bolsheviks had shot him. So, here was that cross behind me of which I was unaware.

Soon thereafter my husband had me and the children sail to Sevastopol, where we spent a few days. We then moved on to Odessa, where my husband took up his duties.

The White forces were constantly arriving and passing through Odessa from the front. On one occasion I was going, for some reason, to see the head of the White Cross Department, Colonel Dmitrievskii. I was struck by the appearance of one officer standing at the door to the office. He was without his cap, no shoes on his feet, and an overcoat covering his naked body. He was pale, emaciated, and barely able to stand. I let him go in first, and when he left I went into the office and asked Dmitrievskii who that officer was. "He just returned from the front," answered Dmitrievskii. "Their supply wagon with their things and food rations were taken by the Bolsheviks, and those who got stranded on the front wound up without food or clothing and still tried to hold their position." Here was a true hero, I thought.

Activities in Odessa were moving at a feverish pace. When we arrived in Odessa, we again, like the first time, wound up in the hotel "France." For about two or three months everything went well, and news from the front was fairly comforting. But suddenly the allies began to rush about and fuss, and they informed my husband they were about to evacuate. An English officer, a commander of a minesweeper, offered my husband to have me and the children transported to Constantinople. I declined his kind offer, deciding to stay with my husband, since I knew if we were separated we might never see each other again, thanks to this hellish situation.

The regional commander of Odessa and Novorosiisk, General Shilling, a friend of my husband's from their days at the cadet academy, recommended that we get ready to evacuate, and this indeed happened with great haste, as the Bolsheviks had broken through the lines at the front and were advancing on Odessa.

Many allied warships were docked, but suddenly they weighed anchor and moved out to sea. My husband directed all his subordinates to meet that evening where the ship *Vladimir* was docked since that was the ship that would be leaving in the morning. I stayed at the hotel, packing what few things we had, and my daughter ran around to warn all the personnel who reported to my husband of his order, as most of the junior officers had dispersed and there was nobody else to send. My husband was in constant touch with General Shilling, but several times he rushed to the hotel to find out how we were doing. I asked him not to do that because Bolsheviks who were already secretly in the city were searching hotels. So I asked him only to take our son and daughter. I asked for a horse-drawn sleigh cab, but the cabbies refused to take officers and their families, not even their baggage. Hotel employees also began to act hostile and, in general, the city was already experiencing a Bolshevik spirit. It was thanks only to the hotel concierge, who told the cabbie that I was the wife of one of the residents of the hotel, that I was able to get a sleigh for our baggage. Having packed our things onto the sleigh, I dragged myself walking behind the sleigh, because hooligans were already attacking people who were leaving and robbing them of their things. So, this is how I made it to the ship *Vladimir* late that night and was able to catch up with everyone, including my husband and children. Once we were on the ship, I pleaded with my husband not to go back into the city, where there was rifle fire and the Bolsheviks were already executing people.

In the morning my son ran into my cabin all agitated to tell me that my husband, along with two of his officers and purser, had left for the city. I became very frightened, because cannon volleys had grown louder and there was not a single allied ship in port—only the *Vladimir*, swaying in the tide. People on board were nervous; the ship was overloaded with eleven thousand people. Many were lying on the deck suffering from typhoid fever, and in the salons and dining room it was absolute chaos. The Bolsheviks were firing on the ship from shore, and two colonels who were on the deck were killed. To my horror, I saw that the *Vladimir* was beginning to move away from the pier. The captain, whose name I don't remember, was giving some kind of orders in a hoarse voice.

I ran over to the captain in great fear and tried to talk him into not sailing without my husband, who had gone into town under some kind of order from General Vitnivitskii, who was in charge of the ship's passengers.

The captain was straining, trying to shout over the noise and shooting that was going on. He said the ship would not leave without General Globachev. However, the ship had already begun to move away from the pier to free itself from the surrounding ice. Everyone on board was anxious to leave and was hurrying the captain to get under way.

I ran back to our cabin, where all my husband's subordinates were, and prepared to get off the ship with my children, not wanting to leave without my husband. Suddenly there was shouting on deck that General Globachev was running toward the ship, the stern of which had already moved away from the pier. The naval counter-intelligence officers, who were on deck, threw him a line, on which he was able to clamber onto the ship, as were the bank director and paymaster. Everybody's nerves were frayed; some of the men wept when they saw that my husband was alive.

As it turns out, General Vitnivitskii was so frightened that the sailors of the *Vladimir* would refuse to sail if they were not paid in advance, that he forgot that the money to pay them was on board all the time, so he sent my husband into town to get the money from the bank even though he knew that the Bolsheviks were nearly in control of the city. My husband told us that arriving at the bank with the paymaster, and leaving two of his officers wait-

FIGURE 29.1. One of the evacuation ships overloaded with Russian refugees. From W. Chapin Huntington, *The Homesick Million* (Boston: The Stratford Company, 1933).

ing in the car, he asked the bank director to give the money to the paymaster and he would sign for the transfer. The bank director fulfilled the request. As my husband and his group were ready to leave, local Bolsheviks were gathered around the bank, threatening anyone who dared to try to leave, saying the first person to show himself at the door would get a bullet in the head.

So, the money had to be left behind. The bank director took them, via a back entrance, to his apartment, where my husband put on a civilian overcoat over his uniform and, with the bank director's sister joining them, they all hurried out into the street through a back door and ran toward the ship. The officers who were supposed to be waiting in the automobile for my husband had taken off, seeing that Bolsheviks surrounded the bank.

Already, many dead bodies were lying in the street on the way to the ship. As the ship began to move away from the dock, the Bolsheviks began to fire on the ship. We could hear one cannon shell and then another as they exploded nearby. The panic on board the ship was awful, and some officers who were unable to get on the ship because there was no more room shot themselves on the dock. This was hell in reality. An unseasonable frost and stormy weather was rampaging here in the south, and it seemed as if all of hell's forces were working to aid the Bolsheviks. Even when we finally arrived in Sevastopol, in the frenzy to get off the ship, two people were crushed to death.

In Sevastopol we stopped at a hotel, but it was not heated, and my children almost froze there. I was going to try to locate some of my acquaintances to see if I could get some warmer clothes for my children, who had fallen asleep from the cold and exhaustion. Luckily, my acquaintances came over and were able to wake my children up, but with some difficulty, and began to warm them.

The next day my husband decided we should move to Constantinople, since there was nothing for him to do in Sevastopol. The problem was to find a ship bound for Constantinople, and so my husband contacted an English admiral to negotiate our entire family going, as well as my husband's subordinate officers and their families. The admiral invited my husband aboard his ship and gave orders to the captain of the cargo ship *Mercedes* to take all those designated by my husband, about twenty-four people, for passage to Constantinople.

All the men and women of our group on the *Mercedes* were lodged in common cabins together, and only my daughter and I were given a small cabin as a privilege. We were fed well at the start, but quite soon the ship's captain, apparently hoping to rid himself of us, and to disembark at any port on the Asiatic side, walked around telling us, "No more food, no more food," meaning there was no more food for us on his ship.

30

Refugees on the Prince's Islands

General Globachev

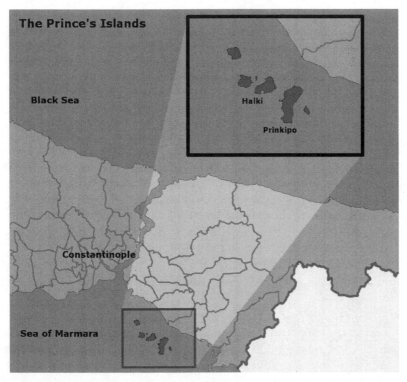

MAP 3. Constantinople could be seen from the Princes' Islands, which are between one and two hours by ferry from the city. The largest island is Prinkipo; the second largest is Halki. (Source: Wikimedia Commons.)

The Prince's Islands. Accommodating the refugees. General Shvartz' staff. The refugees' plans. The arrival of General Denikin's representative. The transfer of Russian refugees to Russia. Departure to Novorossiisk.

All the refugees from Odessa and Crimea, who had to be evacuated by the British at about the same time, were disembarked on the Prince's Islands and were distributed thus: most who were evacuated by the French—the military and civilian staffs of Odessa's government—were settled on Halki Island, which was under French authority. Refugees from Crimea were settled on Prinkipo, which was under British authority. Considerably fewer refugees were settled on Antigone, in the Italian zone, and on Proti, the American zone. Each of these countries requisitioned the necessary living accommodations and supplied provisions according to the ration standards for soldiers of each respective country.

I wound up on Halki, where the largest facility for living accommodations was the Greek seminary, which could hold six hundred people. Those who wished could find their own living accommodations on the island, but had to pay for them out of their own pockets. Order was maintained by the foreign military commands of each country, but assisted by Russians. Credit must be given to the foreigners for feeding and caring for the Russian refugees in a very tolerable way. At the same time, they did insist that refugees respect the order and the existing regime. Some of the refugees, who either had some independent means or were able to get work, were allowed to go to Constantinople unimpeded, and the foreign powers were glad to get these people off their hands.

All the government agencies that had been in Odessa were disbanded, and all the officials were now just plain refugees. Only General Shvartz's staff and the Defense Council remained, but it was not clear what purpose these two organizations served. Once there was no longer a territory, there was no need for a Defense Council; once there was no longer an army, there did not seem to be any need for a staff. The army, by the way, was left to its fate and fought its way independently, with few resources, to Rumania [Romania] after Odessa's evacuation. However, Shvartz was able to get some valuables and money out, and this allowed him to support these two organizations for about two months.

Shvartz seemed to have no long-term plans. It is true that he did not break off relations with the French command, but as time passed he did not realize that he would not get further help from the French. The Defense Council concluded that its continued existence would not be productive, and so it decided to disband. All members of the Defense Council each received one thousand Turkish lire and emigrated to other countries to begin new lives. The remaining money that had been withdrawn from the Odessa government bank, about nine million Ukrainian karbovanets, was given to Bernadskii, who was the head of finance of the Volunteer Army, to transmit to Denikin's government.

General Shvartz's staff continued to exist with General Prohorovich as Chief of Staff. He was authorized to give financial aid to certain refugees from sums that had been left under General Shvartz's authority.

Except for those refugees who planted their roots in Constantinople, it became clear that the Russian High Command could not support the refugees in terms of any future possibilities. It was no longer possible to depend on foreign charity, so the refugees began to group and organize to emigrate to other countries or to return to Russia. By May it was evident that the Volunteer Army was beating the Bolsheviks and was enlarging its territory. Reports were also coming from the Far East that Kolchak's army was gaining in the Urals, and that he was asking for specialists and officers to join him via Vladivostok. Registration procedures were initiated for groups that volunteered to go to Novorossiisk, Vladivostok, Siberia, Bulgaria, and other places. General Benzinger, the representative of the High Command of the Volunteer Army, arrived in Constantinople and offered assistance to those willing to join the Volunteer Army, and from that moment the free transportation of the Russian refugees to Novorossiisk began. There was only one specially equipped and supplied ship arranged by Shvartz—this was the *Jerusalem*, which was able to take about three hundred of the volunteers.

With General Benzinger's arrival, General Shvartz began to lose credibility with the foreigners. After the departure of the *Jerusalem*, he had no choice but to give up the title of Commander in Chief and to disband his staff. A large number of the refugees from Odessa who had been transported by the French began to return to Russia, especially when Denikin's forces had retaken Odessa and the Crimea.

I left Constantinople for Novorossiisk on the ship *Kherson* in late June. The mood of all those who were returning to Russia was joyous; each person believed in the liberation of Russia, each person went planning to put his efforts to this cause that was dear to him, each person hoped that he would be met, if not with outstretched arms, then at least would be welcomed to be in his homeland. Everyone believed in working together for the future. Alas, for so many there was total disappointment.

The following is Globachev's letter to his wife.

Tsaritsyn is finally taken—June 1, 1919, Novorossiisk

Dear Sonia,

I am writing to you from the ship, since we have been ordered to disembark and go directly to the train station to catch the 9 o'clock train, so I probably won't be able to see the city. We left Constantinople only at 4:30 p.m. on Saturday and got to Novorossiisk on Monday at 6 o'clock without any incidents or adventure. The weather was perfect, and there was not even the slightest rolling or pitching the entire trip. We were docked from Monday until 5 o'clock Tuesday, and it is just now that we are allowed to leave. Judging by what we hear on the pier, the activities of the Volunteer Army are going perfectly.

Everybody is noticeably animated. Kharkov is taken, as is Ekaterinoslav, and all of Crimea. Advance units are nearing Kursk. The Bolsheviks are pretty well being destroyed. All the commissars in Kharkov were hanged. Dybenko was hanged in Yalta. Tomorrow the ship with the refugees from Crimea is sailing for Yalta.

Now, regarding money: only Don, Kerenki, and best of all Tsarist money is exchanged here. Other money is not used. Bread costs 2.5 rubles a pound, and I don't know about other products because I have not been in the city, and this information I have only from Ekaterinodar. So, Sonia, that is all the news I have about myself. I am sending this letter along with letters of the Polianskiis via Colonel Dobrovol'skii, who is going to Prinkipo with his family in two days and will stop off at Halki on the way.

The ship will not be going to Vladivostok, at least that is what the officers at the pier said, and everyone will be ordered to go to Ekaterinodar.

I ask you not to be nervous and not to worry; I feel that everything will be all right for you and me. In general, I am happy to be back in Russia. All the stories that you hear from you-know-who on Halki are nonsense. God willing we will see each other in a month.

I send you my kisses and my love. Kiss the children. I am your loving Kostia.

There's been a change. Dobrovol'skii is not going, so I am sending this through the agency.

31

Our Homeland Deteriorates

GENERAL GLOBACHEV

Novorossiisk. Ekaterinodar. Rostov. The reception of those who returned to their homeland. The investigative commission. Denikin's government. The administration. The front. The seizure of government property. The situation at the rear. Denikin's slogans. The mood of the population. The officer corps. Administration of supplies. Military achievements and Denikin's strategy. The Makhno insurrection. My departure to Odessa.

We found out in Novorossiisk about the gains of the Volunteer Army over the Reds that had cleared out of Crimea, and that Tsaritsyn would fall to us any day. Upon arriving in Ekaterinodar, which was the headquarters of the Commander in Chief of the Volunteer Army, every new immigrant rushed to either join the army or join one of the administrative units and, as I stated before, to participate in liberating Russia, but this was not as easy as it seemed. The immigrants were received coldly and even with animosity if they were monarchists or had the misfortune of even having worked one day in Ukraine during the Hetman's regime. All the government organizations were in the hands of Kadets, S.R.'s, and others whose political views were unprincipled. Among the military were those who participated in Kornilov's campaigns—that is, individuals who were in the Volunteer Army from the beginning. These were people who thought of themselves as the most capable, the only ones who could save Russia. Those who had not been able to get to the south of Russia at the opportune time because of geographic factors or for some other reason were considered unsuitable and unworthy and deserved only charity and leniency.

All the generals who had returned were investigated. A special investigative commission was set up, and all generals and commanders of special units had to go through it. Even if the commission found that you had not been involved in any criminal or compromising situations in your former career, this did not mean that you could get into the Volunteer Army. The Commander in Chief had to approve your appointment. Here is where Denikin's bias toward certain categories of people, and that of his Chief of Staff, General Romanovskii, showed itself.

There were individuals who had served in the Special Corps of Gendarmes during the Tsarist regime, police, those who served anywhere but who were monarchists, those who served under the Hetman in high positions, and finally anyone serving under General Shvartz in Odessa. All these individuals were treated offensively. If any such persons were hired, it was only in lesser positions. Most of the major administrative positions were held by former activists, journalists, or lawyers—that is, by individuals not well suited for administrative work. This is why the secondary positions, which carried the weight of the administrative work, were filled by competent people with prior experience. As examples: a former barrister was appointed governor, and the vice governor was the aged governor; the commander of the municipal police brigade was a line officer, and his assistant was either a former police chief or head of a Gendarme administration. Thus it was everywhere. When it came to political and criminal

FIGURE 31.1. General Anton Ivanovich Denikin. Wikimedia Commons.

investigations, which for some reason were both put into one department, most of the personnel had judicial backgrounds. The director of the so-called division of political and criminal investigation was the former Nizhni Novgorod region prosecutor, Zubelevich, who turned coat to become an S.R. He was neither capable nor competent and had no sense of his job. He simply appointed people to be in charge of various regional investigative agencies who might have had some judicial experience. Gendarme and police officers were not able to get these positions under any circumstances. The municipal guard, or in other words, the police, was made up entirely of line officers, and if a gendarme or police officer happened to get an appointment, it was in the most menial job. In other words: the same thing. The best positions went to individuals who had republican leanings and who were not stained by any previous support of the old Tsarist regime. Generals who had gotten through the investigative commission and were thought to be of some use were enrolled into the reserves. However, young individuals, even if they were raring to go to the front, were first enrolled in the commandant's company, because it was too dangerous to make them combat soldiers too quickly. The only ones of the reserves who received positions in the government were those who had connections or whose political views met the standards of the Commander in Chief and his chief of staff.

The following is Globachev's letter to his wife.

24 June [Old Style calendar]
Ekaterinodar

My dearest Sonia!

I arrived at Ekaterinodar five days ago, buy I didn't write immediately because I was involved in personal bustling about. I went to the general in charge with a list of questions and was told that my matter would be forwarded to a certain commission. It was only today that I met the chairman of the commission, where my matter would be examined, which would take at least a week, after which a report would be made to Denikin and he would decide whether or not to accept me into the Volunteer Army. All generals who come to Ekaterinodar are subjected to this ordeal; but staff officers and senior officers are immediately assigned to combat units or to administrative duties. Former gendarme officers, and especially generals, are treated with prejudice and are not given higher-level responsibilities, especially in government security. I saw Mr. Nikol'skii, but based on what was said it was obvious to me that I would not be serving under him because I could not count on having a more or less decent position given the current political situation. A. I. Pilts is away and will be back in five days, so I haven't seen him, but I have high hopes when I meet with him.

My late arrival played no significant role. Shredel' and Mezentsev are still unemployed. In any event, don't you worry, as soon as I get through the Commission I will be settled, but I don't know where, since the territory is expanding and all the major administrations intend to transfer to the south. I think that I will be employed either as the Chairman of the Requisitions Commission or, maybe, in the civilian administration. In any event, it is better that you did not come, and unpleasant as that is, you must wait (until I have a definite job) and until I write to you to come.

There are no apartments at all. I am staying at Malenovskii's in a really small room in the courtyard of a foul building, and thank God even for that. Living conditions are pretty expensive. The most expensive are textiles, and they are scarce, so they have to be gotten from Turkey. For example, women's white stockings of very poor quality cost 275 rubles. Further, sugar—100 rubles per pound, chocolate—100 rubles per pound, candy—the same, a box of matches—5 rubles, bread—2 rubles, 50 kopeks per pound, beer—6 rubles for a bottle. I eat in the building dining room, two courses—10 rubles. So, food is less expensive than in Turkey, but other things are more expensive. When you do leave, stock up on sugar, tea (100 rubles per pound here), linen goods, and shoes. One can't get any uniforms here.

I gave your message to E. N. Pilts and E. L. Beletskoi's letter to Colonel Tikhobrazov. The weather here alternates between very hot and pouring rain. The city is not bad. It's big and decent enough; there are several theatres and good movie houses, and a big city park.

I must admit to you that I lost the enthusiasm I had when I came here because this place smells of a Kerensky-type government. In general my mood is not that good now, and who knows, maybe it will improve, but maybe it would have been better to go elsewhere.

All the lower-ranked people have already found work in various government duties. Moskvin is in Novocherkask. Podgornitskii is here on duty with the railroad. In any case, don't be lonely and don't worry about me, I will write to you as often as I can, but in the meantime stay in Halki until I send for you, since coming here with living accommodations as they are and not knowing for how long isn't possible. I will send this letter either with General Mustafin or some other way. You probably already got my first letter (the letter from Novorossisk).

Give my regards to Ekaterina Leonidovna and to all our other acquaintances. I embrace you and kiss you and love you.

I kiss the children, your loving Kostia.

Denikin's government, which was also called "The Special Council," was made up mostly of leftists, and besides that, of many different political parties, so there was a constant struggle within the government that could not but be felt in the course of its activities. The government was afraid to lean too much to the left or to the right—it sat, as one would say, on the fence, and so it was incapable, spineless, and lacking in will. The government did not have a clear or firm course of action. All the local governments and establishments had the same leftist complexion and were filled by the same ill-assorted staffs.

The composition of the commissions that were responsible for produce, apartments, and other domestic matters were interspersed by smart Jews who also worked out their own deals. Selfless obligation to duty to the homeland was a rare occurrence; most saw the current situation from the perspective of making a personal profit.

The situation at the front was not any better. Most of the line officers looked on the Civil War as a means of enriching themselves quickly. As the army regained territory, it captured government property, not to mention the treasures seized from the Bolshevik commissars. The unprincipled officers considered seized items to be their personal property, and it was not only the rank-and-file officers who thought this way, but also command staff and commanders themselves. It was often the case that generals returning from the front had wagonloads of government property that was seized from the Bolsheviks sent to their home addresses. Military leaders and the government itself looked the other way, but when these activities went beyond all bounds and the government took measures to abolish these practices, it ran up against resistance from army commanders.

Those who enriched themselves at the front wanted to get back to the rear in most cases—to Rostov or Ekaterinodar, where they indulged in binging and other disgraceful activities as they enjoyed their ill-gotten loot. Both of these major cities of the Volunteer Army were overpopulated, but there was an unusual segment of the population that did not go to the front nor participate in the government, but focused solely on speculation; these were mainly very capable young people who should have taken up arms, but who preferred to remain at the rear and enjoy life. Ekaterinodar, Rostov, and Novocherkask were so overpopulated with newly arrived people that there was a major problem with housing accommodations and great increases in the prices of necessities.

The following is Globachev's letter to his wife.

1 July 1919
Ekaterinodar

My dear Sonia!

My file is still in the hands of the Commission, and I cannot be assigned a duty until Denikin finally decides. I got a job in the main department of military supply, and in all probability I will be the Chairman of the Inspection Commission, or so I've been promised. I already go to work and am getting acquainted with the job. A. N. Pilts arrived just today and was very happy to see me, but he didn't offer me anything, and I did not ask, because if they do have something for me, it wouldn't be suitable for me. It would be better for me to serve in a military capacity, and when I am accepted, then maybe I can have some choices of work, and it is a fact that it will happen.

In the next few days all the major administrative offices and the Commander in Chief's staff will be moving to Rostov and Taganrog; I don't know where I will be, so that is why I am not asking you to come yet. Ekaterinodar is awfully overcrowded; all our people live in communal accommodations under terrible conditions. Food rations are less expensive, but everything else is terribly expensive; for example, men's shoes—1,600 rubles. I gave mine to have new soles and heels, and it cost 160 rubles. So stock up on shoes and dresses, the prices here are exorbitant.

Nikol'skii gave me a magnificent reference, which is why I was accepted into the supply staff. E. N. Pilts sends her regards and is appreciative that you had her in your thoughts. When you do leave, buy some more chocolate—sweets are very expensive. I suggest that you also buy and bring coffee; there is none at all here.

All the Odessa inhabitants who were on Halki are slowly coming here from Turkey. Gornostaev gave me your greetings, and I got your letters from P. A. Ivanov. Write to me at the following address: Dmitrievskaia, No. 76, Government Staff Office, care of S. V. Savitskii to be transmitted to me, because if you write to me at my apartment, where I am staying (Kotliarovskii, No. 90) and I wind up moving to Rostov, it won't be forwarded to me, but Savitskii will always notify me.

I want to see you all very much and soon, but what to do, since I still am not settled and do not have particular duties. I think something definite will be known in about two weeks, and then I will write to you immediately.

The general situation here is unchanged, but according to newspaper reports, things are very bad in the Caucasus. Give my regards to E. L. Veletskaia and all our acquaintances of whom, I hear, there are fewer—they all left for Vladivostok. Tell Kostia Polianskii that the conscription age is nineteen. Until we meet, I hug you, kiss you, and love you. Kiss Lialia and Kolia.

Your loving Kostia

So, this is what I encountered during the early days upon my arrival at the Volunteer Army territory. On the political side of things, Denikin had issued a rallying phrase: "For a united indivisible Russia." This was the banner of the Volunteer Army, but this catch phrase did not explain the future nor was it understandable to the masses. What kind of Russia would there be, what kind of government, and who would govern? All of these were unanswered questions, and that is why the catch phrase did not get support from the population.

If we look at the political state of affairs of the entire Volunteer movement, it would be important to note that the Volunteer Army supported the
interests of a democratic republic and was under the influence of the Kadet
and S.R. parties. In truth, the founders of the Volunteer Army, Alexeev and
Kornilov, were republicans. Their successor, Denikin, was a republican. They
all spoke of the blessed homeland, but they did not say what this homeland
would be like, because they were not able to distinguish between the common good and their own political views and personal ambitions. They were
not like the Minin and Pozharskii of old, who brought their all to the altar
of their homeland and stood for a monarchical idea that they saw as Russia's salvation. These people wanted to see a rebirth of the Russia of Lvov,
Miliukov, and Kerensky so that they could take their place. The masses of
the population, especially the peasants, did not participate in the war, so it
really could not be called a national war. The war was strictly party oriented:
the Kadets and S.R.s disputed over who would wield power over the Russia
that was subjugated by the Bolsheviks, and the Bolsheviks were luckier and
more capable, which was proven by how quickly they seized power after the
fall of the monarchy.

One may ask why the officer corps joined the Volunteer movement.
Simply put, the officer corps was a professional military class that was run out
of Soviet Russia, removed from responsibilities, and tortured. Naturally the
officers of the corps went where their services were needed, where their rights
were respected, and where they were paid for their services—that is, the Volunteer Army. Moreover, a new kind of officer popped up, one with republican
leanings, and these were named "the colored forces." These were the followers
of Kornilov, Alexeev, Markov, and Drozdovskii. Some had never served nor
were officers during the Great War. In general, it must be said that of the
entire corps of the Volunteer Army, not more than 25 percent were for the
liberation of Russia and did not represent any political ideology; the rest were
for saving a democratic republic or simply to promote their personal interests.

The mood of the population toward the Volunteer Army can be seen
by how the people reacted to the army as it reoccupied territories anew. The
arrival of the Volunteer Army in some cities and villages was greeted by the
chiming of church bells, tears in peoples' eyes, and people kissing the stirrups
of the cavalry horses, but within about two weeks, the people wound up hating the Volunteer Army as much as they hated the Bolsheviks. The people did
not understand the army's catch phrases, and the army's behavior engendered
hatred. Many of the officers of the Volunteer Army, in their lack of principles,
unruliness, and vicious behavior, were not much different from the Reds and
would probably have fit in better on the Reds' side. They were in the Volunteer
Army by mistake—the Civil War just happened to catch them on this side.

The relationship between the appointed administration of the regions that were occupied by the Volunteer Army and the populace was not good. The actions of the new bureaucrats were often capricious and even illegal, since these actions were often based on self-interest. As an example: some administrators were appointed to regions where they had owned estates, and the first thing they did was to reestablish their property that had been ruined by the revolution, and they dealt harshly with the peasants, whom they blamed for their ruination. Others, who were completely irresponsible, robbed the populace just as front-line soldiers did. Thus, the laws and orders of General Denikin's government engendered no trust from the people, so the people neither supported nor joined the Volunteer movement.

Denikin's propaganda apparatus, called Osvag, was extraordinarily cumbersome. It required a colossal sum of money to function, and salaries to the whole army of workers, but its productivity was nil. Osvag's efforts were focused almost exclusively on the territories that were occupied by the Volunteer Army, and whose purpose was to convince the population that the Volunteer Army's regime was better than that of Soviet Russia. This was usually demonstrated through the use of posters that highlighted all the unfavorable features of the Soviet regime, and in contrast, the Volunteer Army's favorable features. Osvag did not display any spiritual educational activities. Osvag did not promote any propaganda on Bolshevik held territory; such was the strong hold that the Bolsheviks had. In a word, Osvag did not justify its own existence. After all, how could it operate a unified robust propaganda operation when its very organization was replete with people of all different political leanings?

After I had looked around and observed that Denikin's government was no different than Kerensky's had been, that it was all "Kerenskyism," I decided to step back from any political investigative work and sought employment completely outside the political environment. I attained work with the Central Administration of Supply. The immediate head of its administration was happy to hire me, and appointed me Chair of the Interdepartmental Commission to inventory government property that had been seized from the Bolsheviks. It was necessary only to record those things ordered by the Commander in Chief, and to confirm that this had been done. Here is where the High Command's political intolerance showed itself.

Within a two-month period, I worked unpaid in the Supply Administration, first in Ekaterinodar and then in Rostov, and regardless of the number of times that I applied to join the Volunteer Army, I was rejected, with no reason given. I finally decided to find out personally the reason for my rejection from Chief of Staff, General Romanovskii. My meeting with him reinforced my assumption. I was told the Commander in Chief could not agree to my joining the Volunteer Army "on the totality of my former service in political investigation"—that is, during the Tsarist regime and later in Kiev and Odessa. I asked him to note that I did not choose my type of work to specialize in and that I was totally apolitical. He answered that the prevailing thinking was such that it had to be taken into consideration, and although the Commander in Chief had nothing personal against me, nevertheless, given the character of my past political service, he could not agree to my appointment. This answer showed the timid character of the High Command's politics in ingratiating itself to leftist elements and the harmful influence that they played. Nevertheless, as subsequent conditions showed, and in spite of being blamed by Denikin and Romanovskii for my past service, in September, when I was in Rostov, I received a telegram from staff headquarters inviting me to be the assistant to the head of counter-intelligence on the Commander in Chief's staff. I declined the offer. I was already in Odessa in December when I received a second telegram inviting me to be the head of counter-intelligence. I declined this too.

The following is Globachev's letter to his wife.

Rostov, Romanovskii 122
25 August [old style 1919]

My dear Sonia!

Things are not going well for me; it's no wonder that I had a foreboding about going to Novorossisk. In the last letter I wrote to you that I had already been appointed to Kiev as the Chairman of the Interdepartmental Requisition Commission, and that I had no doubts about going. Things worked out differently—Denikin turned me down. I went to Taganrog to find out why—it seems that the issue is my former duties in the Corps of Gendarmes and the Security Bureau. The Chief of Staff promised that he would resubmit, and I await the result. Of course, I won't get to Kiev, but it's important to me to be enrolled in the reserves, since I don't have anything to live on, without pay. If I am turned down again, I will be finished with the Volunteer Army, and I will try to get work in any other place. All these unpleasantries have exhausted me. The boredom is terrible, I do nothing, and I sit in my little room or wander the streets. In general my life is unenviable. Could anyone have thought that I would have been treated this way? Besides that, I am worried about you; only two letters in all this time, via Terehov and Sotiri. How are all of you? I don't know anything, and I can't even write to you to let you know where you should come. It's simply awful. I will finally find out in the next few days whether I will serve in the Volunteer Army, but I have to write you without waiting since today is the opportunity to go to Novorossisk.

As soon as I find out something, I will write immediately. Everyone who came from Turkey has been appointed jobs, except generals, and especially those from the Corps of Gendarmes.

Rostov is a nice city, but twice as expensive as Ekaterinodar. I miss you all very much, how good it would be to be united. Well, let's not lose our good spirit, maybe everything will work out for the best.

I kiss and embrace you all, lovingly Kostia.

The end of September 1919 was a turning point in Denikin's military fortunes. The extremely thin and fluid front line did not allow the army to take any quick offensive operations. The Reds, who had beaten back Admiral Kolchak in the east, and were forcing him to retreat deeper into Siberia, were free to coordinate their forces in the south and could now threaten Denikin's front at any point.

From this moment on, the Volunteer Army retreated along the entire front. At first it was a battle-by-battle, slow and stubborn retreat, but later it became a rush to evacuate the entire territory held by the Volunteer Army, with the exception of Crimea, which was being held by General Slashchev's forces.

I do not sort through nor judge the reasons for Denikin's defeat, but it does seem to me that he did not follow one of the major principles of strategy: the consolidation of forces at a decisive point. The capture of the very important point on the Volga—Tsaritsyn, back in June, should have indicated a major operational direction toward Saratov and Samara to join with Admiral Kolchak's forces, which had already reached the Volga, and not to widen the front in the west and head for Orel and Moscow, leaving the Red Army to defeat Kolchak separately. The inopportune occupation of Ukraine and the desire to take Moscow defeated Denikin.

At about the same time, there was a peasant insurrection at the rear of the Volunteer Army under the leadership of Ataman Makhno, who completely unexpectedly, for the Volunteer High Command, seized Berdiansk, Mariopol, and almost captured the High Command at Taganrog. It was totally inexplicable how such a danger could pop up so suddenly at the rear. I attribute this complete lack of information to the wretchedly organized intelligence and counter-intelligence staff of the High Command, who missed this entire movement.

By October it was clear to anyone that neither Rostov nor Taganrog could be held. The Kievan front began to retreat to Odessa, and the Kharkov front to Rostov, which allowed the Bolsheviks to pursue in any direction.

In November, I accepted a job offered by the Navy Department to be the head of the Odessa region naval counter-intelligence. I was content with this, and here is why: I had been very negative about counter-intelligence work in the Volunteer Army, and especially in its staff, which, as I have mentioned, was not much different from the Cheka. Here I was in a unique situation. Naval counter-intelligence had been organized anew, and I was to organize matters in Odessa my way and, most importantly, I could staff it with people I knew—honest, decent, and competent in investigative work. I left Rostov for Odessa in the middle of November, and did not arrive until the beginning of December. This was how difficult travel had become in the rear, even by sea.

32

Return to Odessa and to Turkey

General Globachev

The situation in Odessa. The Odessa front and its defenders. The conditions and setting up the naval counter-intelligence function. General Shilling and his entourage. Political work of the regional staff. Kirpichnikov. The mood of the population. Defense of the city. The British. The orders of the regional staff and evacuation. The siege on the bank. Departure. Sevastopol. The situation in Crimea. Departure for Turkey.

I found the situation in Odessa as cheerless as it was in Rostov. The city was extremely overpopulated with refugees, mainly from Kiev. The lack of living accommodations increased the cost of living considerably. What was really disturbing was the mass of officers that gathered in Odessa. I think about 70,000 of them here were unemployed. Many of them were apparently financially comfortable, because they were living well, but there were also those who barely had shirts on their backs. This entire rear-guard army was what was left of the Kiev front that had already broken down, had retreated in separate groups, and on its way pillaged the local population as it hastened to Odessa to sell its ill-gotten loot.

The Kievan front retreated in disorder and carried some of the Odessa group with it. Slashchev's Odessa group retreated to the Crimean peninsula. Whoever was left in Odessa retreated in disorder just like the Kievans. By January 1920, Odessa was virtually without military cover.

Lieutenant General Shilling, who was the commander of the Novorossiisk region, had already written to Denikin that there was little point in defending Odessa, and a plan to evacuate to Crimea should be developed, but Denikin categorically ordered that Odessa should be defended at all cost. This order, given the absence of a front, created a catastrophic situation within a month.

Shilling told me that, already in December, after the fall and retreat from Odessa, the Odessa front did not really exist and it was impossible to form a new force from the kind of material that was available, namely the officer corps that had inundated Odessa.

In truth, the efforts of the staff were useless. In December and January efforts were made to form new units: officer registration was begun, staffs were formed, uniforms and arms were distributed, and German colonists were encouraged to join up, but nothing came of this. Even units that were newly formed could not be sent to the front lines because they deserted along the way, ran off, and, in most cases, never even arrived at the rendezvous points. Definitely, nobody wanted to fight. The only unit that was established was a detachment of a thousand officers to defend the city, who were able to defend Odessa from riots up to the last days. This detachment was commanded by an energetic and brave Colonel Stessel, who did not abandon the city until its complete evacuation and who, with his entire detachment, could not get onto a single ship leaving Odessa. So the detachment had to fight its way overland to Rumania.

On my arrival in Odessa I had to organize my operation under extraordinarily difficult conditions. I was able to pick my staff quickly and luckily, but the biggest problem was finding office space, which took over two weeks. Here I faced a second problem—to find office equipment and heating fuel for the office. This last issue was one that even the requisitioning commission could not solve, and it was their job to provide service to government agencies. We had to get our equipment through purchases and requests—where to find a chair, where to find a desk? The large office that we were authorized to have was without furniture or heat, which prevented any possibility of conducting our work productively. The cold could really be felt. The temperature was never higher than 2 or 3 degrees. It must also be added that there was no faith in the work, as it was felt that everything would have to be abandoned, and quickly. The thing that was more depressing than anything else was the sense that the work, the energy, and resources were being spent needlessly.

It was the same with the administration as it had been in Rostov. At the helm of the local government were individuals who were unprincipled and lacked any ideology. General Shilling was a very decent man and an extreme monarchist by conviction. I knew him from our younger days—this was a very kind, honest, and responsive person, as he had remained. For someone occupying such a high position, his shortcoming was that he was too soft, and was more focused on his private life than someone in his position should have been. Military and civilian officials around him took advantage of his shortcomings and worked their own personal interests in the name of the Commander in Chief. So, all of the censure that was brought against Shilling in Odessa and its disgraceful evacuation were not entirely fair. Just like Denikin, he was put in a very difficult situation. His Chief of Staff, General Chernavin, sensing the collapse, left early on for Crimea, supposedly on business, but he never returned. By the middle of January, the remainder of the command staff did not involve themselves in military matters, but were more concerned with a successful evacuation. The civilian staff did no better and handed matters over to a young man who had little administrative ability and made many mistakes, some of his own choosing, but he covered himself by doing them in Shilling's name.

The struggle against Bolshevism and political investigation was under the authority of a certain individual named Kirpichnikov, the chief of the counter-intelligence division of the Novorossiisk regional staff. He was a smart man, but not a specialist and, being a Socialist Revolutionary, he saw everything from a socialist perspective. He released many of the more important Bolshevik workers who had been arrested with great difficulty after the Volunteer Army took Odessa. He saved many of them from the death sentence by getting their sentences commuted to lighter ones. His motivation was not quite clear to the public, and he became suspect. Perhaps he was trying to win over the sentenced individuals to become agents, and this could have been justified, but the public did not understand this humane treatment of the communists who were arrested, and so the public cast a suspicious eye for his sympathy and protection of the Bolsheviks. Kirpichnikov put himself in a bad light with the Volunteers, and this led to his tragic end. He was murdered in January by unknown persons while on his way from staff headquarters to Shilling's apartment to give him a report. The investigation turned up no perpetrators, but from all available information, Kirpichnikov was the victim of a secret, pseudo-monarchist organization that harbored ill will against him.

The mood of the Odessa population was heightened; each person felt that he would have to re-live Bolshevism. Some awaited this with fear, while others were overjoyed—the Volunteer movement's regime had been too much to bear. Besides, there were many Soviet agents in the thick of the population who were agitating and corrupting. The police, or as it was called, the Government Guard, was wretched, starting with the City Prefect, Baron Shtempel and right down to the rank-and-file guards. As I have stated, the upper ranks of the guard and the City Prefect were of military background and not experienced in administrative work, while the lower ranks, the guards, were a politically unstable element. These lower ranks did not come from the best people, such as the former police, which had former line soldiers, but now these were the worst who had nowhere else to go. The economic conditions for being in the guards were so bad that even under such conditions many soldiers and workers did not want to compromise themselves by joining the government guards. The

City Prefect, Baron Shtempel, apparently saw his position as a sinecure given to him as an award for his previous combat service, from which he returned as an invalid. He showed no energy or initiative. Nobody knew anything about him nor heard from him nor counted on him, but saw him simply as a person who spent his days counting numbers. At a time like this, such a guard could not keep order in the city, and it was therefore fully understandable that an officer militia unit was formed under Stessel, upon whom was placed the internal security and defense of the city. It must be said that he coped with these responsibilities brilliantly.

The British, who had lent moral and some material support to the Volunteer Army, had their own military legation in Odessa that included some forces, as can be seen by their having one or two destroyers and minesweepers in dock. The British were very preoccupied that the Volunteers not hold on to Odessa, and they made every effort, although not realistically, to make that happen. As an example: they had the completely insensible desire to hand Odessa over to Galicia, not counting on the fact that these places were completely devastated and of no value. They proposed to form a special Ukrainian army, but could not find the necessary experienced cadres. They banked all their hopes on Stessel's detachment, which they hoped could hold Odessa, but even this was not fated. In general, the British command wanted to assure everyone that Odessa would not be surrendered, but they could not say how this could be done.

After Kirpichnikov's murder, I was offered the position of head of the regional counter-intelligence department that I had turned down before, as I already mentioned, but I gave in to General Shilling's and others' insistence, and agreed to accept the job. I was in this job for not more than ten days, but all the assumptions I had made that had led me to decline the job before were borne out. The staff, and its jurisdiction, was an ill-assorted group who assembled in Odessa and were a pain in the neck, and we had to attend to them and use their services. It seems that state funds and property were handed over to these people or lost or abandoned under the pressure of the sudden retreat. All this had to be dealt with, and in most cases these things had to be taken on faith; nothing could be proven. Everybody stuck to promoting their own interests and not the government's.

Around January 20 the regional staff made definite plans to evacuate, as there was not a single soldier at the front, and two Red divisions were moving on Odessa. From that moment, the entire city government was transferred to Colonel Stessel's staff.

On January 23, I arrived for work, as usual, at the regional staff office and found nobody in my department. It turned out that the officer on duty, General Vitvinitskii, did not consider it necessary to notify the department heads, and during the night ordered that the staff and its equipment be loaded onto the ship *Vladimir*. So, this was how things were, the evacuation was kept secret from the personnel. It was so secret that the city's population found out about the Volunteer evacuation only on January 24, and that was through an announcement made by the British. This was such an unscrupulous act that many who were slow in getting ready to be evacuated wound up paying with their lives. What astounded me was that none of my closest subordinates even tried to warn me of the last order of the last duty general of the regional staff. Once more I was convinced about the composition of the counter-intelligence staff. What could one expect when the civilian personnel of the counter-intelligence staff were Bolshevik agents who were on the Bolshevik payroll; and some of them were even found guilty and shot.

As soon as I found out about the evacuation, I immediately took steps to get the naval personnel onto the ship *Rumiantsev*, and to get the ground forces onto the *Vladimir*. By the evening of January 24, there was not a single subordinate of mine on shore. During the day I left the ship to go into the city, where a heightened anxiety was already noticeable; police were not at their posts, and officer detachments were retreating and gathering at staff headquarters and on the Nikolaevsk Boulevard. The city was about to explode.

By January 25, all the ships had been loaded, were overcrowded with soldiers and refugees, and were set to sail, but they remained at docks and inlet piers. That winter was cold, and the water was frozen. The departure of the ships was a problem, and some could only get out with the help of an icebreaker tugboat. The *Vladimir*, the ship that I was on, was at the very end of the pier. At nine in the morning the head of our echelon, the very same duty general of the Odessa region, General Vitvinitskii, asked me to go to the government bank with the staff paymaster to get two million of Kerensky money to pay the ships' company, without which the ships would not raise anchor. Even though it was risky to go into the city, and the ship was to sail at 1 p.m., I nevertheless went into the city. Besides me, there was the paymaster, two armed officers from my department in the car, and the chauffer. When our automobile approached the bank we saw that its entrance off Pol'skii Street and the main entrance on Zhukov Street were overflowing with a diverse crowd awaiting the bank's opening to get their money out—some were depositors wanting their money, and others were workers wanting their wages. It was pretty hard to get into the bank, but after I had ordered the automobile to wait for us, with some difficulty the paymaster and I were still able to get into the bank. The assistance of the bank director made it easy to get the money; it only remained for us to get back. The bank director was supposed to be evacuated on the *Vladimir*, and in finding out that I had an automobile, he asked if he and his sister could come along. I gladly agreed. In order for us not to push our way through the throng, the bank director suggested that we go through his apartment and exit onto Zhukov Street via the main entrance. Given that, I went out to signal the automobile from Pol'skii Street, but as I rounded the corner, the automobile was not there, and when I returned I asked some people in the crowd if they saw the automobile. I got smug smiles and rude answers that the automobile had left. The mood and composition of the crowd had completely changed; there were now almost exclusively former reserve soldiers who were ready to go over to the Bolsheviks at any moment. The signs were clear: unruly behavior, defiant smiles, and rudeness. It became necessary to return and warn my companions that we had to get to the pier quickly on foot in order to avoid a subsequent worse situation.

By the time we were ready to get out, we were not able to; all the exits from the bank, including the director's apartment, were occupied by rioting reserves that flatly refused to let me pass. It also became clear that they were ready to use their firearms. For example, we heard the phrase, "Whether it's a soldier or general, whoever shows up first gets a bullet in the head." Our situation was now very serious and difficult. We rushed to the telephone to try to get help from the defense staff—the telephone did not work, as the connection had been broken. We realized that we were trapped with no way out. Looking out the windows, we could see armed people on passing trucks, rifle and machine gun fire could be heard. There was fighting in the city, and we expected that the bank would be taken any minute, and, of course, that would mean our deaths. We finally found out why the reserves occupied all the exits and were not letting anyone out. It seems that they were supposed to get paid by the head of the reserves, who was to get the funds from the bank. They were afraid that the bank director would leave with all the funds, and they would wind up with no money. After a quick discussion, we decided to hurry up and give the money to a recipient of the reserves, and let him out the gates. This decision of ours was carried out quickly, and it turned out to be miraculous. Everyone who was in the street rushed to the money, and that freed our exit. We took advantage of that and got out of our trap. It is hard to describe what we went through in that one hour in which we were prisoners in the bank. On the one hand, the reserves could have been replaced by Bolsheviks who, of course, would have dealt with us mercilessly. On the other hand, we thought that the ships might sail away, and we would inevitably be stuck in Odessa. This generated a feeling of horror and anger that we wound up in this stupid and useless trap because of General Vitvinitskii's cowardice and loss of composure in sending me to the bank to get the Kerensky money when the money, according to the bank director, had for the most part already been loaded on the *Vladimir*, which surely Vitvinitskii was aware of.

Fighting in the city streets had already erupted when we exited onto Pol'skii Street and began to run to the pier to get on the *Vladimir*. Rifle and machine gun fire were intermixed with that of revolvers being fired from the building windows. The bullets were whistling past us from both sides of the street, and we had to run full speed across the street intersections. We passed wounded and dead on the streets. When we finally got to the pier, all the ships docked there in the morning had already sailed, and only the *Vladimir*, which had cast off, still had its stern to the pier. Several hundred officers had gathered on the dock. This was Colonel Stessel's detachment, which had retreated under pressure from the Bolsheviks, who had taken Nikolaevskii Boulevard and set up their artillery there. This group of officers could not get on the totally overloaded ships that had already sailed, and they now awaited any kind of vessel to take them. This did not happen, so they had to return to the city and fight their way through to the Rumanian border. I and my companions, that is, the bank director, the staff paymaster, and the bank director's sister, were all hoisted aboard by having cable thrown to us from the stern of the *Vladimir*, which was already slowly moving away from the dock under machine gun fire from the adjoining dock and cannon fire from Nikolaevskii Boulevard.

These few nightmare hours really tested me—no thanks to General Vitvinitskii, who forgot the order he gave me, the captain of the *Vladimir*, who wanted to hurry and sail away, and my brave subordinate officers who were willing to leave me to my fate.

The *Vladimir* headed for Sevastopol. The trip was short, but awful, owing to the overcrowded conditions. The cabins, decks, and holds were all overflowing with people, many of them with typhoid. Others had been wounded by machine gun fire as the ship passed by the Odessa docks. There was an unprecedented frost at night that was twenty-six degrees on the Reaumur scale and lasted until six in the morning. On January 26, a strong storm hit us that we were unable to avoid as we entered the southern bay of Sevastopol. Those vessels that had left Odessa for Constantinople were hit by the storm at sea, and some of them were lost.

So, this was how the nightmare of Odessa's evacuation went, put off to the last moment by the High Command that led to even worse consequences than would have happened had General Shilling's recommendations of a planned gradual retreat been heeded.

I was in Sevastopol for only a week, but even in that short time it was clear to me that the cause of the Volunteer Army was lost. Crimea was still holding on by General Slashchev's Odessa forces that had withdrawn to Perekop, where Slashchev was reinforced, and was able to hold back the Red advance. Sevastopol was overflowing with officers and refugees and presented

FIGURE 32.1. The White Army evacuating Crimea. expert.ru

the same picture as had Odessa. There were ships at the Sevastopol piers that were ready to remove the belongings of the Naval Department and of sailors' families. The latter took care to load their personal and domestic belongings onto the ships in a timely manner. The situation was that Sevastopol was going to be abandoned in a day or two. The troop commander, General Shilling, arrived only on January 27, and General Slashchev was in the north of the Crimean peninsula. There was no order; confusion and panic reigned. General Shilling arrived on the 27th on the ship *Molchanov*, but even he could not alter the situation or the mood of the populace, whose one wish was to stubbornly oppose General Slashchev. My entire operation had been evacuated from Odessa so, since Crimea had its own counter-intelligence agency, I considered myself not needed anymore. Moreover, I had accepted my job reluctantly, so it did not bode well for me that I had been involved in liquidating and transferring of property during the evacuation. So, I decided to decline to do any more, and sent my resignation to General Shilling on February 2. He accepted it, and I left Sevastopol for Constantinople on the British coal tender.

33

Life on Prinkipo and in Constantinople

SOFIA GLOBACHEVA

We were moored on the Asiatic side near Tuzla. Here there was a disinfecting sanitation station for people, and their belongings, coming from Russia, where typhus was raging. The ship's captain tried to talk us into taking all our belongings, apparently thinking that he could then depart without us. It was clear that his responsibility for us, and the inconvenience that we were occupying some of the cabins of the ship's company, honestly annoyed him. However, we did not take his bait and left our heavier belongings on the ship, knowing the admiral's order to the captain of the *Mercedes* was to get us to Constantinople.

After a long and tedious twelve days of sailing, since the *Mercedes* sailed very slowly and stopped often at one place or another to take on or to unload coal, we got off at the Turkish port of Tuzla. We were glad to finally wash off the coal dust, and after a long time of not bathing, we were delighted to take a shower in a Turkish bath house. Old genial Turkish women painstakingly washed us and chatted to us about something or other, which we did not understand at all.

It was curious, but sad too, that having survived the disinfection, many of our clothes were returned to us shrunken—especially leather jackets, trousers, overcoats, and gloves that had been left in pockets. They seemed to have been re-sewn into clothes for children or midgets, and they certainly were of no further use to us.

The *Mercedes* finally dropped anchor a few miles from Constantinople and sent a radiogram of our arrival. A large motor launch was sent for us into which we had to climb down a rope ladder late at night, which really frightened us women.

As soon as we arrived in Constantinople, my husband wanted to see the British admiral right away. An adjutant informed my husband that the admiral had already retired for the night and would see my husband in the morning. A little later, two British officers arrived and did not know what to do with us, since we had already disembarked from the launch onto the pier. One of the officers left and returned shortly, saying that the admiral ordered us to return to the *Mercedes*.

"That is impossible," I said.

"Why?" asked the naval officer.

"Because this order is tantamount to sending us to the moon!"

The officers glanced at each other and smiled.

"It's night, the sea is turbulent, we risked enough getting off the ship and we have children who don't even walk well yet, and to try to climb that ladder again at night and at sea is impossible," I said.

After my response, the British officer asked me what we planned to do. Since I was the only one who knew some English, I said, "Nothing. We will stroll along the dock until morning, until my husband meets with the admiral." The officer left and returned in a while and asked if we would agree, under

FIGURE 33.1. Russian refugees arriving at Prinkipo. Library of Congress, catalog number 2010650570.

the circumstances, to spend the night on board a British warship, which was docked. We certainly agreed; our belongings were put in a storage area, and we set off for the ship. All of the women were put up in some large room where beds had been arranged, and we were brought a huge tank of tea, black in color as coffee, and sandwiches. In general we were treated kindly. Having spent the night aboard, my husband went to see the British admiral. It was decided that we would all depart for the island of Prinkipo,[1] which was under British authority. We were very happy about this, since we knew, even from our first arrival to the islands when we wound up on Halki, that the British treated and fed Russian refugees well.

Upon arriving on Prinkipo by motor launch, we spent the first few days in some house near the dock. We had to squeeze into a small room, which was given to us by the former Governor General of Siberia, A. Pilts. Our few days in this room were awful. The house was full of people who frankly did not have to be evacuated; they could have stayed under the Bolsheviks. They were rude, slovenly, and foul-mouthed. They organized themselves into some kind of a commune, assigning people staying in this house to cleaning tasks and all kinds of other responsibilities. We were able to escape this situation, thanks to the British. They set us up in a beautiful estate surrounded by gardens, a separate bath house, and a stairway that led down to the beach, where we bathed. Besides us, there was only one other family living above us. This estate belonged to some rich Greeks. The British had organized everything well; at each estate a refugee tenant was elected who went at an appointed time every day to the British commissary for provisions. Upon his return, these would be distributed equally among the tenants. The British fed us refugees well and abundantly; they gave us meat, cheese, preserves, butter, bread, and even kerosene, matches, and kindling for heat.

Prinkipo was under the authority of a commandant who was a Dutch colonel and under whom Russians were invited to function as interpreters for negotiations with Russian refugees. At first people were allowed to go to Constantinople and even work there, but later those who worked in Constantinople had to forego their ration allocations. Others could only go to Constantinople with the commandant's approval, but that never stopped anyone. In general, credit must be given to the British: life under them was good.

Prinkipo was the most beautiful of the four Princes' Islands, which are very close to one another, and communication between them was by small steamboats that operated out of Constantinople. Prinkipo had a hilly terrain covered with forests. It had a wonderful road along which stood beautiful estates belonging to rich Greeks and Turks, and the British settled the Russian refugees into these. There was a good restaurant right on the seashore on Prinkipo with a large terrace frequented by Greeks, Turks, and Russians. A string orchestra played every evening. There were Russians on Halki too, and the French administered Halki. The Russians were fed mostly rabbit and beans. The French treated the Russians well. On the island of Antigone[2] Russians found themselves under the Italians, who fed the Russians mostly sardines and macaroni.

Proti[3] was the smallest of the islands and the Russian refugees were under American jurisdiction. Nobody wanted to wind up there, since people were fed poorly, which surprised everyone because America was always generous in providing funds for food and rations. The explanation for this was that on the three islands mentioned earlier, the supplying of provisions to the Russian refugees was handled by the military. On Proti, this was run by civilians, who apparently did not know how to handle the large sums of money to organize supplying provisions to Russian refugees. However, the Americans did provide great help through the American Red Cross and other charitable organizations that set up free dining facilities, supplied indigent refugees with food, clothing, linens and footwear, and offered educational services to children and helped young people to continue their education in secondary schools and universities in Europe.

My husband did not stay on Prinkipo very long. He left for Constantinople before us, having gotten a job as head of the passport bureau of the Russian Embassy, representing the Commander in Chief of the White Russian Army in Constantinople, General Lukomskii, who was a thoroughly decent, honest, and smart man who loved Russia passionately. The Russian Embassy was on Pera, the main avenue, and my husband had an office of three rooms upstairs in the area that was also occupied by translators and interpreters. One of these rooms had a door that led out onto a large terrace where, having arrived recently from Prinkipo, I often strolled or sat, enjoying the beautiful view of the Bosporus and the Sultan's Palace below. It seemed so mysterious to me when I remembered reading long ago of the lives of sultans and their harems and all the things that went on there.

Our Turkish acquaintances were happy to see us arrive, and just as during our first evacuation, they treated us very well and with respect, and often visited us on Prinkipo while we were there. When we moved to Constantinople they took us sightseeing everywhere. They took us to the Hagia Sofia during a service and our Turkish acquaintances removed their shoes and held them in their hands as they entered the mosque, while we were allowed to put straw slippers over our feet at the entrance. The officiating mullah, seeing us nonbelievers in the mosque during a service, became anxious and sent someone to find out who we were. After some whispering between our Turkish guides and the mullah's messenger, who reported back to the mullah, the mullah smiled and continued with the service. The Turks also showed us their oldest

FIGURE 33.2. Main entrance to the Russian Embassy in Constantinople. Marinich collection.

FIGURE 33.3. The Globachevs with friends on a quay in Constantinople, August 1921. Marinich collection.

cemetery, which was very well maintained. When it was necessary to go on the bridge that crossed over the Golden Horn, which connected the two parts of Constantinople, the old Turkish toll keepers on both ends of the bridge never took any tolls from the Russian refugees.

We frequented the bazaar known as Galata with the Turks, which was in the market section of the city. Entire suites of stores were filled with brocades, old gold and silver cups, and handmade articles. The merchants displayed all these things for us even though they knew we would not buy anything. Still they would bring out, from somewhere in the backs of the stores, beautiful fabrics embroidered with gold and gold items. They proudly laid them out before us, and they treated us to their specially brewed coffee served in miniature cups since it was the Turkish custom that merchants treated customers and visitors to their stores with coffee.

During their holiday known as Bairam, the Turks invited us to all kinds of festivities and to restaurants where Turkish musicians played some kind of pipe instruments and sang doleful songs, as the Turks listened thoughtfully in complete silence and smoked their water pipes; later they explained the songs to us. The Turks did not let us pay for anything, saying that we were their guests.

One time we told some Turkish naval officers that we would like to see the Sultan's processional carriage ride from his palace to the mosque, which occurred on certain holidays, and onlookers were allowed only if they had tickets. The Turkish officers took care of this for us. At the entrance to the palace we were met by a Turkish colonel, the Sultan's adjutant, who escorted us into a modest-sized hall with windows through which we could watch the ceremonial precession. An open carriage arrived drawn by white horses, and the Sultan came out surrounded by all his ministers. He sat in the carriage while all the ministers walked behind and on the sides of the carriage as the procession began to move slowly toward the mosque, but when the Sultan's carriage moved faster, then all the ministers had to run to keep up with it. This ended our visit to the palace, since waiting for the Sultan to return was not allowed. I think that this may have been the Sultan's last processional from the palace to the mosque, considering the imminent events that Turkey would experience soon.

Constantinople really impressed me with its colorfulness. You could see the red fezzes everywhere, and beautifully dressed pashas. Turkish women strolled about in black attire and veils, and mullahs calling the people to prayer from minarets. Constantinople (Istanbul) was divided into two parts. One was higher, called the European part, Pera, where one found the embassies and consulates of European governments, good stores, restaurants, and gardens where one could listen to music and actors tread the boards on an open stage. One time we went to one of the gardens and watched with sadness some Russian

FIGURE 33.4. The Galata Bridge. University of Michigan Library Digital Collections, Michigan Quarterly Review Images.

refugees who were homegrown acrobats perform. We trembled for them as they performed their stunts, which were beyond the bounds of their abilities. We feared that they would fail—that is how uncertain they were. The need to have a job forced them into this kind of work.

The other part of the city was considered the commercial side, called Galata. Greek and Turkish merchants lived there. Banks, money-changing shops, and other commercial activities operated there. Communication between the two parts of the city was either via the wide and long stone stairway in Galata, on both sides of which were shops of all kinds and cafes, or by cable car. During the early part of our stay in Constantinople, I was stunned but also liked the noise and din that one heard along the Galata stairway. Little Turkish children in their red fezzes ran around and loudly begged passersby for money, and merchants yelled out their merchandise, and all this was so extraordinary that I felt sorry when the allies demanded that all this noise and din be stopped. The city volunteer fire department really surprised me when they hurried to a fire. The firefighters, half dressed and barefoot, would run yelling, as they carried litters with small pumps on their shoulders.

34

The High Command in Turkey

General Globachev

My arrival in Turkey. The transfer of the High Command to General Wrangel. The representative of the High Command in Turkey. His deputies. My appointment as head of passport control. Procedures for dispatching and prohibiting travel to Crimea. Relationship of the allies with the Russian refugees. The foreign intelligence in Constantinople. Supplying Crimea. Russian life in Constantinople. Abandoning Crimea.

The passage on the *Mercedes*, including stops at quarantine points, lasted nine days, and compared to previous travel on the Black Sea, was a pleasant outing. There were seventeen of us Russians, including families; we were put up in the officers' cabins and fed very well, thanks to the civility and hospitality of the ship's company and officers. We all disembarked at Prinkipo (Prince's Islands), where there were already about two thousand Russian refugees from Odessa and Novorossiisk, and were put up in various dachas, completely at British expense. The British must be given full credit for their fairness. Even under their strict discipline, they treated the Russians perfectly well and made us feel content.

By March, reports came in of the complete evacuation of Novorossiisk, and in addition the remnants of the Russian Army were thrown back to Crimea. Some of the army withdrew to the Caucasus and even into Persia. The families of the Volunteer Army rank-and-file were evacuated to Turkey, Bulgaria, Serbia, Greece, Cyprus, Malta, and even Egypt. The Commander in Chief, General Denikin, laid down his title and transferred it to General Wrangel, who was sent for from Constantinople, where he happened to be. His first task was to save the remnants of the army. As a first step, he began to reorganize it, calling it the Russian Army, and securing and strengthening the Perekop Peninsula so that the Reds could not attack unexpectedly. This could easily happen, given the disordered state of the remnants of the army that had been evacuated from Novorossiisk. I cannot describe the activities of the Russian Army in Crimea, or the character of the administrative work of the High Command, since I was not there. I can only note information from newspaper articles and what was told by those who came out of Crimea, so I will limit myself to an account of Russian life and the work of the Russian representative agencies of the army in Constantinople. I was witness to all of this when the representative of the High Command under allied authority, General Lukomskii, asked me to be the head of the Passport Control Department under him.

General Lukomskii replaced the former military representative of the Volunteer Army, General Agapaev, with new authority. All Russian military establishments reported to him now, because before that, many of them were autonomous, including the Russian naval base, Russian naval agencies, the port captain, finance officer, the representative of the artillery department, various procurement and purchasing commissions, and the special refugee department. The diplomatic and Russian consular bureaus were under the diplomatic representative, A. A. Neratov, who was independent of General Lukomskii but had to operate cooperatively with him.

I was a member of General Lukomskii's office and was in charge of passports—that is, granting visas, control of transportation to Crimea, and information coming out of the Middle East regarding Bolshevik propaganda and activities. My job required me to give General Lukomskii daily reports. I had known him when he was a second lieutenant, and we were both in class at the Nikolaevsk General Staff Academy. Now, after twenty-five years, I got to know him in an official working relationship in Constantinople. He was without a doubt an honest man who carried out the interests of the High Command and its treasury dutifully. One could see that he had considerable administrative competence, which he had acquired from long experience at the staff level in St. Petersburg, and later on the staff of the Special Council of the Commander in Chief of the Volunteer Army. In 1920, while a bit of Russian land was still in the hands of the Russian Army, the foreign heads of allied governments and occupying forces in Constantinople interacted mostly with the Russian military representative rather than with the diplomatic one. Thus, maintaining good relations with the foreigners took on major importance; nevertheless, the dependence on the Entente affected the morale of the Russians. In this regard, General Lukomskii truly fulfilled his duty. He established an excellent relationship with the Entente and maintained the honor of the Russian Army with dignity.

Not all of the officials under General Lukomskii were irreproachable. Of course, most did their jobs conscientiously, but there were those who saw everything in terms of their own personal interests. As an example: two naval agents embezzled government money, and one of them, who had accumulated a large sum, had foreseen being caught and vanished.

At this time the work of organizing a government in Crimea was begun. General Wrangel began to recall certain people from foreign countries whom he thought would be helpful to him. At the same time, Crimea also drew people who were not invited. These latter individuals counted on joining in the rear so that in the event of military victory, they would be in a solid position in the future. Moreover, in accomplishing its goal in reinforcing the army, the High Command established the requirement that those returning from overseas had to be battle ready. This measure, however, produced passive resistance. Thanks

FIGURE 34.1. General Alexander Sergeevich Lukomskii. Wikimedia Commons.

to these conditions, the rear grew excessively, while the reinforcement of the front was weak. This forced General Lukomskii to initiate some very decisive steps to compel the young battle-ready officers to go to Crimea, even to the deprivation of his own staff and material support. There was one category of people who rushed to Crimea, come what may, in spite of the High Command's prohibitions: these were the families of those serving in Crimea who had been evacuated and now wanted to be reunited, no matter what. This prohibition led to tough economic conditions, a crisis in living accommodations and food provisions.

On May 3, I was unexpectedly appointed by the order of the Commander in Chief as something like the Director of the Police Department on the Commander in Chief's staff—in other words, the head of the political and criminal investigation in Crimea. This appointment did not suit me. First, I doubted that Crimea could withstand the Bolshevik onslaught; the matter had been lost by General Denikin, and judging by the first order that General Wrangel issued while he was still in Constantinople, Crimea was one phase in a long-term evacuation of the army to other countries. Second, working under conditions similar to those under General Denikin and with the same people was unacceptable to me; the experience I had in Odessa was too much of an object lesson. That is why I declined the appointment without hesitation and stayed at my modest position in Constantinople. However, I was still able to observe the activities of our Crimean intelligence and counter-intelligence agencies, and I must say they were not exactly the best. For instance, most of the intelligence agents who came to Constantinople were either scoundrels or imposters. Their only goal was to get funds for some operation and to flee abroad, where they felt they would be untouchable. Even former regular army officers were not clean. As an example, the former commander of a cavalry regiment, Colonel Fuss, an honorable man, was dispatched to Constantinople to establish communication between Crimea, Constantinople, Belgrade, and Sofia. He was to get about three thousand English pounds from General Lukomskii to give to the Commander in Chief on his return trip. Having received these funds, he did not go to Crimea—he hid overseas, and it was only a year later that we got word that he was living well in Paris on the appropriated money. Another example is Colonel Siminskii of the General Staff, who went over to the Reds, taking some secret documents with him. And this was the colonel who had been head of intelligence on the staff of the High Command. These facts merely reinforced my opinion of the lack of moral standards of my comrades-in-arms in the White Movement, especially those who worked in counter-intelligence.[1]

As the person who controlled and authorized departures to Crimea, I constantly had two issues to deal with. On the one hand, I had to endure the aggressiveness and tearful pleas of families that wanted to be reunited with their relatives in Crimea in spite of the High Command's prohibitions, and, on the other hand, to exert almost heroic efforts to convince young combat-ready soldiers to go to Crimea. This latter category of individuals was the most intolerable. In most cases this was the worst social element of the army: they were out of the habit of working and, with nothing to do, they hung around Constantinople, drank, brawled, and besieged the refugees by asking for handouts.

In addition to all these people, Crimea also attracted small merchants and speculators. These were Greeks, Turks, and Russians who brought with them all kinds of goods, mostly manufactured, and tried to make a 100 percent profit after expenses. At this time the value of the High Command's currency kept falling. The stock exchange in Constantinople began betting on the currency's decline, and in Crimea efforts were made to curtail the depreciation of Russian money. I recommended some practical measures to raise, or at least to stabilize, the value of Russian currency, but unfortunately my project, which General Lukomskii sent to the Commander in Chief's deputy for civilian affairs, Krivoshein, was not given its due attention. The measures proposed were that every individual leaving for Crimea on business had to pay ten Turkish lire for a visa, but the fee must be paid in Russian currency. This would create a demand for Russian money in Constantinople and thus would strengthen and stabilize the ruble. This fee on passports in Russian currency had to be under the authority of the Commander in Chief and would have minimized the need to print additional new money. Every ship sailing to Crimea would have returned millions in Russian money to the Russian government bank. I do not know why Krivoshein turned down this project.

The British treatment of the Russian refugees after the evacuation of Novorossiisk and Odessa was more protective of the refugees, compared to the other allied powers occupying Constantinople. After General Denikin, the Commander in Chief of the Volunteer Army, departed for London, the British continued to maintain Russians in camps and communal living accommodations until June 1920. From that time on, Lloyd George's policy toward the Bolsheviks took a sharp turn, and instead of intervention, a policy that Britain had in place since 1918, negotiations began with Soviet Russia on the possibilities of trade relations and on ending aid to the White Movement. The communal living accommodations and camps that had been supported by the British were liquidated, and very soon after the first trade agreement was concluded with the Bolsheviks, a Soviet trade mission was established in Constantinople.

At about the same time, France recognized the government of General Wrangel in Crimea. Although France did not provide material support, it did ensure significant stability and protection during this unfortunate period. Italy, the third occupying power in Constantinople, remained neutral in Russian affairs.

I must add that France and Italy continued to offer aid to the Russian refugees, taking them under their authority on the Prince's Islands, while Britain continued to support the refugees on Cyprus, Malta, and Egypt for another year. The American Red Cross provided colossal aid to Russian refugees, as did other American charitable organizations in arranging free meals; providing the indigent refugees with food supplies, clothing, laundry, and shoes; and sending children and young students to Europe for education. This assistance deserves the profound gratitude of the Russian nation to America.

The allied intelligence and counter-intelligence organizations were quite useless, mainly because each country had its own agencies, but no unifying coordination, which was a serious flaw. There were the following counter-intelligence organizations: British, French, Italian, Greek, Russian, Polish, Japanese, Ukrainian, army, navy, and more. It was completely justifiable that the Russian poet Miatlev, who was in Constantinople, wrote in one of his poems, "and forty three counter-intelligence organizations encircle the new Babylon." Another reason for the unsatisfactory organization of investigative work was the composition of the staff. The heads of these foreign agencies were incompetent people, mostly rank-and-file officers with little knowledge of the details of the job, so unscrupulous people were chosen to be agents, mostly from among unreliable Russians, about whom I already spoke. All the work of the counter-intelligence organizations was directed against the oncoming of the Bolsheviks, but there was little action taken. This is not to mention the Russian, Ukrainian, Polish, and other counter-intelligence organizations, which were incompetent, and those of the occupying forces, which fought communism in a wait-and-see manner. If someone was found who had spread propaganda among the allied forces, the matter would be settled with an arrest and trial, but in the presence of clear evidence of communist origin, the matter was sometimes not pursued at all.

Owing to such conditions, the Bolshevik intelligence organizations and propagandists were able to operate easily, and communist propaganda in Constantinople increased progressively.

35

Last Days in Constantinople

SOFIA GLOBACHEVA

As I have mentioned, my husband was already working under the Commander in Chief of the White Army in Constantinople, General Lukomskii. My husband's job as the head of the passport bureau put him in charge of issuing passports, controlling transportation to Crimea, and processing information about Bolshevik propaganda and activities in the Middle East. Quite unexpectedly, my husband received orders appointing him director of the police department on the staff of the Commander in Chief in Crimea. I was really stunned by this order. After all the horrors that we experienced in Russia, and after my husband almost wound up under the Bolsheviks in Odessa, I shuddered at the thought that my husband would have to go back. To my delight, General Lukomskii wrote to the Commander in Chief, General Wrangel, and requested that it was necessary that my husband remain at his post, since he had no one to replace him. So, we stayed in Constantinople, and my husband continued to work, maintaining constant contact with the allies, who valued his information and advice, and who never gave anyone permission to leave without my husband's signature. As time passed, rumors began again from the south of Russia that the Bolsheviks were winning. Everyone was still hoping that General Wrangel would be able to hold on to at least some of the territory in the south, but then the news arrived of the complete evacuation of the entire White Army and fleet. The Bosporus became a sorrowful and shocking sight for us as the Russian warships and passenger ships came one after the other and dropped anchor. We did not want to believe that this was the end, but fighting outside of Russia was impossible.

My husband was busy day and night. The allies did not permit anyone to leave the ships, and so the Russians were dependent on them and not on themselves. My husband would send his subordinates, with approval from the

FIGURE 35.1. The Globachevs in Constantinople, 1920. Marinich collection.

allies, to get some generals and other officials off the ships. He got requests from the ships for bread, as most people on board had not had any for some time—all the bread there was had been distributed during the voyage. All my husband's subordinates were busy, so I volunteered to my husband that I would take a motor launch to the ships with bags of bread and buns. My husband agreed, and assigned an Armenian orderly to assist me. I took my daughter and a friend of hers, and we loaded a Greek launch with bags of bread and buns and motored from one ship to another. We were thrown a line with a hook, and we would attach the bags of bread for them to be hoisted onto the deck. Sometimes we would just throw bread up, and the soldiers on deck would catch it with their hands. Everyone's faces were sad, staring, and emaciated.

Several days later, my husband received a note from one of my brothers, a regimental commander, that he was on one of the ships. I took a launch, with permission, to get him. He was horribly emaciated, sad, and had aged, and was terribly worried about being separated from his family. His wife had visited him for several days at his camp at the front, and not knowing about the evacuation, had left the day before. She returned home with her young daughters to Simferopol, not far from Sevastopol. My brother was ordered to go to Sevastopol with his regiment and board ships. His sense of duty and honor would not allow him to leave his regiment to go after his family, so he sent an orderly to bring them to Sevastopol. The orderly was not able to get to them because all the roads were overflowing and blocked by troops and vehicles. My brother, who was now disembarked in Constantinople, could find no peace and was searching for ways to return to Russia to get his family out. He even wanted to sail back to Russia in a small Turkish boat, but we tried to convince him in every possible way that he would fall into Bolshevik hands before he reached his family. So, he stayed. My oldest brother and his cadet son were also on one of the ships that had initially sailed for Romania, but the refugees were not accepted there, and the ships had to turn around with all on board. My brothers stayed in Constantinople for some time, but then decided to leave. My oldest brother went in search of his family in Lithuania, and my other brother tried to make his way back close to Russia so that with luck he could get his family out of there. He wandered for three years, searching ceaselessly. He was in Poland, then in Lithuania, trying to get closer to Russia, and finally he wound up in Finland, where he settled in the home of an engineer from whom he also obtained a job.

My brother's family had moved to Petrograd from the south of Russia, and my brother began to work to get them to Finland. After several months, his efforts paid off. He got a telegram from his wife that she and the children were on their way. They were an ideal married couple and truly loved each other. Having received the telegram, my brother was elated and became very excited and could not sleep at all that night. In the morning he did not feel well, and he died of a heart attack, before seeing his loving family. His wife was sent a telegram telling her not to come to Finland. Without my brother there was nothing for her there, whereas she had a mother and a brother with whom she and the children lived in Petrograd. I learned all this from the engineer in whose house my brother lived. And he told me more—that my brother was buried with great honor because he was a holder of the Order of St. George. His funeral was held in the evening because every factory worker where he was employed wanted to attend the funeral, as my brother was so well liked. His family's tragedy continued even after his death. A few years later, his oldest daughter, having completed her secondary education and being engaged to an engineering student, caught a cold, and at seventeen years old died of galloping consumption on the day that her engagement was to be announced. I never heard any more news from the family, and all my letters to them and money that I sent went without reply.

The White Army's evacuation from Crimea was under the most nightmarish of conditions. The worst was the passengers' extraordinary tedium, even on the larger ships of the volunteer fleet. Some of these ships had up to 11,000 passengers and, if you add to that a lack of provisions, it becomes understandable what the Russian refugees experienced during the several days of their voyage.

While the entire Russian flotilla stopped at the port in Constantinople, all the Russian and foreign charitable organizations, and even some private individuals, distributed food, mainly bread, to the hungry refugees. The entire naval fleet and its complement of sailors were sent to the French colony of Bizerte in north Africa. The rest of the freight ships, after all the passengers and cargo were removed, were taken by the French for their use as compensation for their expenses in the transport and upkeep of the Russian army and civilian refugees. With the arrival of the White Army, Constantinople came alive and filled up with military uniforms of all kinds, making a strange picture of

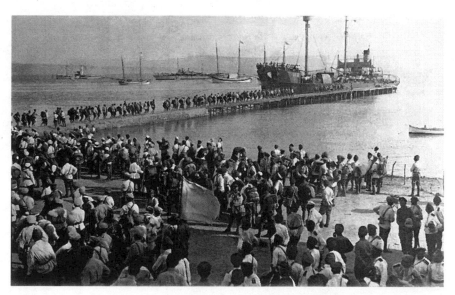

FIGURE 35.2. Evacuees boarding a ship, dates from 1919 to 1921. Royal Russia.

FIGURE 35.3. Baron General Peter Wrangel, the last Commander in Chief of the White Army. alchetron.com.

the city. Constantinople was conquered by the Russians, who had inundated every street in the city. Life was in a feverish full-swing.

The Commander in Chief, General Wrangel, maintained his residence on the yacht *Lukul* and only came to the embassy in Constantinople on business. The *Lukul* was anchored in the Bosporus quite far from the embassy. When the Italian ship *Adria* sank the *Lukul* due to an accidental or deliberate collision, General Wrangel had to move into the embassy. Investigation by port officials of the sinking of the *Lukul* did not uncover the reasons for the collision, but all the Russians believed the yacht was sunk by the Bolsheviks with the intent of killing the Commander in Chief, General Wrangel.

Not far from the embassy was a big field where a group of young students had settled, and since the weather in Constantinople was generally beautiful, they lived under the open sky where they slept and cooked. When it got colder they asked my husband to get them a tent. My husband turned to the Americans with this request, and they provided a huge tent in which the students lived the whole time they were in Constantinople. In the evenings

FIGURE 35.4. The ship *Constantinople* that brought the Globachevs to the United States. Wikimedia Commons.

we could hear their magnificent choral singing and melancholy melodies, and while I was on the embassy terrace listening to them, I felt pangs of longing for my homeland and the past.

The Russian Army began to disperse little by little, lacking any material or moral support, and the allies were preoccupied with the coming menace of Kemal Pasha. Turkey became an uneasy place, and Russians began leaving in droves for Serbia and Bulgaria. Those with money left for France and Italy. Many especially left for Serbia, where King Alexander treated the Russians very well. The Serbian king himself was educated in Russia at the Corps of Pages, and he loved Russia very much. The Russians were able to exchange the worthless money that they had from the southern Russian command for Serbian currency. The Russians lived very well in Serbia; almost everyone was able to get a government job, and others found work for themselves everywhere.

My husband stayed at his job until the last minute, and not only was he the chief of the passport bureau, but he was also the assistant to General Chertkov. When General Wrangel and his staff left Turkey, leaving the White

Army still in Constantinople, my husband decided to go to America. Having completed his duties, we left on the Greek ship *Constantinople* for New York, along with many other Russians. We spent an entire month traveling on this ship under the most horrible conditions. My daughter, my friend, her daughter, and I were given a small cabin, but all the men were put up in holds. We were fed disgusting food, even though all the ship's passengers had paid their own way. Fortunately, the weather was beautiful and the sea was calm. If there had been a storm, with such a mass of people and disgusting sanitary conditions, it would really have been horrible. During our voyage, the Russian cook on board, who was going to America with his wife and child, died suddenly and was buried at sea, which really depressed the passengers.

Everyone was saddened to part with the Turks and Constantinople. Although many Russians had lived poorly there in a material sense, nearly everyone retained fond memories of their life in Turkey. Our voyage finally came to an end as the Statue of Liberty appeared, as did the skyscrapers—the likes of which we had never seen. The ship stopped at Ellis Island, and after inspection sailed on to New York, where we arrived on September 30, 1923.

36

Waning Hopes

GENERAL GLOBACHEV

Evacuation of Crimea. Distribution of evacuees to other countries and camps. The fate of the fleet. Reorganization of authority and local Russian organizations. The liquidation commission. The transition to refugee status and flight from camps. Constantinople during the influx of Russian refugees. The Russian embassy and its security. The sinking of the "Lukul." The Commander in Chief General Wrangel.

All the Russians who left Crimea under the Commander in Chief were accepted under French protection and were assigned as follows: the Cossack units went to camps on the island of Lemnos and to a camp on Chatalgi on the Thracian shore of the Sea of Marmora. All the infantry units under General Kutepov, cavalry units under General Barbovich, and an artillery unit were assigned to the Gallipoli peninsula. Civilian personnel were assigned to camps in the environs around Constantinople and in the city itself, in barracks and in hostels. Thus were formed the large camps: St. Stefan, Lan', Karober, Seliame, Tuzla, Dolmabakhche, Halki, Buyuk, Terapia, and others. Twenty thousand were sent to Serbia via the port Kataro without even disembarking in Constantinople. About ten thousand went to Bulgaria through Varna, and one thousand went to Greece. Rumania refused to accept even a single person.

Based on what was said by the evacuees, the voyage from Crimea was under the most awful conditions. The worst was the incredible overcrowding, even on the larger ships of the Volunteer fleet. Some of the ships carried up to eleven thousand people. If you add to this the lack of provisions, it can certainly be understood what the Russian refugees endured during these several days. When the flotilla stopped at anchor in Constantinople, Russian and foreign charity organizations, and even individuals, brought provisions, mostly bread, to the hungry refugees.

The entire fleet, including the Russian sailors, was sent to the French colony in Africa, Bizerte. The rest of the commercial fleet, once it had disembarked passengers and unloaded its cargo, was taken over by the French as compensation for their expenses incurred in transporting and caring for the Russian army and civilian refugees. Only two vessels were temporarily left for use by the Russians; one was the steamship *Mikhail Alexandrovich*, and the other was the yacht *Lukul*, on which General Wrangel was staying.

The restructuring of the local Russian organizations and governmental authority began right after the assignment and relocation of the refugees. The Commander in Chief had laid down his title as head of southern Russia, and thus his government had to be reformed. At that point in time it was necessary only to keep the following administrations: the refugee bureau assigned to S.N. Il'yin; the finance bureau, at first assigned to Professor Bernardskii, but after his departure to A. I. Pilts; and finance control went to Savich. The military bureau was organized as follows: the Commander in Chief's staff was under General Shatilov, and the commission on the reduction of forces was under General Stavitskii. The position of the military representative to the Allied Command was abolished and replaced by a military agency, the head of which was General G. G. Chertkov. (The passport division, as before, was left under the military agent).

The largest was the refugee department, with its several bureaus: general, sanitation, nutrition, relief, and others. The Constantinople bureau initially coordinated all the refugee bureaus in the Balkans. At first this bureau had the largest personnel staff, but as refugees were resettled and resources diminished, the bureau gradually got smaller, and by January 1922 it was abolished. Its functions were picked up by the diplomatic representatives and consisted only in providing a little aid and support for the emigration of refugees to other countries.

Initially, the finance department was quite big too. Eventually it was reduced to only one finance agent, and when the Commander in Chief left for Serbia in February 1922, the Constantinople bureau was abolished, as was the Control Department.

In the beginning, the staff had abolished the entire quartermaster general bureau and left only the duty general, justice unit, military line unit, and information unit. Even this was reduced. Only two units remained: the operations/line unit and the information unit. From within these units the staff and Commander in Chief left for Sremski Karlovei in Serbia. The reduction in force commission, counting on operating for just three months, lasted for half a year.

The ships that came to Turkey carried not only the cash on hand of the government bank in foreign currency, but also a cargo of valuables that could be converted into money and help to fill the High Command's meager treasury. There were many claims by creditors for various orders and deliveries to Crimea that had to be satisfied in one way or another. All this was assigned to the commission on reduction in force with the cooperation of the finance and control bureaus. A special committee, the composition of which included representatives of the finance, control, and reduction in force commission, approved every expense. The outstanding debts were far greater than the cash on hand, so it was not possible to satisfy all the creditors; thus, for the most part, the finance committee affirmed its debts to the creditors and declared they would be paid once Russia was restored. Unfortunately, the finance committee did not come to this conclusion at the start, but had spent great sums satisfying contractors and speculators who made huge profits during the Civil War. The money would have been better spent on supporting the refugees.

At the same time that the Russians were disembarking and being relocated to camps, there was also a major exodus from the camps of refugees who wanted to be self sufficient in the city and who did not want to be part of the refugee army. Under such circumstances, the Commander in Chief gave them their freedom. Nobody was forced to stay in the army. What were these people striving for? Some felt inhibited by the routine of camp life and wanted to have jobs, others who had some savings got into trade and commerce, and quite a few who did not want to stay in Turkey, for whatever reasons, obtained visas and headed for other countries. The French, who had accepted the responsibility for evacuating and protecting the Russians at first, tried to keep the Russians from running off from the camps. In their attempt to resettle the refugees back into their original camps, they introduced many passport regulations and prohibitions. As an example: there were French patrols that checked Russians in the city for documents, detaining any who were suspect and sending them to an assembly area at the Sirkedja camp. These measures came to nothing, and the flight of the Russians from the camps continued. France subsequently relaxed its regime and began to look at the Russian exodus from the camps as a perfectly normal phenomenon. Even later, France's change in its policy regarding the Russian issue led it to assist the Bolsheviks in every way possible to disperse the Russian émigrés.

Constantinople presented a strange picture in these days—it was absolutely overrun by Russians who inundated the city's streets. Most of the refugees were homeless. They wandered about, looking for work; they sold the few belongings they had left from their homeland at markets and in the streets; and they slept at the entrances to the mosques or in bath houses. On Pera, near the Russian embassy, huge crowds of Russians would gather to sell their belongings and to sell Russian money, which was worth nothing at the time. The embassy courtyard and all the offices of the embassy were overcrowded with Russian refugees. Some were there for passports, and others for aid, but many had no business there and simply felt drawn to be on Russian territory. Within this mass of people were also those who could just as easily have stayed with the Reds; there would have been no threat for them in that because their ideologies were closer to that of the Bolsheviks, so it was surprising that they left Crimea. This latter element of society stole from the embassy, spread false rumors that any day now the embassy would be seized by the Bolsheviks, and after disturbing the public with this danger, they proposed that they could protect the embassy with the help of some secret organization. All this led to the need to provide order and security for the embassy by creating a security detachment and establishing the authority of its commandant. By order of the Commander in Chief, General Chekatovskii was appointed commandant and half a mounted guard squadron was assigned to protect the embassy. The same squadron guarded the Russian consulate and the Nikolaevskii military hospital. With the establishment of this security, some degree of order was achieved and ensured that neither the Bolsheviks nor any other sinister organization would seize the embassy. It must be said, however, that the mounted guard was not up to the task. Thefts continued, sometimes even with the help of the very same security guard. When mention was made that the mounted guard should be replaced by regular troops, one of the mounted guards, who was at his post in front of the gate to the Translators' building, threw a grenade to provoke a crisis. Although the grenade caused no harm to anyone, the rumor was spread that the Bolsheviks wanted to seize the embassy, which of course meant it would not be wise to replace the mounted guard, since they were trained in guarding the embassy. An inquiry was conducted, and it was determined that the Bolsheviks had nothing to do with the grenade explosion. The mounted guard was replaced by a regular army squadron, under which security was much improved.

The main building of the Russian embassy was packed. The embassy held: the diplomatic representative, his chancellory and his entire staff, the waiting room of the Commander in Chief and his personal secretary, the embassy church, and the embassy infirmary for all the wounded evacuees from Crimea. The translators' area was occupied by the military agency, passport bureau, and all the post-evacuation organizations and their personnel; moreover, this last group was packed with families, who occupied one room each, and single people, assigned to several individuals per room. Subsequently, when staff personnel left for Serbia aboard the *Alexander Mikhailovich*, the remaining staff of the High Command, even in its diminished number, overcrowded the translators' bureau even more.

The Commander in Chief had accommodations on the yacht *Lukul*, and came to the embassy only on official matters. The *Lukul* stood at anchor in

FIGURE 36.1. Alexander Vasilievich Krivoshein, assistant to General Wrangel for civilian affairs, General Peter Nikolaevich Wrangel, General Pavel Nikolaevich Shatilov, Chief of Staff to General Wrangel. Wikimedia Commons.

the Bosporus, quite far from the embassy, which created major problems in terms of efficiency in communication and reports.

Later, when the *Lukul* sank as a result of the Italian steamship *Adria* crashing into it, either intentionally or by accident, General Wrangel moved into the embassy. An inquiry conducted by the port authorities regarding the sinking of the *Lukul* did not come up with the true reason for the collision, but all the Russians believed the yacht was destroyed with Bolshevik backing, with the aim of killing Commander in Chief General Wrangel. General Wrangel accomplished a great deal; he got the army and civilians out of Crimea, thereby saving them from Bolshevik brutality. But the question was, what to do with the army? Everybody had the right to ask this question. What were the Commander in Chief's plans; what was his vision for the future? Each person, especially those who chose to stay in the army, awaited an answer. Everyone knew that General Wrangel wanted to save the army, come what may, but for what and when he would use the army, nobody knew and I think that Wrangel himself did not know. Wrangel did not have a definite plan. However, to sum up Wrangel's activities in Constantinople, his attention to the condition of the army in the various camps and his wish to improve the material conditions, along with the emigration of parts of the army to Serbia and Bulgaria, led people to think that Wrangel was carrying out a plan for some kind of future action in Russia. Thus, it is perfectly clear why the Bolsheviks who had run the Russian army out of Russia were alarmed, and from the start felt a threat from beyond the sea at the prospect of having to fight again over a piece of Russian territory. The population in southern Russia had already felt the weight of the Bolshevik regime and waited and looked across the sea with hope for this army beyond its borders. Alas, those hopes were not to be realized. Wrangel had no plans for future operations and, given the political situation, no foreign country wanted to help him enter into hostilities with the Bolsheviks to free Russia and to deal a crippling blow to communism as a world threat.

So, perhaps it is justifiable that there are those who reproached Wrangel for needlessly soothing the remnants of the army with vague hopes of a speedy return to Russia, instead of telling them that this time the cause was completely lost and that some kind of new ways were needed to free the homeland that was enslaved and had poured out its life blood.

END

K. I. Globachev
December 1922

Epilogue

VLADIMIR G. MARINICH

In July 1923 Globachev's position with the Russian Embassy in Constantinople was abolished, as were many other positions at the embassy. "In 1922 and 1923, 1,771 Russians went from Constantinople to France; 2,011 went from Constantinople to the United States."[1] The Globachevs considered several countries to which they might immigrate; they had visas to Bulgaria, France, the United States, and even Spain. Their decision to go to the United States was based on their assessment that it was there that they could survive the best. Globachev and his family left Constantinople in 1923 on the British ship *Constantinople*, arriving at Ellis Island on August 1, 1923. Their son Nicholas had left sometime earlier to study voice in Italy. He had an opera-quality bass-baritone voice. He joined them later in 1923 in New York, where he continued his lessons and performed in several concerts. For the next several years, Sofia, Konstantin, and their children rented rooms in a boarding house on St. Nicholas Avenue on the upper west side in Manhattan. They did this because they were somewhere between certain and hopeful that communism would be overthrown in Russia and that they would be returning home. For this reason Konstantin did not seek to make a career in the United States. As a matter of fact, he had several temporary jobs, including one mowing lawns in a cemetery, which he enjoyed because it was peaceful and quiet. He and Sofia even kept a suitcase filled with Tsarist paper money and stock certificates under their bed. As time went on it became clear that things would not change in Russia and that they would never return. Sofia and Konstantin became United States citizens in August 1929.

After the February and October Revolutions of 1917, and the Civil War between the Reds and Whites of 1918–1921, those who were part of, or loyal to the old regime, and who lived to flee, evacuated Russia as political refugees and scattered all over the world, often forming Russian enclaves, or "colonies," as some of these Russians referred to their communities. Paris was one such place with a large community of Russians; they had not only their own stores, restaurants, nightclubs, and churches, but also political organizations. One such organization was the Russian All-Military Union (*Russkii Obshche-Voenskii Soiuz*), often referred to by its initials, ROVS. The Grand Duke Nicholas (an uncle of Tsar Nicholas II), who had been the head of this émigré organization, died in 1929. General Peter Wrangel, who had been the last and most heroic of the White Russian leaders during the Civil War, took his place. When he too died in 1929, the rumors spread that Soviet agents had poisoned him. Such a possibility has to be considered, because ROVS was active in anti-Soviet propaganda, and in various other counter-revolutionary efforts in the hopes of bringing down the Soviet regime. A new leader was selected: ex-Tsarist cavalry commander, General Alexander Pavlovich Kutepov.

FIGURE 37.1. General Evgenii Karlovich Miller. Wikimedia Commons.

On January 26, 1930, he disappeared in Paris. It was generally concluded that he had been abducted and done away with by Soviet agents. His replacement was another Tsarist officer, Lieutenant General Evgenii Karlovich Miller. In an attempt to thwart the infiltration of Soviet agents and others who might harm it, the ROVS organization decided that a bureau had to be set up to deal specifically with intelligence and security issues. As chief of the Secret Political Bureau, Miller chose General Abram Mikhailovich Dragomirov who, in turn contacted Globachev. Dragomirov offered Globachev the job as his assistant. Under the circumstances, this meant that Globachev would really be in charge of the Bureau, since Dragomirov's entire military experience had been primarily as a line officer, with no experience in the area of security.

Globachev's daughter speculated on why her father was selected for this work, since there were other former Gendarme officers still around who were quite capable and competent. In her view, Martynov was somewhat of an intriguer

FIGURE 37.2. General Abram Mikhailovich Dragomirov. ww2awards.com.

and had been quite outspoken about some of the Tsarist leaders, especially his animosity toward Dzhunkovskii, which was no secret. Indeed, Martynov himself admitted to having had past personal difficulties. During the Civil War, Martynov had applied for a position with the White Movement, was not hired, and was told, "Your very name is odious."[2] Spiridovich was very capable, too, but he tended to have a bit of an abrasive personality, and there were still people who were troubled by his involvement in the Stolypin assassination. There was also Colonel Pavel Zavarzin, who had been the Chief of the Warsaw Okhrana, and later of the Moscow Okhrana. Of Zavarzin, Globachev's daughter knew only that he was a pleasant, gregarious man, and a great storyteller.

Globachev accepted Dragomirov's offer, and on August 18, 1930, Dragomirov sent his new assistant a check for $350 and a cover letter that stated that, regrettably, the ROVS could not afford more. The money was enough for two one-way tickets to France, second class; and so, Globachev and his wife left shortly for Paris. Their son Nicholas, their daughter Lydia, and her husband George had to pay their own way. Lydia had recently married George Marinich, who had been a young officer in the 9th Kazan Dragoon Regiment during World War I.

Dragomirov's letter mentions that Globachev's salary would be two thousand francs per month, and if members of Globachev's family could gain employment, life could be much easier for all of them. Dragomirov also states that knowledge of English could yield better jobs. His letter speaks of the difficulty of finding apartments in Paris. Finally, Dragomirov states that he would be willing to help Globachev get settled, although Dragomirov writes that he still fumbles about Paris and endures the bustling and nervous life of the city with difficulty.[3]

In 1930 Globachev accepted the offer to come to Paris and work as a deputy director of intelligence for ROVS. This para-military organization of Tsarist officers functioned to help White Russian émigrés and to gather intelligence on other Russian émigrés who may have been in the employ of Soviets and whose purpose was to infiltrate and disrupt ROVS. Over the years Globachev had maintained contact with former colleagues and émigré organizations.

It is estimated that the Russian population in France in the early 1930's "probably did not much exceed 120,000," and "[t]he capital and its surrounding districts certainly harboured more one-time subjects of Nicholas II than did any other region in France"[4] Further, some data show that in 1930 there were over 43,000 Russians living in the twenty arrondissements, with an additional 9,500 in the suburbs. It would be Globachev's job to keep track of all, or as many as possible, of these Russians. Once in Paris, Globachev threw himself into his work.

Life in Paris was not bad for Globachev and his family. The family's move to Paris in 1930 allowed it to escape the great depression that hit the United States in October of 1929. Globachev was now employed by ROVS, and his son-in-law was able to get work there also as a maintenance worker in the building that ROVS occupied, and as an occasional chauffer for ROVS personnel. The family rented a decent apartment at 8 rue du Commandant Leandri in the XVth Arrondisement. They even purchased two Whippet puppies, and named them Volga and Ural. Evenings were often spent at restaurants, with acquaintances, and weekends were spent sightseeing in Paris, visiting friends who lived in the suburbs, and going to the horse races. There were also the Sunday services at the Cathedral of St. Alexander Nevskii on the Rue Daru, followed by tea, pirozhki, and other familiar and favorite foods at the several Russian restaurants in the neighborhood of the church. Conversations often focused on current events, especially those happening in Russia, reflections of days gone by, who was to blame for what, and what some of the émigrés were doing these days.

While Globachev initiated intelligence and surveillance operations against Soviet agents and GPU operatives, there were other problems that affected

Figure 37.3. Outside the St. Alexander Nevskii Cathedral in Paris on a Sunday. From *The Homesick Million* by W. Chapin Huntington (Boston: The Stratford Company, 1933).

ROVS operations. One was that ROVS was running out of money, and another was some of the personality conflicts among the ROVS leadership. There were ex-Tsarist officers who held grudges against one another over some disagreement or slight during World War I, or during the Civil War following the revolution. This did not make things easy, even though Globachev was not involved in such squabbles.

Among the top echelon of leaders in ROVS were Miller, Dragomirov, General Fedor Fedorovich Abramov, General Pavel Alexeevich Kussonskii, Major-General Nikolai Vladimirovich Skoblin, General Pavel Nikolaevich Shatilov, and some others.

Some detailed information about ROVS can be found in Shatilov's memoirs, which are in the Bakhmeteff Archives of Columbia University. Shatilov had been a cavalry commander in the Tsar's army, and was Wrangel's Chief of Staff during the Civil War. His reputation as Wrangel's immediate subordinate was one of a capable officer, but prone to get involved in intrigues. He had antagonized some White general officers, and now they were senior members of ROVS. From Shatilov we learn that, beginning in the summer of 1930, Miller began to have weekly meetings with his senior staff. Shatilov states that from the outset "all these people . . . immediately demonstrated ill will toward me."[5] This perception was shared, at least in part, by others. Shatilov's relationship with Dragomirov was not good. Miller noticed that there seemed to be animosity between the two, and when he asked Shatilov about it, the latter did not know why Dragomirov harbored ill will toward him. Miller then confronted Dragomirov, who admitted there was a problem and said it went back to the Civil War, at which time Shatilov was responsible for keeping Dragomirov from getting an official position in Wrangel's government. Shatilov's antagonism apparently did not extend to Globachev, however.

Much of Globachev's intelligence work was keeping track of those Russian émigrés who either showed some suspicious side or wanted to join ROVS. In either case, ROVS needed to be watchful for Soviet operatives infiltrating the organization. A number of émigrés, wanting to join ROVS, claimed past positions in the Tsarist government or military and, since most records were lost, or certainly still in Soviet Russia and thus not available to ROVS, verifying the loyalty and reliability of many émigré applicants was a difficult chore.

In 1932, one such émigré, Pavel Timofeevich Gorgulov, shook the world. He had arrived in Paris and become known as someone who preached anticommunist rhetoric and a return of Russia to its glorious past. He did not seem to draw much attention, and when holding meetings he did not draw much of a crowd. It seemed that his presence in Paris was that of an eccentric, so Globachev "did not seem concerned and failed to warn the French police. A short while later Gorgulov assassinated the French President Paul Doumer."[6]

A recent historian, writing about the White Russian Army in exile, clearly sees Globachev as failing to recognize Gorgulov as dangerous, and, thus, not thwarting this major catastrophe.[7] Shatilov's view of this is different. Shatilov states that it is hard to blame Globachev, as he never had any corroborating information about Gorgulov, and often when there was corroborating information from informants, it was unreliable. It should also be pointed out that Globachev's operation consisted of just himself and one office-staff worker.[8]

As early as 1932, Globachev had been given information by an agent, who had received it from an OGPU informer, that a certain general who was very close to Miller was in the pay of the Bolsheviks. The informer had not named the general, but said that if he mentioned the name of the general, everyone would be thoroughly shocked. Globachev told Miller what he had learned, and Miller became very upset. He replied to the effect that he refused to believe such a thing about one of his colleagues. Thus, Globachev was unable to get Miller's support in attempting to locate the traitor.

In 1933, Abramov recommended that Globachev's operation should be discontinued and intelligence work be transferred to other personnel. Miller disagreed, stating that transferring Globachev's duties to another, who lacked Globachev's experience, was not the best decision.

By 1934, however, the financial condition of ROVS forced the organization to reduce its expenses and, therefore, its staff. By the early summer of 1934, the Secret Political Bureau was disbanded. General Dragomirov, who was its head, left for Yugoslavia, and Globachev was given notice. During their last meeting, Globachev asked Miller how the work of security and intelligence gathering would continue. Miller answered that he would be taking on those functions himself.[9]

The entire Globachev family returned to the United States in mid-1934 on the popular French ship, *Ile de France*. Globachev would have to start anew in seeking employment in the States. He was able to use other skills. Even in his youth Globachev was talented. He was good at playing the accordion, and was quite an accomplished artist. During his years of service in the Tsar's government, he devoted his few hours of leisure to oil painting. He particularly enjoyed painting landscapes and portraits. So, upon his return to the United States, it was a fortunate happenstance that he was able to get a job as a commercial artist.

Sergei Sergeevich Krushinskii, a former Tsarist officer himself, was the owner and operator of a small company that produced batik art on scarves and clothes. Krushinskii, as other Russians who became somewhat successful in this new land, gave employment preferences to his compatriots.

By now the Globachev family had already increased. Their daughter Lydia had given birth to her first son, Oleg, in Paris several months before their return to the United States. Thus, the choice of living in a boarding house and simply occupying rooms, as they had in the mid- and late 1920s, was no longer practical. They rented an apartment on the upper west side of Manhattan in New York City. This section of the city was a Russian enclave. Not only did a number of Russian families live within a twenty-block area, there were also two Russian delicatessens that carried a full range of foods that Russians bought for "zakuski." As Russian Orthodox Easter approached, these stores also made sure that Kulich and Paskha were available. Also nearby were a Russian pharmacist and an east European butcher who spoke Russian. The neighborhood Russian Orthodox Church of the Holy Father was hardly a church in the usual sense. It was a large room in the unfinished basement of an apartment building. The iconostasis could not reach the ceiling, as the building's water and heating pipes were in the way. The congregation was small, but faithfully attended services, and the priest was Alexander Krassnaumov, a former Tsarist officer.

A local public library, on 145th Street, between Broadway and Amsterdam Avenue, had a decent Russian collection, and on Saturday mornings lessons were offered to pre-teen and teenage first-generation Russian Americans in reading and writing in Russian. There was also religious instruction (Zakon Bozhi). The instructors were most often Russian Tsarist émigrés.

This little Russian colony consisted mostly of ex-officers, Tsarist government officials, and individuals who had been successful merchants and businessmen in Russia. They all saw themselves as members of the intelligentsia, and most of them were bilingual, and some even trilingual. Within the Globachev family, Konstantin spoke French, and Sofia was fluent in French, German, and Polish. Their daughter and son, Lydia and Nicholas, were fluent in French and German. Lydia's husband, George Marinich, was fluent in Ukrainian and Serbian. They were all fluent and literate in their native Russian, but with the exception of Lydia, they spoke English badly.

Globachev enjoyed his employment as a commercial artist, and, in the evenings at home, he continued his landscape and portrait painting, except now he worked exclusively in watercolor and pastels. He liked chess and working on picture puzzles. About once a week he and his son-in-law would get together with acquaintances to play bridge. Globachev was a good bridge player. He also enjoyed going to the movies, which he tried to do at least once a week.

Sofia had a number of acquaintances and friends; most were Russian ladies of her generation and background, educated and cultured. But she also had a close acquaintanceship with a German couple by the name of Hiber. This was a German émigré couple that had left Germany after the end of World War I and lived a few city blocks from the Globachevs. They were particularly delighted to be able to converse with Sofia in German. Everyone

FIGURE 37.4. Samples of Globachev's watercolors. Marinich collection.

in the household was employed except for Sofia, who the family had decided should stay home and care for the household. They all pooled their money to take care of household expenses, and each took an allowance for personal expenses and entertainment, including Sofia.

The entire family lived together in an apartment in New York City. Konstantin Ivanovich had a job as a commercial artist, Sofia kept the house and cooked for the family, and their children both worked outside the home. By the end of 1936, Sophia had two grandsons to take care of and, as they grew, she taught them to speak, read, and write Russian.

Globachev maintained contact with the ROVS operation in Paris, advising and consulting with General Miller and his assistant, Kussonskii, on various matters pertaining to ROVS activities. ROVS was a thorn in the Soviet's side, and it is possible that Globachev's continuing contact with ROVS was an irritation to the Soviets. What follows comes from Globachev's daughter Lydia, who recounted this incident.

Her father, as mentioned, was working as a commercial artist. During a coffee break at work in the early spring of 1935, the office boy at the studio went for coffee. This young Hispanic man was an ardent communist, according to Globachev's recounting of the event, who often and openly expressed his views. On this particular day, he brought coffee for everyone, and passed the cups around. As soon as Globachev finished his coffee he doubled up with severe cramps and literally rolled on the floor in pain. His coworkers rushed to him and began to assist and comfort him as best they could. In the confusion and concern for the agonized general, nobody noticed the young Hispanic man. He disappeared that day from work and was not seen again, either at his apartment or in the neighborhood. No one could ever locate him.

Globachev was brought home, and his condition had worsened. The doctor who was summoned was unable to determine the cause of the illness. As a long shot, the doctor administered a powerful dose of castor oil, which caused violent nausea and a respiratory reaction, and also saved Globachev's life. His convalescence took over two months, most of which time he was too weak to leave his bed. He did recover and returned to work. He was sixty-five years old, and his close brush with death did not diminish his vitality or his mental alertness. He continued to correspond with Paris, and it was only after the abduction of General Miller in 1937 that contact between the general and ROVS petered out. However, even in one of Globachev's last letters to Kussonskii, he voices his disappointment that Miller, who had been informed by an agent that Skoblin was a Soviet plant in ROVS, had never relayed this information to Globachev. Globachev speculated that, had he known, perhaps Miller's abduction could have been prevented.[10]

One of the last references to Globachev's work for ROVS comes from Kussonskii, who states, "fairness requires me to say that Globachev's intelligence documents, which I still use, are without a doubt valuable, insofar as he was able to operate under his given conditions and budget."[11]

FIGURE 37.5. The last portrait photo of the General, ca. 1940. Marinich collection.

On December 1, 1941, Globachev woke up at about five in the morning complaining of a severe headache. He went to the dining room and sat down at the table. He mentioned to his wife that he just was not feeling well. Finishing that statement, he slumped over dead. He was seventy-one years old. His funeral was held in the Russian cathedral in the Bronx, with Archbishop Vitalii conducting the service. Globachev's coffin was draped with the Russian national flag. There were no hyacinths at his funeral. He was buried in the Russian Orthodox section of the Rutherford, New Jersey, cemetery.

Sofia Nikolaevna outlived the general by nine years. His death was a particular shock to her, as he had been in good health for the previous several years. In her remaining years, Sofia Nikolaevna continued to be a member of the Russian Orthodox Church, but she explored other denominations of Christianity, and she also formed some new personal acquaintances, especially with a woman whose last name was Tarasenko, who was an evangelical Baptist. Sofia Nikolaevna also studied Christian Science and would go to their local reading room in New York City for discussions. Likely she was looking for some kind of meaning and answers.

FIGURE 37.6. Sofia Nikolaevna Globacheva in 1947. Marinich collection.

Sofia died of cancer on November 3, 1950, at the age of seventy-five. Her funeral was at the Russian Church of the Holy Father in New York City, with Father Alexander Krassnaumov presiding. She is buried next to her husband in the small Russian Orthodox section of a cemetery in New Jersey. Their son Nicholas died in 1972, at the age of sixty-nine. He had spent most of his adult life employed by the publishing company Charles Scribner's and Sons, where he was in charge of the stock room. His rich bass singing voice allowed him to perform in local concerts in the New York area. Lydia, Globachev's daughter, spent most of her working life in the United States as a supervisor in various perfumeries, such as Prince Matchabelli and Schiaparelli. She died in 1997 at the age of ninety-six.

Appendix A

Globachev Timeline

April 24, 1870	Born into a family of hereditary nobility in Ekaterino-slav. Educated at the Polotsk Cadet Academy.
1875	Sofia Nikolaevna Popova born in Warsaw.
1890	Completed the Pavlovsk Military Academy and began his military career as a junior lieutenant in the Keksholm Life-Guards Infantry Regiment stationed in Warsaw. He continued his education in 1890 at the Nikolaevskii General Staff Academy in St. Petersburg, after which he returned to his regiment.
1897	Temporary assignment to St. Petersburg to be part of the greeting of the Austrian Emperor Franz Joseph, who was the honorary commander of the Keksholm Regiment. Globachev received a commendation medal.
January 1898	Marries Sofia Nikolaevna Popova.
May 1, 1899	Appointed staff officer of the regimental court.
September 25, 1900	Appointed head of the regimental training command. Shortly thereafter promoted to Captain.
February 1903	Applied to transfer to the Special Corps of Gendarmes.
September 23, 1903	Transferred to the Special Corps of Gendarmes with the rank of Captain.

September 30, 1903   Appointed Adjutant to the Petrokovsk Province Gen-
                      darme Administration.

May 29, 1904   Transferred to Grodinsk Province Gendarme Adminis-
                      tration headquartered in Bialystok, and appointed head
                      of the Okhrana.

September 5, 1905   Appointed head of the Lodz and Lassk region's Gen-
                      darme Administration.

April 2, 1906   Promoted to the rank of Lieutenant Colonel.

April 22, 1907   Awarded the St. Vladimir Cross, fourth degree, for
                      meritorious service.

December 29, 1909   Appointed head of the Warsaw Okhrana.

April 18, 1910   Promoted to the rank of Colonel.

November 20, 1912   Assigned as head of the Nizhni Novgorod Provincial
                      Gendarme Administration.

April 14, 1913   Awarded the St. Vladimir Cross, third degree, for meri-
                      torious service.

February 1, 1914   Appointed head of the Sevastopol Gendarme
                      Administration.

March 1, 1915   Appointed head of the Petrograd Okhrana.

January 1916   Promoted to the rank of Major General.

March–Nov, 1917   Under arrest.

Early 1918   Worked in the anti-Bolshevik underground.

Summer 1918   Flight from Petrograd to Kiev.

1919   Various jobs within the White Movement; Rostov,
                      Odessa.

1920–1923	Evacuation to Constantinople. Appointed head of passport control and intelligence at the Russian Embassy in Constantinople.
1923–1930	Emigrated with family to the United States. Worked several menial jobs in New York.
1930–1934	Moved to Paris on invitation to be employed by ROVS to be in charge of counter-intelligence.
1934–1941	Returned to New York and worked as a commercial artist specializing in batik.
December 1, 1941	Died in New York at the age of 71.
November 3, 1950	Sofia Nikolaevna Globacheva died at age 75 in New York.

Appendix B

Globachev's Transfer to Nizhni Novgorod

Globacheva's statement about her husband's appointment as Chief of the Gendarme Administration in Nizhni Novgorod is accurate, but it was not a promotional transfer for him. There was more behind his transfer from Warsaw to this city.

Globachev's career in the Corps of Gendarmes had progressed nicely. His leadership while in Bialystok, followed by his appointment to head the Lodz office, was recognized in St. Petersburg, and he was appointed to head the Warsaw Okhrana in December 1909, just six years after his transfer to the Corps of Gendarmes from his infantry regiment. This was a promotional appointment. The three most responsible and prestigious security offices in the empire were Moscow, St. Petersburg, and Warsaw. Within four months of his appointment, Globachev was promoted to the rank of full colonel.

Globachev's transfer to Warsaw happened at the same time as the Department of Police was conducting a major investigation and review of the personnel of all the offices involved in political investigation that came under the supervision of the Vice Director of the Department, who at this time was Sergei Evlampovich Vissarionov. Born in 1867, Vissarionov was university educated in law, and between 1889 and 1908 he held various positions within the judicial system.

The review that Vissarionov embarked upon was quite in depth. Not only were there the fairly routine matters to be looked at, such as the education of employees, their debts, family situations, knowledge of departmental rules and regulations, and so on, but also whether the employee who was responsible for investigations knew the history of revolutionary movements and revolutionary groups within the empire. A major matter of review was to determine the number of secret agents these employees had personally brought into the system and with what parties these recruits were affiliated.

In the spring of 1910 the Warsaw Okhrana operations were reviewed, and the result was documented in a report that pointed to several deficiencies in the operation of the Warsaw office. Some of the criticism was that Globachev had met with only eleven of thirty-seven agents and that secret agents were under the supervision of two of Globachev's subordinate officers. Globachev concurred with the report, but as he had been on the job for only five months, the report acknowledged that fact and scheduled a second review for some months later. The second review was conducted in February 1911, and it was reported that over the year that Globachev had now been in office he was unable to turn things around. The report stated that the operation of the secret agents was weak, that Globachev was slack as a leader, and some of his subordinates criticized him as lacking energy, being too soft, and not interested in his work.

Vissarionov's system-wide review led to fourteen Chiefs of Gendarme Administrations to be fired, among which were the heads of Moscow, Nizhni Novgorod, Smolensk, Riazan, Minsk, Kherson, and other security offices. Globachev was not among those fired. While the negative evaluation he had received was serious, he had very strong backing from the Governor General for Poland, General M. Kaznakov, and from the general's deputy for police matters, Lieutenant General Lev Karlovich Utgof. The latter not only questioned some of Vissarionov's criticisms, but took the offensive and wrote directly to the Director of the Department of Police, who at that time was Stepan Petrovich Beletskii. Utgof recommended that Globachev be awarded a decoration as soon as possible, and he reminded Beletskii of Globachev's promotion to the rank of colonel in 1910 for meritorious service. Utgof went on: "[S]ince Colonel Globachev carries an excessively difficult responsibility for the Security Bureau (of Warsaw) and for the entire region, I consider the award of a decoration not only for his service but as a necessary incentive to a person who is heavily burdened in his work."[1]

Vissarionov's review of security offices and operations was followed with memos and orders to the various offices to tighten their operations, and particularly to increase the recruitment of secret agents. This produced an interesting result. Some security chiefs, having experienced this system-wide review and wanting to avoid any further inquiries and investigations, recruited friends, local clerks, old people, and others, just to increase the numbers. Globachev did not do this.[2]

The Department of Police decided to transfer Globachev to another post. Initially, a recommendation was made in June 1912 to assign him as head of the Gendarme Administration in Yaroslavl,[3] but several months later, in November, this was changed, and Globachev was transferred from Warsaw to Nizhni Novgorod to be chief of the Regional Gendarme Administration.[4] His transfer from Warsaw may have had more to it than the negative evaluation he had received. He had been in Poland for a long time, and it might have been time for a change.[5] Thus, toward the end of 1912 Globachev took his new post. In the United States, Woodrow Wilson had just been elected President.

Nizhni Novgorod was a major commercial, industrial, and transportation center at the confluence of the Oka and Volga Rivers. Like so many other cities in Russia, it had its ancient fortress, its Kremlin, looking over the river. A very important institution of the city was its market, and especially the summer trade fair that brought tradesmen from as far away as Central Asia in the east and Europe to the west. This made the Gendarme Administration a key government agency. The year 1913 was the 300th anniversary of the House of Romanov, and Nizhni Novgorod was on the Tsar's itinerary of touring major Russian cities. This meant that the Gendarme Administration had the added task of coordinating security operations even more than usual with the local constabulary of the city, with the Tsar's personal security, and with the Chief of Staff of the Corps of Gendarmes, who was responsible for railway security. It must also be mentioned that as part of the anniversary celebrations, the Tsar amnestied many political prisoners, which increased the city's Gendarme Administration workload.

Upon his arrival in Nizhni Novgorod, Globachev immediately asserted his authority. Documents of the Moscow regional Okhrana (within which Nizhni Novgorod fell) showed that Globachev quickly got to know his subordinates and local gendarmes, and his reports to his superiors demonstrate his activity and grasp of the region's revolutionary parties and the mood of the population.

Preparations for the Tsar's stop in Nizhni Novgorod in May included an inspection visit in March by General Vladimir Fedorovich Dzhunkovskii, who was the Assistant Minister of the Interior for political matters. He was, in effect, in charge of all security issues. His inspection visit included meetings with the governor and various other heads of local government. One of those who he met was Globachev. Dzhunkovskii's assessment of the city's gendarme administration was that "it was organized in an excellent manner, thanks to Colonel Globachev, who was in every way an honest and irreproachable officer.[6] He further comments on Globachev: "He impressed me greatly and that was fully confirmed as I got to know him better. He was an outstanding officer in every way, he understood fully investigative matters; he was calm, he had a gentle disposition, honest, modest, and did not try to stand out. I later promoted him to the responsible position of Chief of the St. Petersburg Okhrana, a position he held until the very revolution. When I met him for the last time in 1918, this was still the honest and noble person that I had known before."[7]

Globachev's relationship with his superiors in St. Petersburg, who were now a different set of persons, was not only back on track but was also one in which he was trusted and respected. He was doing his job well in Nizhni Novgorod, although his wife was not enamored with the city.

Notes

Introduction

1. Peregudova, Z. I. (Ed.) *Pravda o Russkoi Revolutsii*. Moscow: Rosspen, 2009, pp. 5–8.

Chapter 2

1. Roman Globachev to V. Marinich (emails), July 14, 2011, and August 9, 2011.

Chapter 3

1. Globacheva does not explicitly state that the ten were executed, but they most likely were.

Chapter 4

1. Memo Beletskii to Martynov, November 28, 1913. GARF f.102.00.
2. Idem.
3. Dzhunkovskii memo to Martynov, December 6, 1913. GARF f. 102.00.
4. www.australiarussia.com

Chapter 16

1. Blok, Alexander A. *Poslednie Dni Imperatorskoi Vlasti*. Moscow; Progres Pleiada, 2012, p. 16.
2. Spiridovich, A. *Velikaia Voina I Fevral'skaia Revolutsia 1914–1917*. New York, 1960. Vol. 3, p. 79.

3. GARF, f. 1788, op.1 d.74. II, pp. 34–35.

4. Peregudova, *Pravda,* pp. 31–39.

5. Spiridovich, A. I. *Velikaia Voina i Fevral'skaia Revolutsia, 1914–1917, Tom 1.* New York; All Slavic Publishing House, 1960, p. 184.

6. Peregudova, Z. I., and J. Daly. Introduction to memoirs of K. I. Globachev and S. N. Globacheva.

7. Cited in Martynov, A. P. *Moia Sluzhba v Otdel'nom Korpuse Zhandarmov: Vospominaniia.* Edited by Richard Wraga. Stanford, CA: Hoover Institution Press, 1972, p. 315.

8. Kolokolov, Boris. *Zhandarm s Tsarem v Golove.* Moscow: Molodaia Gvardia, 2009, p. 451.

9. Globachev's promotion to head the Department of Police was unusual, but not unheard of. Prior to Vasiliev, there was General Klimovich, "the first and only gendarme officer to head the Police Department," from Jonathan Daly's *The Watchful State.* DeKalb: Northern Illinois University Press, 2004, p. 184.

10. Paleologue, Maurice. *An Ambassador's Memoirs.* New York: Geo. Doran, Co., 1925, Vol. 1, p.243.

11. Trotsky, Leon. *The History of the Russian Revolution,* Vol. 2. New York: Simon and Schuster, 1932, p. 108.

Chapter 23

1. Kolokolov, Boris. *Zhandarm s Tsarem v Golove.* Moscow; Molodaia Gvardia, 2009. p. 494.

Chapter 28

1. The modern name of Halki Island is Heybeliada.

Chapter 33

1. The modern name for Prinkipo is Buyukada.
2. The modern name for Antigone is Burgazada.
3. The modern name for Proti is Kinaliada.

Chapter 34

1. The new Commander in Chief, Wrangell, lamented, "Our badly organized police and counter-intelligence systems are a great help to the Bolshevist agitators in their subversive work behind-the-lines." Wrangell, General Baron Peter N. *Always with Honor.* New York: Robert Speller & Sons, 1957, p. 113.

Chapter 37

1. Hassell, James E. "Russian Refugees in France and the United States between the World Wars." *Transactions of the American Philosophical Society,* Vol. 8, Part 7, 1991.

2. Martynov, A. P. *Moia Sluzhba v Otdel'nom Korpuse Zhandarmov.* Stanford, CA: Stanford University Press, 1972, p. 53.

3. Letter, Dragomirov to Globachev, 18 August, 1930.

4. Johnston, Robert H. "New Mecca, New Babylon," *Paris and the Russian Exiles, 1920–1945.* Montreal: McGill-Queen's University Press, 1988, p. 25.

5. Shatilov, Pavel Nikolaevich, *Memoirs.* Bakhmeteff Archives, Columbia University, New York, Box 9, 10, p. 1736.

6. Robinson, P. *The White Russian Army in Exile 1920–1941.* Oxford, 2002, p. 162.

7. Idem.

8. Shatilov, *Memoirs*, p. 1755.

9. Letter, Globachev to Kussonski, November 3, 1937.

10. Idem.

11. Letter, Kussonskii to Abramov, February 22, 1937

Appendix B

1. Peregudova, Z. I. (Ed.) *Pravda*, p. 27.

2. Idem.

3. Memorandum from S. Beletskii to V. A. Tolmachev. GARF f. 102.00, June 11, 1912.

4. Memorandum from S. Beletskii to D. K. Gershel'man. GARF, f.102, November 22, 1912.

5. Ibid., p. 28.

6. Dzhunkovskii, V. F. *Vospominania.* Vol. 2. Moscow, 1997, p. 218.

7. Ibid., p. 169.

Glosssary

Admiralty. The headquarters of the Russian navy. The Admiralty Building was in St. Petersburg (Petrograd).

Bolshevik. The derivation of the word is from the Russian *bol'shinstvo*, meaning "majority." The Bolsheviks were a faction within the Marxist Russian Social Democratic Workers' Party, the RSDWP (in some sources the party is named the Russian Social Democratic Labor Party, the RSDLP). The Bolsheviks won a series of issues at the Second Party Congress in 1903; hence they became the majority. The opposition became known as the Mensheviks, from the Russian word *men'shinstvo*, meaning minority.

Central War Industry Committee (CWIC). The role of this committee was to organize and coordinate local War Industry Committees in providing arms and munitions to the military. The Central Committee was responsible for the management of distribution of money, contracts, and materials to support the war effort.

Cheka. Acronym for the Soviet Extraordinary Commission (*chrezvychainaia komissiia*) established in December 1917, whose function was to combat counterrevolution and other forms of dissent.

Corps of Gendarmes. The official name was Special Corps of Gendarmes. Army officers who had transferred from their regiments administered the Corps. The Chief of Staff was usually a major general, and the commander of the Corps was the Assistant Minister of the Interior for Political Affairs. The functions of the Corps were the maintenance of state security, railway security, security of the royal family during their travels, public safety, riot control, investigation of political crimes, as well as working with local police when necessary.

Dacha. A dacha was a summer residence other than the main residence of a person. It was often in the country and away from the city.

Department of Police. This department reported directly to the Minister of the Interior. With few exceptions, the Directors of the Department of Police were civilian men trained in law and with experience in judicial areas. The functions of the Department were to coordinate and supervise the operations of the Gendarme Administrations and Okhrana Bureaus.

Durnovo's Dacha. Following the February Revolution, anarchists and revolutionaries seized the dacha of P. Durnovo, who had been the Governor General of Moscow in 1905. This villa was a symbolic target for the revolutionaries. The villa was converted into a "house of rest" for the people.

Entente. This term refers to the Triple Entente, which was an alliance between Great Britain, France, and Russia. Its purpose was to counter the Triple Alliance of Germany, the Austro-Hungarian Empire, and Italy. By 1919, references to the Entente by Globachev meant Great Britain and France.

Extraordinary Commission of Inquiry for the Investigation of Illegal Acts by Ministers and Other Responsible Persons of the Tsarist Regime. As the name states, this commission was established in August 1917 to investigate possible illegal acts of the tsarist regime. This commission should not be confused with the Soviet Cheka.

Gatchina. A town approximately thirty miles south of Petrograd that was the site of one of the royal family's palace and parkland/hunting grounds.

Hetman. Originally this was the title of an elected Cossack military or village chieftain. During the Civil War the title applied to the head of the Ukrainian government of Pavel (Pavlo) Skoropadkii.

Kadet Party. Acronym for the Constitutional Democratic Party. During the Russian Revolution of 1905 the Russian historian, Paul Miliukov, founded the Constitutional Democratic Party and was its leader in the State Duma. Members of the Kadet Party were mostly middle class professionals and intellectuals. Following the February Revolution, Miliukov was Foreign Minister in the Provisional Government.

Kronstadt. A naval base about twenty miles west of Petrograd and the headquarters of Russia's Baltic Fleet. During the February Revolution, the sailors of Kronstadt rebelled against their officers killing a number of them.

Maliuta Skuratov. This is a reference to the sixteenth-century henchman of Ivan the Terrible, who was infamous in history for his oppressive and cruel execution of Ivan's orders.

Menshevik. The derivation of the word is from the Russian, *men'shinstvo,* meaning minority. Mensheviks were a faction within the Marxist Russian Social Democratic Workers' Party, the RSDWP (in some sources the party is named the Russian Social Democratic Labor Party, the RSDLP). The leader of this faction, Martov, lost in a disagreement over membership to Lenin at the Second Party Congress in 1903, hence this faction became known as the minority.

Mogilev. During World War I Mogilev was the staff headquarters of the Russian Army's high command. Upon Nicholas II's assumption as Commander in Chief, he spent much time there. Mogilev, which today is in Belarus, was over three hundred miles south of Petrograd.

Octobrist Party. Following the January 1905 revolution, the Octobrist Party was established in October 1905 following the publication of the October manifesto, hat was a document signed by Nicholas II giving some limited civil rights to the population. The Octobrists were led by Rodzianko, a leader in the Duma, and Guchkov, a Moscow banker. The party was generally conservative and influenced by landholders and capitalists.

Okhrana. This word is a noun that means security. It was not used in Tsarist times as a designation for the institution. Modern English authors use it to designate the agency. The official title of the agency was "Bureau for Public Security, Safety, and Order in Petrograd." There were three major offices of this agency, Petrograd, Moscow, and Warsaw. The majority of the Chiefs of the Okhrana offices were military men who came from the Special Corps of Gendarmes.

Old Believer. A faction of the Russian Orthodox Church in the mid 1600s that split with Patriarch Nikon, who introduced liturgical and ritual reforms to have the Russian Church more in line with the Greek Church. This group continues to this day

OSVAG. Acronym for Osvedomittel'no-Agitatsionnoe Otdelenie (Bureau for Surveillance and Agitation). A civilian propaganda bureau of the Volunteer Army, established in late 1918 during the command of General Denikin, whose purpose was to operate in areas held by the Volunteer Army.

Pale of Settlement. This was an area of over 450,000 square miles within which Jews were required to live by law. The area stretched from Crimea in the south, almost to Riga in the north. It stretched from the provinces of Chernigov, and Ekaterinoslav in the east to what is now Belarus in the west. Even within the pale there were cities prohibited for Jews to live, such as Kiev and Sevastopol. Following the February Revolution, the Provisional Government abolished the Pale.

Petrograd. The original name of the capital, from its founding in 1704 until 1914 was St. Petersburg. With the start of World War I, having the capital's name with a German suffix, "burg," was unacceptable. The name of the capital was Russified. In the Soviet period the name of the city was Leningrad, and following the collapse of the Soviet Union the name was changed back to St. Petersburg.

Progressive Bloc. This was a coalition of several parties in the Fourth Duma that was organized to seek reforms from the Tsar. Several of the parties involved were the Kadets, Octobrists, and some individual representatives in the Duma.

Provisional Government. Following the turmoil of the February Revolution and the abdication of Nicholas II, senior leaders of the Duma formed a temporary government whose function was to establish order until free elections could be held to form a Russian Constituent Assembly, thereby forming a stable republic. The Provisional Government existed from the beginning of March 1917 until the end of October 1917 when the Bolsheviks overthrew it.

ROVS. Abbreviation for *Russkii Obshchevoinskii Soyuz*. This organization's title has been translated into English in slightly different ways (Russian All-Military Association, Russian General Military Association, and Russian Para-Military Association). ROVS was established in the late 1920s under the leadership of the Grand Duke, Nikolai Nikolaevich. Its function was to support White Russian refugees, but also to maintain information on Soviet infiltrators into the organization, and to promote counter Soviet activities. ROVS headquarters were in Paris. ROVS activities continued up to World War II.

Social Democrats (SDs). The full name was the Russian Social-Democratic Workers' Party that was the predecessor of the Communist Party of the Soviet Union. By 1903 there were two opposing factions within the party, the Bolsheviks and the Mensheviks.

Socialist Revolutionaries (SRs). The full name was the Russian Socialist Revolutionary Party. The ideology of the Party was that a true revolution would require the uprising of peasants, workers, and liberal to radical thinking intelligentsia. In the early 1900s the Party employed terrorism as a means of destabilizing the government. By the beginning of World War I the Party split between those members who opposed the war and those who supported it. A number of SRs held leadership positions in the Provisional Government.

Soviet of Workers' and Soldiers' Deputies. This was a council during the period March through October 1917 that was a rival and in a power struggle with the Provisional Government. Most of the members of the Soviet were socialists, Mensheviks, and Socialist Revolutionaries.

Spala. Nicholas II's hunting lodge in central Poland. It is approximately between thirty and forty miles from Lodz. In addition to the Tsar's lodge there were also guest accommodations for government officials on vacation and foreign visitors.

Special Corps of Gendarmes. This organization is often identified also as the Separate Corps of Gendarmes in historical literature. This was the political police of the Russian Empire. It was organizationally under the Ministry of the Interior, and its commander was the Deputy Minister of the Interior for Political Matters. Its functions were severalfold: investigating political crimes, security of borders and railroads, and cooperating with other police and investigative agencies. Most of its personnel entered this service from the army.

State Council. This institution was somewhat comparable to the upper house in a parliamentary system. The Council could only make recommendations to the Tsar. There were one hundred members in the Council, half of who were appointed by the Tsar, as was the Chairman of the Council, and the other half through elections. The Council was dissolved after the February Revolution.

State Duma. This was the "lower house" of a system that approximated a parliamentary one. This was a legislative body whose actual authority was very limited. The Tsar could dissolve the Duma if the Duma's recommendations and attempts at influence were perceived as a threat to the autocracy. Between 1905 and 1917 there were four Dumas; the first two were dissolved by the Nicholas II, and the third was reorganized to be subservient to the Tsar. It lasted its five-year term. The fourth Duma was dissolved by the Provisional Government.

Trudoviks. This was a faction within the Socialist Revolutionary Party that broke away from the party due to their more moderate views.

Tsarskoe Selo. The translation is "Tsar's Village." This was the summer and preferred year-long residence of Nicholas II and his family, about fifteen miles from Petrograd. It was a compound of several palaces. The royal family lived in the Alexander Palace. The compound is most famous for the Catherine Palace.

Union of Republican Officers. A small group of socialist officers organized to support the Soviet. The group's major intent was to prevent the restoration of the monarchy.

Union of Russian People. A nationalist, pro-monarchy party that was established following the Revolution of 1905. Its function was to be a counter-revolutionary influence.

Union of Zemstvos and Cities. An organization established upon the start of World War I whose function was to assist the Russian army with the provision of supplies, transportation, and assistance to wounded soldiers and displaced persons in war zones.

Volunteer Army. This was the Russian counterrevolution army established late in 1917 to combat the Bolsheviks. It was composed mostly of tsarist officers. Also called the White Army.

White Army. Another name for the Volunteer Army.

White Movement. A generalized term describing the efforts of former senior tsarist officers to create an army and a government to counter the advances of Bolshevik power. This included fund raising, enlisting various Cossack units, Russian frontline units in the south, attempting to attract Czech units, and organizing a government.

Winter Palace. The official residence of the royal family in the capital. Today it is the Hermitage Museum.

Zemgor. Acronym for the Union of Zemstvos and Cities.

Zemstvo. A system of local self-government with an elected representative council. The Zemstvos had the authority to deal with local matters concerning agriculture, education, welfare, roads, and medical resources. They also had authority to collect taxes.

Zimmerwald and Kiental Conference. An international conference of socialists held in September 1915 in Zimmerwald, Switzerland.

Annotated List of Names

There were several sources for the people identified below. The noted and highly respected Dr. Zinaida Ivanovna Peregudova of the Government Archives of the Russian Federation provided very detailed glossaries in her works on Globachev's Russian language memoirs and those of Alexander Blok. Jonathan Smele's *Historical Dictionary of the Russian Civil Wars, 1916–1922,* was thorough and useful also. There are a number of names mentioned by the Globachevs for which there is little information. These are sometimes some subordinate of Globachev's, an acquaintance, or just a mention of someone in passing about whom there was no further information. Unknown or unverifiable birth or death dates are indicated by a question mark (?).

Abramov, Fedor Fedorovich (1870–1963). He was a line tsarist officer in World War I and an active senior officer (Lt. General) during the Civil War. In 1930 he became deputy chairman of ROVS. In 1948 he emigrated to the United States. He was killed in a car accident in 1963 and is buried in a Russian Orthodox cemetery in New Jersey.

Agapaev, Vladimir Petrovich (1876–1956). Lieutenant General and cavalry commander during World War I. He joined the Volunteer Army in 1918 and in 1920 he was the Volunteer Army's representative in dealing with the French and British commands in Constantinople. He emigrated to Serbia and then to Buenos Aires.

Akerman, Petr Alexandrovich (?). Prosecutor of the Vilensk District Court.

Alekseev, Mikhail Vasilievich (1857–1918). Infantry general. At the beginning of World War I, was commander of the Southwestern Front. From 1915 to 1917 was Chief of Staff of the High Command. Following the revolution he was one of the organizers of the White Movement. He died in September 1918 of heart failure.

Alexander I Karageorgievich (1898–1934). King of Serbia from 1929–1934. He was educated in Russia and supportive of Russian refugees following the Civil War.

Anastasii (birth name: Alexander Alexeevich Gribanovskii) (1873–1965). Ordained into monastic orders in 1898. In 1901 he was promoted to archimandrite and then to bishop of the Moscow Episcopate. In 1916 he was elevated to archbishop. In Constantinople in 1920 he was head of the Russian Orthodox community. He was chosen to be Metropolitan in 1935 and in 1936 he was elected by the Synod of the Russian Orthodox Church Outside of Russia to be its head. From 1950 he resided in the United States.

Andre (de Langeron), D. F. (?). During World War I he was a supplier of bread to the army. He claimed to be a descendant of a famous Odessa family—the Langerons. He worked his way into the Odessa government during the Civil War. On March 5, 1919 General Denikin ordered General Sannikov to put no trust in Andre.

Avksenteev, Nikolai Dmitrievich (1878–1943). Political journalist and member of the Social Revolutionary Party. Between 1905 and 1907 he was arrested, but fled Russia. He returned after the February Revolution and served as Minister of the Interior under Kerensky. At the end of 1918 he emigrated to France and then to New York.

Axenov, Leonid (?). Step-brother of Globachev. Spent his life in the medical profession specializing in ophthalmology. He died in the late 1940's in Germany.

Badmaev, Petr Alexandrovich (1851–1919). A Buriat native who specialized in Tibetan medicine. He occasionally used his home as a neutral place for Rasputin to meet people. Badmaev was also physician to Alexander Protopopov, the Minister of the Interior.

Balk, Alexander Pavlovich (1866–1957). Major General and the last City Prefect of Petrograd from November 1916 until February 17, 1917. After the revolution he emigrated to Serbia and then to Brazil, where he died in 1957.

Baranov, Petr Petrovich (1843–1924). Cavalry general. He was a regimental and brigade commander until 1898, when he was appointed commandant of Grand Duke Michael Nikolaevich's palace. He also served on various investigative committees. After the revolution he emigrated to Estonia.

Bark, Petr Lvovich (1869–1937). The last Minister of Finance from 1914 to 1917, and he was a member of the State Council. He was arrested by the Provisional Government, but was released soon after. He emigrated to Great Britain in 1918 where he spent the rest of his life managing Russian financial accounts outside of Russia. He became a British citizen in 1935 and was knighted.

Beletskii, Stepan Petrovich (1872–1918). Director of the Department of Police from 1909 to 1912. From September 1915 to February 1916 was Assistant Minister of the Interior. He was arrested in March 1917 by the Provisional Government and following the Bolshevik Revolution of October 1917 he was executed in the fall of 1918.

Beliaev, Mikhail (?). Minister of War, January to February 27, 1917.

Benzinger, Alexander Vasilievich (?). Major General. He was Russian Military representative of the Volunteer Army to the Allied Command in Constantinople.

Bezobrazov, Vladimir Mikhailovich (1857–1932). Cavalry general. In 1916–1917 he was commander of a guard unit.

Blok, Alexander Alexandrovich (1880–1921). A poet who was invited in 1917 to edit the various reports of the Extraordinary Commission of the Provisional Government. The result was his publication entitled "The Last Days of the Old Regime," that included a number of Globachev's reports and testimony.

Braikevich Mikhail Vasilievich (?–1940). Engineer and art collector. He was a member of the Kadet Party and Minister of Trade and Industry in the Provisional Government. Emigrated to England in 1920, where he lectured at the University of London and was active in a Russian émigré group that supported Russian refugees.

Budnitskii, Mikhail Titovich (1882–?). From 1903 to 1908 a junior officer in the Iaroslav Infantry Regiment. He transferred to the Special Corps of Gendarmes in 1908 and held staff positions in various security offices. In 1915 he was assigned to the Petrograd Security Bureau. At the time of his arrest by the Provisional Government, he held the rank of captain.

Burtsev, Vladimir Lvovich (1862–1942). Originally a publicist and publisher of various political magazines, he was arrested several times. His best-known activities in the early 1900's were exposing agents of the Okhrana. After the revolution he emigrated to Paris where he died.

Chaplinskii, Georgii Georgievich (1865–?). Trained in law. From 1912 to 1914 he was prosecutor of the Kiev Court. After 1914 he was senator and in 1917 a member of the State Council.

Chebykin, Alexander Nesterovich (1857–1920). Member of the Tsar's Suite. He was deputy under General Khabalov and in February 1917 he was responsible for the reserve forces in Petrograd.

Chekatovskii, Ignatii Ignatievich (1875–?). General and commandant of the Russian Embassy in Constantinople.

Chernavin, Viktor Vasilievich (1877–1956). Major General. He joined the Volunteer Army in 1918. In 1920 he was appointed as chief of staff under Lieutenant General Shilling.

Chernevskaia (?). Briefly mentioned by Globachev as having an apartment that allowed Rasputin to meet with A. N. Khvostov.

Chernov, Viktor Mikhailovich (1876–1952). A member and theoretician of the Social Revolutionary Party. In 1917 he was Minister of Agriculture in the Provisional Government. He emigrated in 1920.

Chertkov, Grigorii Grigorievich (1872–1938). Military attaché in Turkey.

Chkheidze, Nikolai Semenovich (1863–1926). In 1898 he joined the Russian Social Democratic Labor Party and in 1903 became a leader of the Menshevik faction. He was a representative in the Third and Fourth State Dumas. After the October Revolution he emigrated to Paris and was active in the Georgian SD émigré society in France. He committed suicide in 1926.

Denikin, Anton Ivanovich (1872–1947). Lieutenant General as of 1916. He took over command of the Volunteer White Army in 1918 and replaced Admiral Kolchak as Supreme Commander in 1919. After the failed campaign to take Moscow from the Red Army, he relinquished command to Baron General P.N. Wrangell. He emigrated to France where he lived from 1926 to 1945. He then moved to the United States.

Dobrovol'skii, Nikolai Alexandrovich (1854–1918). Senator appointed Minister of Justice at the behest of Rasputin. Voluntarily submitted to arrest during the February Revolution. He was released but was arrested after the October Revolution and was shot by the Bolsheviks.

Dobrovol'skii, Nikolai Vasilievich (?). Major General in command of an engineering battalion in St. Petersburg.

Dolgorukov, Alexander Nikolaevich (1872–1948). Lieutenant General. Replaced General Keller to command the defense of Kiev. Emigrated to France.

D'Overk, Count (?). According to Globachev, there was a criminal by the name Overko, the son of a janitor. Overko presented himself as Count d'Overk.

Dragomirov, Abram Mikhailovich (1868–1955). Cavalry general during World War I. During the Civil War he held major commands in the Volunteer Army and was a close advisor to General Wrangel. He emigrated to Paris and was one of the senior leaders in ROVS.

Drozdovskii, Mikhail Gordeevich (1881–1919). Career officer. He saw combat in the Russo-Japanese War and World War I. After the October Revolution he joined the Volunteer Army. As Major General he commanded the Third Infantry Division. He was wounded in October 1918 and died on January 1, 1919.

Durnovo, Petr Nikolaevich (1845–1915). Minister of the Interior in 1905–1906. He suppressed revolutionary groups, but because of the turmoil he was dismissed and later appointed to the State Council where he served until his death.

Dzhunkovskii, Vladimir Fedorovich (1865–1938). General and Governor of Moscow 1905–1913. He was appointed Assistant Minister of the Interior 1913–1915. He was dismissed by Nicholas II for submitting a negative report on Rasputin. From 1915 to 1917 he was a division commander in the war. He remained in Russia after the revolution. He was arrested by the Soviet regime and shot in 1938.

Efremov (?). Colonel and military commander of the Pletz District.

Frederiks, Vladimir Borisovich (1838–1927). Cavalry general who became Minister of the Imperial Household in 1897 and a member of the State Council in 1905. He was arrested in March 1917 but was soon released. In October he was granted permission by the Soviet Government to emigrate to Finland.

Freidenberg, Henri (1866–1975). Colonel in the French Army. During the Civil War was commandant of Odessa. He was recalled to France in 1919.

Furs, Petr Ilyich (1857–?). A gendarme officer since 1883. He held various positions of leadership, either as deputy or as head of gendarme administrations in major cities such as Perm, Peterhof, Warsaw, and St. Petersburg.

Fuss (?). A cavalry commander in the Tsarist army, he was in the Volunteer Army during the Civil War. He was responsible for maintaining courier services between Constantinople and Crimea, Belgrade, and Sofia. According to

Globachev, he fled to Paris with approximately 3,000 English pounds of the army's funds.

Gepner (possibly Ievelia G.) (?). A member of the governing board of Russian sugar refineries.

Gerardi, Boris Andreevich (1870–?). Colonel in the Special Corps of Gendarmes. Served as deputy head of the Moscow Security Bureau in 1903. From 1905 to 1917, he was head of the Palace Police.

Gerasimov, Alexander Vasilievich (1861–1944). A gendarme officer. From 1889 on he served in various deputy head and heads of gendarme and security bureau administrations. He was successful in thwarting a number of assassination attempts on government officials by revolutionaries. He resigned in 1914 and was promoted to lieutenant general. He emigrated.

Golitsyn, Nikolai Dmitrievich (1850–1925). A member of an old princely family. He held several governmental positions, the last of which was Chairman of the Council of Ministers. The Provisional Government arrested him in February 1917 but later released him. He remained in Russia and was arrested and released several times by the Soviet Government between 1920 and 1924. He was arrested again in 1925 and shot.

Golovina, Liubov Valerianovna (1853–1938). Wife of the Royal Chamberlain, Evgenii Sergeevich Golovin.

Gorgulov, Pavel Timofeevich (1895–1932). Lieutenant in the army during World War I. Joined the Volunteer Army during General Wrangel's tenure. He emigrated to France where he practiced medicine illegally. He claimed to be the leader of the Russian Nationalist Fascist Party. He assassinated French President Paul Doumer and he was guillotined in Paris.

Grigoriev, Georgii Nikolaevich (1868–?). Major General and City Prefect of St. Petersburg in 1904.

Grishin-Almazov, Alexei Nikolaevich (1880–1919). Artillery officer who rose in rank during World War I commanding various Siberian army units. He joined the White Army in 1918 and commanded the defense of Odessa. In May 1919 he headed to join Admiral Kalchak in Siberia. A Soviet destroyer attacked his ship in the Caspian Sea. Rather than be captured, Grishin committed suicide.

Groten, Pavel Pavlovich (1870–1962). Major General and member of His Majesty's Suite. He was acting commandant of the Tsarskoe Selo when General

Voeikov was at Staff Headquarters with the Tsar. Groten emigrated to France after the revolution.

Guchkov, Alexander Ivanovich (1862–1936). One of the founders of the Octobrist Party. He was chairman of the Third Duma in 1910 and was Chairman of the Central War Industries Committee during World War I. He supported the idea of a palace coup to depose Nicholas II. He was Minister of War and Navy in the Provisional Government. He was active in anti-Bolshevik movements between 1917 and 1921. Emigrated to Paris.

Gurland, Ilia Iakovlevich (1863?–?). Academically trained author of various articles, who became an unofficial advisor to Interior Minister B.V. Sturmer. After the revolution he emigrated to Paris.

Guseva, Khionia Kuzminievna. A peasant woman from Simbirsk. She was originally an admirer of Rasputin, but later grew to hate him. In 1914 she attacked him and stabbed a knife into his stomach. She was confined to a clinic for the insane and in 1917 Kerensky ordered her to be released.

Gvozdov, Kuz'ma Antonovich (1882–1956). Member of the Mensheviks in the 1914. The following year he was a member of the workers' faction of the Central War Industries Committee. In 1917 he was made a member of the Soviet of Workers' Deputies. He was arrested in 1931 by the Soviet Secret Police and sentenced to ten years in prison.

Iliashenko (possibly Alexander Nikolaevich) (?). An officer of an infantry regiment. He rose through the ranks and in 1917 he was a Major General and commanded the 35th Infantry Division.

Il'yin S. N. (?). Colonel in charge of the Refugee Bureau of the Russian Red Cross.

Ivanov, Nikolai Iudovich (1851–1919). Adjutant General. He participated in the Russo-Turkish War, 1877–1878. From 1905 on he held command positions. Nikolas II appointed him commander of Petrograd forces on February 27, 1917. After the revolution he joined the White Army. He died of typhus.

Kamenev, Sergei Sergeevich (1881–1936). A former police officer who became an adjutant to Interior Minister A.A. Khvostov. After the revolution he joined the Soviet government and served in several capacities.

Karinski, N. S. (?). A prosecutor in the Petrograd Judicial Court of the Provisional Government. On July 23, 1917, he ordered the arrests and incarceration of A.V. Lunacharskii and Lev Trotsky.

Kartsev, Viktor Andreevich (1868–?). Vice Admiral and Director of the Naval Academy. He was arrested in 1930 and sentenced to three years in internal exile.

Kazakov, Matvei, Ivanovich (1858–?). Major General. Held several senior gendarme posts from 1894 to 1917. He was head of the Moscow, Tombov, and Warsaw Gendarme Police Administrations from 1902 to 1907. From 1910 to 1917 he was head of Petrograd Gendarme Division. The Provisional Government arrested him.

Kaznakov (?). He is mentioned in Sofia Globacheva's memoir. He was Governor General of Lodz, and subsequently was Governor General of Poland.

Keller, Fedor Arturovich (1857–1918). Lieutenant General. He was a cavalry regimental commander from 1904 through World War I up to 1918. In that year he commanded troops to defend Kiev from the Petliura forces. He was captured and shot by Petliura's men.

Kerensky, Alexander Fedorovich (1882–1970). A lawyer by training and a political activist, he was elected to the Duma in 1912. In March 1917, he was appointed Minister of Justice in the Provisional Government. He also held positions of War Minister and Prime Minister. As a result of the Bolshevik Revolution in October 1917, Kerensky left Russia and lived in France and Berlin. In 1940 he emigrated to the United States where he wrote and lectured. He died in New York.

Khabalov, Sergei Sergeevich (1858–1924). A graduate of the General Staff Academy. He held the rank of Lieutenant General and in 1916–1917 he was military commander of the Petrograd District and its troops. He was arrested at the outset of the February Revolution but released in October.

Khari (?). Owner of a sugar refinery in Odessa.

Khvostov, Alexander Alekseevich (1857–1922). Minister of Justice from 1915 to 1916. Appointed Minister of the Interior in 1916.

Khvostov, Alexei Nikolaevich (1872–1918). Born to nobility. Between 1904 and 1912 he was Vice Governor of Minsk, then of Tula. In 1906 he became Vice Governor and then Governor of Nizhny Novgorod. In September 1915 he was appointed Minister of the Interior. He was dismissed in less than a year.

Kirpichev, Lev Nilovich (1878–1928). Major General of Artillary. In 1918 he commanded the Kiev Volunteer Military Unit. Around 1919 he went to join Admiral Kolchak and, by one account, he died in 1920. Another account states he died in Luxor, Egypt in August 1928.

Kirpichnikov, Timofei Ivanovich (?–1918). Noncommissioned officer of the Volynsk Regiment who killed the head of the training command of the regiment, Captain I.S. Lashkevich. In 1918 Kirpichnikov tried to join the White Army. General Kutepov had him executed.

Kliachko, Lev Moiseevich (1873–1933). A journalist whose articles appeared in many Russian newspapers. Interior Minister Sturmer considered Kliachko his enemy. Sturmer fabricated a case against Kliachko, which proved baseless.

Klimovich, Evgenii Konstantinovich (1871–1932). A career gendarme officer. He served as Director of the Department of Police in 1916. During the Civil War he was in charge of counterintelligence under General Wrangel.

Kolakovskii, Iakov Pavlovich (?). He was a junior lieutenant who testified against Colonel Miasoedov, who was tried and executed for espionage. Globachev was quite sure that Miasoedov was innocent.

Kolchak, Alexander Vasilievich (1874–1920). Appointed admiral in 1916 in charge of the Black Sea Fleet. After the February Revolution he joined the anti-Bolshevik movement in 1918 and was appointed Supreme Ruler of the Russian State. Military losses over the next year led to Kolchak's transferring power to General Denikin. He was arrested by the Bolsheviks and executed on February 7, 1920.

Kolontaev (?). According to Globachev, a staff worker of the Extraordinary Investigative Commission charged with examining the activities of the Security Bureau.

Komissarov, Mikhail Stepanovich (1870–1933). A gendarme officer who was personally tasked by Minister A.N. Khvostov and S.P. Beletskii to establish a friendly relationship and surveillance over Rasputin. This surveillance would be outside of the official functions of the Security Bureau. After the revolution, Komissarov emigrated to the United States.

Konovalov, Alexander Ivanovich (1875–1948). Active member of the Duma specializing in trade. In 1915 became involved with the Central War Industries Committee. He joined the Provisional Government in 1917 and was made Minister of Trade and Industry. He was one of several organizers of the Kronstadt Rebellion in 1921. Soon after he emigrated to Paris and at the start of World War II he moved to the United States.

Kornilov, Lavr Georgievich (1870–1918). A general in World War I and the first month of the February Revolution he was made commander of the Petrograd Milo District. He continued to be active during the months of the Provisional Government. Following the Bolshevik revolution he joined General Alekseev in establishing the White Army. He was killed during the White Army's attack on Ekaterinodar.

Korolenko, Vladimir Galaktionovich (1853–1921). A poet and writer on current affairs.

Kreiton (?). Governor of Vladimir.

Krivoshein, Alexander Vasilievich (1857–1921). Expert in agricultural matters (1908–1915) and Chairman of the Union of Landholders (1917–1918). In 1919 General Wrangel appointed him to head civilian affairs. Evacuated Crimea to Constantinople in 1920. Emigrated to France.

Kruglov (?). A noncommissioned officer. He was deputy to the head of the guards in the Ministerial Pavilion of the Tauride Palace.

Kryzhanovskii, Sergei Efimovich (1861–1934). Senator in 1907 and State Secretary from 1911 to 1916. He resigned in January 1917 and was detained by the Provisional Government. Later in 1917 he was released, moved to Kiev and then emigrated.

Kukol'-Ianopol'skii, Stepan Alexandrovich (1859–?). Member of the State Council. Served a short while as Assistant Minister of the Interior in 1916.

Kurlov, Pavel Grigorievich (1860–1923). Assistant Minister of the Interior from 1909 to 1911. After Stolypin's assassination he was dismissed. He was appointed to that position again just before the revolution. He was arrested by the Provisional Government but released when the Bolsheviks came to power. He emigrated in 1918.

Kusonskii, Pavel Alekseevich (1880–1941). He was a tsarist office who attained the rank of Lt. General in 1922, during the latter part of the civil are. He was active in the White Movement and after the defeat of the Whites he emigrated to France and became one of the leaders of ROVS. He was arrested by the Gestapo in June 1941 and beaten to death in August of that year.

Kutepov, Alexander Pavlovich (1882–1930). He was a tsarist officer who became one of the most able generals of the White Movement in the south of Russia. After the Whites defeat he moved to Bulgaria and then to Paris where he became the head of ROVS. Soviet agents abducted him in 1930 and he either died of a heart attack or was killed by his abductors.

Lashkevich, Ivan Stepanovich (?–1917). Erroneously referred to as Mashkevich by Globachev. Lashkevich was a captain and head of the training command of the Volynsk Regiment. T. I. Kirpichnikov killed him on February 27, 1917.

Lenin (Ulianov), Vladimir Ilyich (1870–1924). Marxist revolutionary. In 1893 he became a major figure in the Marxist Russian Social Democratic Labor Party (RSDLP). In 1903 he led the Bolshevik faction of the party in an ideological conflict with the Menshevik faction. After the February Revolution he campaigned to oust the Provisional Government and in October 1917 he led the overthrow that established Bolshevik rule and the creation of the Soviet Union.

Leontiev (?). Lieutenant General and Quartermaster General of the General Staff.

Lukomskii, Alexander Sergeevich (1868–1939). A Lieutenant General during World War I and chief of staff of the High Command. Following the revolution he was one of several organizers of the White Movement. After the White defeat he evacuated to Constantinople where Wrangel appointed him head of the White Army in Constantinople. He probably left there around 1923 when the Whites' funds had been depleted and several European countries recognized the Soviet regime.

Lvov, Georgii Evgenievich (1861–1925). A member of the Kadet Party in the First State Duma. After the February Revolution he became Prime Minister of the Provisional Government. He resigned in favor of Alexander Kerensky in July 1917. He was arrested by the Bolsheviks following the October Revolution, escaped and emigrated to Paris.

Machul'skii (?). A tsarist colonel representing the General Staff who, with Major General Potopov, joined the Bolshevik government after the October Revolution.

Makarenko, Alexander Sergeevich (1861–1932). Artillery general who was appointed in 1911 as deputy head of the military justice administration. He soon became the head of the organization. On February 26, 1917 he replaced Protopopov as Minister of the Interior. Around 1920 he emigrated to Serbia.

Makarov, Alexander Alexandrovich (1857–1919). Trained in law. Between 1906 and 1912 held positions in the Ministry of the Interior, and was Minister in 1912. He was Minister of Justice in 1916. The Provisional Government arrested him in 1917. After the October Revolution he was detained by the Bolshevik government and transferred to Moscow where he was shot.

Makhno, Nestor Ivanovich (1888–1934). An anarchist. He began a partisan war against the German occupying forces in Ukraine and against Skoropadskii's government in 1918. He also fought against the Volunteer Army, the Bolsheviks, and Petliura. After the defeat of the Volunteer Army, Makhno's forces were threatened by the Soviet forces. He fled to Paris in 1921, where he died at age 45.

Maklakov, Nikolai Aledseevich (1871–1918). Minister of the Interior from 1913 to 1915. He was dismissed from this position, but was appointed to the Finance Committee of the State Council. Following the Bolshevik Revolution he was arrested and shot.

Manasevich-Manuilov, Ivan(1869–1918). Began governmental work as an agent in Rome maintaining surveillance over Russian revolutionaries there. His next assignment in 1902 was to represent Interior Minister V. K. Pleve in Paris. In 1914 he met and became Rasputin's close associate. In October 1917 he attempted to flee to Finland. He was captured by the Bolsheviks and shot.

Manus, Ignatius Porfirievich (?). A banker and shareholder in several enterprises.

Markov, V. A. (?). The City Prefect of Odessa.

Markov, V. I. (?). Lieutenant General. He was Secretary of State for Finnish Affairs and Vice-Chairman of the Finnish Senate.

Martynov, Alexander Pavlovich (1875–1951). He was the last head of the Moscow Okhrana, serving in this capacity from 1912 to 1917. He fled south with his family at the outbreak of the Bolshevik Revolution. Around 1920 he evacuated to Constantinople where he started a private detective bureau. In 1923 he emigrated to the United States. He died in California in 1951.

Mashkevich, Ivan Stepanovich. See Lashkevich.

Meklenburgskii (?). The only data available identify him being a general who was arrested by the Provisional Government.

Miasoedov, Sergei Petrovich (1865–1915). He was a colonel in the Corps of Gendarmes. He was accused of espionage in 1914, tried in military court, convicted, and hanged. Subsequent investigation concluded he was innocent.

Miatlev, Vladimir Petrovich (1866–?). Lyric poet and satirist. Marshall of the nobility in Kursk Province.

Miliukov, Pavel Nikolaevich (1859–1943). A historian who was politically active. He was a Kadet representative in the Third and Fourth State Dumas in St. Petersburg. He became Foreign Minister in the Provisional Government. He resigned in May 1917. He emigrated to France in 1918.

Miller, Evgenii Karlovich (1867–1939). Cavalry general. During World War I he was Chief of Staff of the Fifth Army. During the early part of the Civil War, Admiral Koluhak appointed him Supreme Commander of the Northern Province. Following defeats by the Red Army, he fled to France. From 1920 to 1937 he was the head of ROVS. Soviet agents kidnapped him in 1937 in Paris, taken to Moscow and executed in May 1919.

"Mishka Iaponchik." An alias. See Vinitskii, Mikhail Iakovlevich.

Mollov, Ruschu Georgievich (1867–1925). Director of the Department of Police, 1915–1916. During the Civil War he argued for the continued support from France and the formation of a Russian government that was not dependent on the White Army.

Muraviev, Nikolai Konstantinovich (1870–1936). Trained in law. Before the revolution he was active in promoting the causes of workers, peasants, and political groups. His anti-government positions led to several arrests. In 1917 he was appointed Chairman of the Extraordinary Investigative Commission of the Provisional Government.

Nadzharov (?). A noncommissioned officer in charge of the guards on Furshtadskii Street.

Nakhamkes, Iurii Mikhailovich (1873–1941). Political activist and journalist. He was editor of the newspaper "Izvestia" (The News) in 1917. His position of being against the October Revolution led to his arrest in 1938. He died in the Saratov Prison.

Naryshkina, Elizaveta Alekseevna (1938–1928). She was lady-in-waiting and head of the Empress' household.

Neidgart, Dmitrii Borisovich (1861–1942). Senator. During the revolution of 1905 he was City Prefect of Odessa (1905–1907).

Nekrasov, Nikolai Vissarionovich (1879–1940). A member of the Kadet party and a deputy representing the Tomsk Province in the Third and Fourth

Dumas. Following the February Revolution he was Minister of Transportation in the Provisional Government. He was arrested by the Bolsheviks in 1921, but released and joined the Soviet government. He was arrested in 1939 and shot by order of the High Court of the U.S.S.R.

Neratov, Anatolii Anatolievich (1863–1929). From 1910–1917 was Deputy Minister of Foreign Affairs. After the October Revolution, he was the head of foreign affairs in the Denikin government. He emigrated to France and then to the United States.

Nikol'skii, Vladimir Pavlovich (1873–1960). Major General. Initially an officer in the Grenadier Artillery Brigade from 1903 to 1913. He also taught military subjects at the Moscow Military Academy. From 1913 to 1917 was Chief of Staff of the Special Corps of Gendarmes. Following the Civil War he held a senior position in the Russian Embassy in Constantinople. Around 1923 he emigrated to Bulgaria.

Orlov, Vladimir Grigorievich (1866–1918). An active member of various right-wing movements.

Papadjanov, Mikhail Ivanovich (1869–1930). A left-wing Kadet representative in the Fourth Duma. In 1917 he was appointed Commissar of the Transcaucasian Committee of the Provisional Government.

Perets, Grigorii Grigorievich (?). Colonel and commandant of the Tauride Palace. He wrote him Memoirs, "In the Citadel of the Russian Revolution."

Pereverzev, Pavel Nikolaevich (1817–1944). A member of the Social Revolutionary Party. In 1917 the Provisional Government appointed him prosecutor and in April he was appointed Minister of Justice. In July 1917, he published information that alleged Lenin's connection to the German General Staff. This highly controversial publication created some furor and forced Pereversev's dismissal. Following the Bolshevik Revolution in October 1917, Pereversev emigrated to Paris where he died some years later.

Petliura, Simon Vasilievich (1879–1926). Leader of the Ukrainian Social Democratic Workers' Party. Overthrew the government of Skoropadskii in 1918. The Soviet government tried to have Petliura handed over. He left Ukraine and after living in several countries, he settled in Paris in 1914. He was assassinated in 1926 by a Ukrainian anarchist.

Pirang, Richard Iulievich (1870–?). Colonel. He was arrested by the Provisional Government and detained in the Tauride Palace.

Pistolkors, Alexandra Aleksandrovna (?). Sister of Anna Vyrubova.

Pitirim (1858–1919). He was a priest who became bishop in 1894 and rose through the clerical ranks to the position of Metropolitan of Petrograd and Ladoga. He was arrested by the Provisional Government in March 197, dismissed by the Synod, and forced to retire in Vladikavkaz.

Pletnev (?). Colonel who was arrested with others by the Provisional Government.

Polianskii (?). Family friend of the Globachevs.

Poluboiarinova, Yelena Adrianovna (1864–1919). Member of nobility. She became publisher of the "Russian Standard" newspaper in 1907 and its editor from 1909 to 1912. She continued to belong to many patriotic organizations. The Bolsheviks shot her in 1919.

Popov (?). Junior officer in charge of the Vyborg prison.

Potopov, Nikolai Mikhailovich (1871–?). Major General and member of the General Staff. With the success of the Bolshevik Revolution he joined the new government and held several responsible military and intelligence positions.

Protopopov, Alexander Dmitriovich (1866–1918). Member of the hereditary nobility and initially a member of the Duma. Appointed Minister of the Interior in 1916. The Provisional Government arrested him, and when the Bolsheviks took power he was shot by the Cheka.

Prutenskii, Vladimir Sevirovich (1879–?). Lieutenant Colonel. In 1904 he transferred from a line regiment to the Corps of Gendarmes. From March 1914 on he was a senior staff officer in the Petrograd Security Bureau.

Purishkevich, Vladimir Mitrofanovich (1870–1920). Member of the Duma and one of several conspirators to kill Rasputin. The Provisional Government arrested him for counter-revolutionary activities. In 1917 he was given amnesty by the Petrograd Soviet. He moved to the south of Russia, where he died of typhus.

Raev, Nikolai Pavlovich (1856–1919). The son of a Metropolitan bishop, he was associated with a number of social institutions such as the Ministry of Enlightenment and Women's Education. He was appointed Head of the Holy Synod in 1916 and dismissed in 1917. He moved to the Caucasus.

Raevskii. See Rzhevskii.

Rakovskii, Khristian Georgievich (1873–1941). His real name was Kristo Stanchev. A member of the Social Democratic Party following the October Revolution. From 1919 to 1923 was Chairman of the Council of National Commissars for Ukraine.

Rasputin (Novykh), Gregory Efimovich (1864–1916). A peasant from Tobolsk who became known to the royal family as a healer and a holy man. The Tsarevich's hemophilia gave Rasputin access and influence with the Empress. Several monarchist conspirators wanted to save Russia from Rasputin, He was murdered in November 1916.

Rennenkampf, Pavel Karlovich von (1854–1918). Cavalry general. Army commander 1914–1915. After a failed campaign he was dismissed. After the October Revolution he was shot by the Bolsheviks.

Reshetnikov (?). An acquaintance of Rasputin's who made his apartment available to Rasputin for the latter's meeting with highly placed persons.

Riman, Nikolai Karlovich (?). Colonel of the Semenovskii Life Guards Regiment. In 1905 he led punitive forces against an uprising in Moscow. The Provisional Government arrested him in February 1917.

Rodzianko, Mikhail Vladimirovich (1859–1924). A member of a landholding noble family, Rodzianko was a politically active member of the Octobrist Party and a leader in the Duma. Following the October Revolution he affiliated himself with Kornilov's and Demikin's White Movement. In 1920, he emigrated to Serbia.

Romanov, Grand Duke Mikhail Alexandrovich (1878–1918). Younger brother of Nicholas II. In World War I he commanded the Caucasus Cavalry Division. On March 2, Nicholas II abdicated on his own and his son's behalf in favor of his brother, Michael. Michael refused the throne. He was arrested by the Bolsheviks in February 1918 and executed in July of that year.

Romanov, Grand Duke Nikolai Nikolaevich (1856–1929). Grandson of Tsar Nicholas I. In 1914 he was appointed Commander in Chief of all Russian forces, but was replaced by Nicholas II and assigned as commander of Russian forces in the Caucasus. He remained in Crimea until 1919 when he emigrated to Italy and then to France.

Romanov, Prince Dimitrii Pavlovich (1891–1942). A cousin of Tsar Nicholas II and one of the conspirators in the assassination of Rasputin. Nicholas II exiled him to the Persian front. After the Revolution he emigrated to England.

Romanovskii, Ivan Pavlovich (1877–1920). Lieutenant General. He was a supporter of General Kornilov in August 1917. He joined the Volunteer Army in December 1917. He was Chief of Staff of the Southern Russian Army. He evacuated Crimea for Constantinople in 1920. He was murdered in the Russian Embassy in Constantinople.

Rubinshtein, Dmitri Lvovich (1876–1936). A banker who was close to Rasputin and helped Rasputin with the latter's business deals. He emigrated to Paris.

Ruzskii, Nikolai Vladimirovich (1854–1918). Infantry general and commander of the Third Army in World War I, and subsequently commander of the army of the Northwestern front. He was captured by the Bolsheviks in 1918 and shot.

Rzhevskii, Boris Mikhailovich (?–1919). A journalist who was secretly employed by Minister A.N. Khvostov in an assassination plot on Rasputin. The matter became public and Rzhevskii was forced to leave Petrograd. During the Civil War, he joined the White Army using the name Boris Raevskii.

Sadul, Jean (1881–1956). French army captain. Member of a socialist party. Following the October Revolution he was an unofficial representative to the Bolsheviks in Odessa. He spread propaganda against allied intervention in the south among the French troops.

Sannikov, Alexander Sergeevich (1866–1931). Major General in 1910. He participated in World War I, earning the rank of Lieutenant General in 1916. During the Civil War he had major responsibilities in supplying the Volunteer Army of General Dennikin. In 1920 he emigrated to Constantinople and then to Paris.

Savinkov, Boris Viktorovich (1879–1925). A Socialist Revolutionary and terrorist. He opposed the Bolsheviks and emigrated. Around 1924 he was enticed back to Soviet Russia, arrested, and probably executed.

Sazonov, Sergei Dimitrievich (1861–1927). Served in the Foreign Ministry since 1883. Envoy to Washington in 1907. Deputy Minister of Foreign Affairs (1909–1910). In 1910 appointed Minister of Foreign Affairs until 1917 when he was ambassador to London. He joined the White Movement and emigrated in 1919.

Schumaher (?). A naval officer in whose apartment the Globachevs lived temporarily following the February Revolution.

Semkin (?). Secretary of the Committee of Workers' and Soldiers' Deputies in Orsha.

Shatilov, Pavel Nikolaevich (?). General. During the Civil War he was Chief of Staff under General Wrangel. Emigrated to France and was one of the leaders of the Russian All-Military Union (ROVS) in the 1930's.

Shcheglovitov, Ivan Grigorievich (1861–1918). Former Minister of Justice from 1906 to 1915 and Chairman of the Council of Ministers. He was arrested by the Provisional Government. Executed by the Bolsheviks.

Shcherbatov, Prince Nikolai Borisovich (?). A deputy in the First State Duma. He was Minister of the Interior from June 15 to September 21, 1915. Emigrated to Germany after the Revolution.

Shevelev (?). Noncommissioned officer who was one of the several guards in the Ministerial Pavilion of the Tauride Palace. He and Globachev recognized each other from their days in the Keksholm Regiment.

Shidlovskii (?). Possibly the Governor of Archangelsk.

Shilling, Nikolai Nikolaevich (1870–1946). Lieutenant General. During the Civil War he first worked on the staff of Hetman Skoropadskii and then he joined the Volunteer Army. He rose to be commander of Military Forces and Governor General of Southern Russia and Crimea. He was blamed for the poorly organized White evacuation of Odessa in 1920. He emigrated that year to Czechoslovakia.

Shingarev, Andrei Ivanovich (1869–1918). Trained as a physician, he was a Kadet representative in the Second, Third, and Fourth State Dumas. He was Minister of Agriculture in the Provisional Government and then Minister of Finance. He was arrested by the Bolsheviks in November and was killed by sailors and Red Guards in January 1918.

Shurkanov (?). An agent of the Security Bureau.

Shvartz, von Alexei Vladimirovich (?). Lieutenant General. He trained as an engineer and participated in the Russo-Japanese War. After the October Revolution he was appointed Governor General of Odessa by the French occupying command. After the French left in 1919, he emigrated to Constantinople, then to Italy, and finally to Buenos Aires.

Siminskii (?). A colonel in the Volunteer Army who went over to the Red Army with some of the Volunteer Army's secret documents.

Skoblin, Nikolai Vladimirovich (1885–1937). During World War I he rose in rank from a junior officer to Colonel. He joined the Volunteer Army and between 1918 and 1920 he commanded battalions, brigades and a division. He emigrated to Paris where his wife Nadejda Plevitskaia, who was a Soviet agent, enlisted him into Soviet service. He joined ROVS and planned the abduction of General Miller. Skoblin apparently fled to Spain and according to rumors, he was murdered by Soviet secret police agents.

Skoropadskii, Pavel Petrovich (1873–1945). Promoted to Lieutenant General in 1916. Spent his career prior to 1917 as a cavalry commander. After the February Revolution he was active in Ukraine and was proclaimed leader of a major local military council. In November 1918 he was removed from power by Petliura. He emigrated to Germany and died during World War II in an Allied bombing raid of Regensburg, where he lived.

Slashchev, Iakov Alexandrovich (1885–1929). Major General. He joined the Volunteer Army in 1918 and held various staff and command positions through 1920. From 1920 to 1921 he was in Constantinople, but returned to Russia in 1921 and taught. He was murdered by the brother of a man who Slashchev had had executed some years before.

Smirnov, Ivan Konstantinovich (?). He held several positions in the Ministry of the Interior with his final appointment to Vice Director of the Department of Police.

Sobeshchanskii, Matvei Nikolaevich (1855–?). A career gendarme officer since 1885. He held commands of various Provincial Gendarme Administrations. He held the rank of colonel. The Provisional Government arrested him.

Sokolov, Nikolai Alexeevich (1882–1924). Trained in law and investigation, he was assigned by Admiral Kolchak to investigate the murder of the Romanovs. Sokolov provided a detailed report on the event. Sokolov emigrated to Paris in 1920.

Spiridovich, Alexander Ivanovich (1873–1952). A gendarme officer who achieved the rank of major general. He was head of the Kiev Security Bureau at the time of Stolypin's assassination. Investigation into the responsibility for inadequate security was dropped by order of Nicholas II. Spiridovich was appointed head of palace security. In 1916 he was appointed City Prefect of Yalta. After the revolution he emigrated to France and then to the United States.

Stavitskii, Ivan Pavlovich (1873–1966). Lieutenant General. He was head of the commission to liquidate assets and reduce forces as Wrangel's government in Constantinople was coming to an end.

Stavrovskii, V. D. (?). An investigator in the Petrograd Judicial Court.

Stessel, Alexander Anatolievich (1876–1933). Colonel in the Volunteer Army tasked with the defense of Odessa. He emigrated to Constantinople.

Stolypin, Petr Arkadievich (1862–1911). Held several provincial governorships: Grodno from 1902 to 1903 and Saratov in 1906. He suppressed a peasant uprising in Saratov in 1906 and won the Tsar's favor. He was appointed Minister of the Interior and at the same time Chairman of the Council of Ministers. A former agent of the Kiev Okhrana Bureau assassinated him in 1911.

Sturmer, Boris Vladimirovich (1848–1917). Began his career in the Ministry of Justice in 1876. In 1892 he transferred to the Ministry of the Interior. In 1916 he held two offices, Chairman of the Council of Ministers and Minister of the Interior. He left office because of suspicion of being pro-German because of his German name. He was arrested in late 1917 by the Bolsheviks and died in prison.

Sukhomlinov, Vladimir Alexandrovich (1848–1926). A cavalry general who rose to the rank of army Chief of Staff in 1908 and in 1909 was appointed Minister of War. He was dismissed in 1915 for abuse of power and for protecting friends from espionage charges. He spent some time under arrest and was released in 1918. He emigrated to Finland and then to Germany.

Suvorin, Boris Alekseevich (1879–1940). A journalist. In 1919 he published the newspaper, *The Evening Times* in Rostov-on-Don.

Terehov (?). Lieutenant Colonel and assistant to the palace commandant at Tsarskoe Selo.

Tiazhel'nikov, Mikhail Ivanovich (1866–?). Major General. He was appointed Chief of Staff of the Petrograd Military District in 1914. After the October Revolution he emigrated to Serbia.

Timanovskii, Nikolai Stepanovich (1889–1919). Promoted to Major General in 1918. Saw active duty in World War I and was a battalion commander in 1917. After the October Revolution he and part of his battalion joined the White Movement. He died of typhus on December 18, 1919.

Trepov, Alexander Fedorovich (1862–1928). Appointed chairman of the Council of Ministers, replacing Sturmer in November 1916. Dismissed one month later.

Trotsky Lev Davidovich (1879–1940). Active Marxist revolutionary. Initially siding with the Mensheviks, he joined the Bolsheviks in July 1917. After the October Revolution he was Commissar of Foreign Affairs and then Commissar of War. On Stalin's orders he was banished from Russia in 1929. He was murdered in Mexico on Stalin's orders.

Tumanov, Nikolai Evseevich (1844–1917). General. At the start of World War I he was commander of several military districts. In 1916 he was appointed commander of military supplies for the western front.

Uritskii, Moisei Solomonovich (1873–1918). Prior to 1917 was a member of the Menshevik faction. Following the October Revolution became head of the Petrograd Cheka in March 1918. He was assassinated in August of that year.

Varnava (1859/1860–1924). A monk and priest, elevated to the position of bishop. His abuse of authority and association with Rasputin damaged his reputation. In 1917 he was reassigned by the Synod to be Prior of the Vysokogorsk monastery.

Vasiliev, Alexei Tikhonovich (1869–1919). The last Director of the Department of Police from September 1916 to February 1917. Formerly employed in St. Petersburg District Court. In 1913 he joined the staff of the Department of Police. After the revolution he emigrated to France, where he died.

Veletskaia, Ekaterina Leonidovna (?). She was an acquaintance of Sofia Globachev. Veletskaia was the widow of a cavalry captain who died in the war. Veletskaia's daughter, Iulia Den, by a previous marriage, was a close friend of the Russian Empress Alexandra Fedorovna.

Vendorff, Oskar Ignatovich (1849–?). Lieutenant General. After military duty from 1868 to 1881, he entered police service. He was Chief of Police in St. Petersburg from 1895 to 1904. From that date to 1917 was deputy to the City Prefect of St. Petersburg.

Venizelos, Eleftherios (1864–1936). Greek political leader of the liberal-democratic party. He was Prime Minister of Greece during the Russian Civil War and the White Army in Constantinople.

Vinnichenko, Vladimir Kirilovich (1880–1951). Ukrainian writer and political activist. From 1907–1914 he was out of Russia, having fled after being arrested by the Tsarist government. After the October Revolution he joined the

Ukrainian Central Party. In 1920 he joined the Ukrainian Communist Party. Subsequently he emigrated to France.

Vinitskii, Mikhail Iakovlevich, alias "Mishka Iaponchik" (1891–1919). A bandit who presented himself as hating the bourgeoisie and robbing them and their banks only. He was probably caught and shot by the Odessa Cheka.

Vissarnionov, Sergei Evlampievich (1867–1918). Trained in law. Served prosecutorial positions from 1889 to 1908. In 1908 he was on the staff of the Minister of the Interior and by 1910 he was Vice-Director of the Department of Police. General Dzhunkovskii dismissed him in 1913. He was shot by the Bolsheviks in 1918.

Vitnivitskii (?). General in charge of the evacuation of White Russians from Odessa to Constantinople on the ship *Vladimir*.

Voeikov, Vladimir Nikolaevich (1868–1948). Cavalry officer and former commander of the Life Guards Hussar Regiment. From 1913 he was Palace Commandant. Emigrated after the revolution.

Volkov, Ivan Dmitrievich (1854–1917). Lieutenant General. Joined the Special Corps of Gendarmes in 1880. Held various positions in provincial gendarme administrations. In 1915 he was assigned to the Petrograd Gendarme Administration.

Vyrubova, Anna Alexandrovna (1884–1964). She was a lady-in-waiting and a close friend to the Empress. She was also a great admirer and supporter of Rasputin. During the tenure of the Provisional Government she was held under arrest and questioned. In 1920 she was able to escape to Finland where she spent the rest of her life.

Wrangel, Baron Petr Nikolaevich (1878–1928). A cavalry officer in the Tsarist Army. He joined the Volunteer Army in 1918 commanding various units. He replaced General Denikin as head of the White forces in April 1920/ Military defeats to the Soviets led to the mass evacuation of Whites, mostly to Constantinople. He emigrated to Brussels where he established the Russian All-Military Union (in Russian Russkii Obshche Voinskii Soyuz and mostly referred to as ROVS).

Yusupov, Felix, Feliksovich (1887–1967). He was a prince and married to Irene Alexandrovna who was a niece of Nicholas II. He was one of the several conspirators who plotted Rasputin's death. The latter was murdered in Yusupov's palatial home in Petrograd. Yusupov was exiled to his country home. After the revolution he emigrated to Paris.

Zamyslovskii, Georgii Georgievich (1872–1920). Jurist and Justice of the Peace. He was deputy to the Third and Fourth Dumas representing the Russian population of Vilensk Province.

Zavadskii, Mikhail Mikhailovich (1876–?). Worked in prosecutorial positions in various cities beginning in 1904. In 1917 he was appointed to do investigative work for the Extraordinary Investigative Commission of the Provisional Government.

Zavarzin, Pavel Pavlovich (1868–1932). Colonel. Entered the Special Corps of Gendarmes in 1898. He served in various Gendarme administrations and Security Bureaus. He was head of the Moscow office 1910–1912, Odessa 1912–1916, and Warsaw 1916–1917. Emigrated to Paris.

Zein, Franz-Albert Alexandrovich (1862–1918). Lieutenant General. In 1907–1909 he was Governor General of Finland.

Zhevakhov, Nikolai Davidovich (1876–?). Religious writer and deputy to the Head Procurator of the Holy Synod. After the revolution he lived in Serbia.

Zlatopol'skii (?). Owner of a sugar refinery in Odessa.

Zmiev (?). a leader in S.V. Petliura's army.

Znamenskii, Sergei Filimonovich (?). Head of the Ministerial Pavilion of the Tauride Palace guards. He was a junior officer of a reserve infantry regiment.

Zubelevich (?). Former prosecutor of the Nizhny Novgorod District Court before the Revolution. During the Civil War he was Director of Political and Criminal Investigation in General Denikin's government.

Bibliography

Balk, A. P. *Poslednie Piat' Dnei Tsarskogo Petrograda* (23–28 Fevralia 1917 g); Dnevnik posledniago Petrogradskogo Gradonachal'nika. Calif.: Hoover Institution.

Baumgardner, Eugenia S. *Undaunted Exiles*. Staunton, VA: The McClure Company, 1925.

Blok, Alexander A. *Poslednie Dni Imperatorskoi Vlasti*. Moscow: Progres Pleiada, 2012.

Bullock, David. *The Russian Civil War, 1918–1922*. Oxford, UK: Osprey Publishing, 2008.

Daly, Jonathan W. *The Watchful State: Security Police and Opposition in Russia, 1906–1917*. DeKalb: Northern Illinois University Press, 2004.

Dzhunkovskii, V. F. *Vospominania*. Vol. 2. Moscow, 1997.

Gurko, V. I. *Features and Figures of the Past, Government and Opinion in the Reign of Nicholas II*. Stanford, CA: Stanford University Press, 1939.

Hassell, James E. "Russian Refugees in France and the United States between the World Wars." Transactions of the American Philosophical Society, Vol. 8, Part 7, 1991.

Johnston, Robert H. "New Mecca, New Babylon," *Paris and the Russian Exiles, 1920–1945*. Montreal: McGill-Queen's University Press, 1988.

Kolokolov, Boris. *Zhandarm s Tsarem v Golove*. Moscow: Molodaia Gvardia, 2009.

Kucherov, Samuel. *Courts, Lawyers, and Trials under the Last Three Tsars*. New York: Frederick A. Praeger, 1953.

Lauchlan, Iain. *Russian Hide-and-Seek, The Tsarist Secret Police in St. Petersburg, 1906–1914*. Helsinki: Studia Historica 67, 2002.

Lincoln, W. Bruce. *Red Victory, A History of the Russian Civil War*. New York: Simon and Schuster, 1989.

Martynov, A. P. *Moia Sluzhba v Otdel'nom Korpuse Zhandarmov*. Stanford, CA: Stanford University Press, 1972.

Paleologue, Maurice. *An Ambassador's Memoirs*. New York: Geo. Doran, Co., 1925, Vol. 1.

Pares, Bernard. *The Fall of the Russian Monarchy, A Study of the Evidence*. New York: Alfred A. Knopf, 1939.

Peregudova, Z. I. (Ed.) *Pravda o Russkoi Revolutsii*. Moskva: Rosspen, 2009.

———. *Politicheskii sysk Rossii, 1880–1917*. Moskva: Rosspen, 2000.

Purishkevich, V. M. Iz Dnevnika V. M. Purishkevicha; Ubiistvo Rasputina. Buenos Aires, 1944.

Robinson, P. *The White Russian Army in Exile 1920–1941*. Oxford, 2002.

Ruud, Charles A., and Sergei A. Stepanov. *Fontanka 16: The Tsar's Secret Police*. Montreal: McGill-Queens University Press, 1999.

Shatilov, Pavel Nikolaevich. *Memoirs*. Bakhmeteff Archives, Columbia University, New York, Box 9, 10.

Smele, Jonathan D. *Historical Dictionary of the Russian Civil Wars, 1916–1922*. New York: Bowman & Littlefield, 2015.

Spiridovich, A. I. *Velikaia Voina i Fevral'skaia Revolutsia, 1914–1917, Tom 1*. New York: All Slavic Publishing House, 1960.

Trotsky, Leon. *The History of the Russian Revolution*, Vol. 2. New York: Simon and Schuster, 1932.

Wrangell, General Baron Peter N. *Always with Honor*. New York: Robert Speller & Sons, 1957.

Zavarzin, P. P. *Zhandarmy i Revoliutsionery: Vospominania*. Paris: Izdania Avtora, 1930.

Zuckerman, Frederic S. *The Tsarist Secret Police in Russian Society, 1880–1917*. New York: New York University Press, 1996.

Index

Page numbers in *italics* indicate illustrations;
(?) indicates individuals whose full name is not given.